European Private Law Beyond the Common Frame of Reference

Europa Law Publishing, Groningen 2008

European Private Law Beyond the Common Frame of Reference

Essays in Honour of Reinhard Zimmermann

Edited by Antoni Vaquer

Europa Law Publishing is a publishing company specializing in European Union law, international trade law, public international law, environmental law and comparative national law.
For further information please contact Europa Law Publishing via email: info@europalawpublishing.com or visit our website at: www.europalawpublishing.com.

Typeset in Scala and Scala Sans, Graphic design by G2K Designers, Groningen/Amsterdam

NUR 828; ISBN 978-90-76871-93-6

Preface

Two decades after the European Parliament called for a European Civil Code in 1989,[1] delivery and publication of the *academic* Common Frame of Reference entrusted by the European Commission to the CoPECL network of excellence is completed in its interim outline edition.[2] It is difficult to predict the *political* use to which the CFR will be put. Parliament and Commission have exchanged several initiatives in search of a more coherent contract law and a way forward.[3] A process that characterized as a half marathon[4] will end in a sprint. Nevertheless, the outcome will be important, judging by the five large volumes produced by the Study Group on a European Civil Code[5] and the sixth volume prepared by the Acquis-Group.[6]

On October 25-26, 2007, a number of outstanding professors from different jurisdictions came to Lleida to discuss drafts of the CFR, a project that has engaged efforts of about one hundred scholars. The conference occurred on the occasion of the conferral of a doctorate *honoris causa* upon Reinhard Zimmer-

---

1 Resolution of 26 May 1989, OJ C 158/400-401. Later, the Resolution of 6 May 1994, OJ C 158/400-401, insisted in the same idea.

2 *Principles, Definitions and Model Rules of European Private Law. Draft Common Frame of Reference (DCFR). Interim Outline Edition,* prepared by the Study Group on a European Civil Code and the Research Group on EC Private Law (Acquis Group). Edited by Christian von Bar, Eric Clive and Hans Schülte-Nölke *et al* (2008).

3 For an overview of the different steps taken by the European institutions, S. Vogenauer, S. Weatherill, "The European Community's Competence to Pursue the Harmonisation of Contract Law – an Empirical Contribution to the Debate", in id. (ed.), *The Harmonisation of European Contract Law* (2006); M. Röttinger, "Towards a European Code Napoléon/ABGB? Recent EC Activities for a European Contract Law", (2006) *European Law Journal* 807. For the viewpoint of an insider, D. Staudenmayer, "Ein optionelles Instrument im europäischen Vertragsrecht", (2003) *Zeitschrift für europäisches Privatrecht (ZEuP)* 828; id., "The way forward in European Contract Law", (2005) *European Review of Private Law (ERPL)* 95; for the viewpoint of active (then) outsiders, C. von Bar, S. Swann, "Response to the Action Plan", (2003) *ERPL* 595.

4 For example, J. Basedow, "Codification of Private Law in the European Union: the making of a Hybrid", (2001) *European Review of Private Law* 48, wrote that twenty or thirty years would be needed to enact a European Civil Code. Evidently, the CFR draft is not –and will not be– a Civil Code, but it certainly looks like it –in only seven/eight years!

5 *Benevolent Intervention in Another's Affaires. Principles of European Law. SGECC.* Prepared by C. von Bar (2006); *Commercial Agency, Franchise and Distribution Contracts. Principles of European Law. SGECC.* Prepared by M. Hesselink, J. W. Rutgers, O. Bueno Díaz, M. Scotton, M. Veldmann (2006); *Service Contracts. Principles of European Law. SGECC.* Prepared by M. Barendrecht, C. Jansen, M. Loos, A. Pinna, R. Cascao, S. van Gulijk (2006); *Personal Security. Principles of European Law. SGECC.* Prepared by U. Drobnig (2007). *Lease of Goods. Principles of European Law. SGECC.* Prepared by K. Lilleholt, A. Victorin, A. Fötschl, B.-E. R. Konow, A. Meidell, A. B. Torum (2008).

6 Research Group of the Existing EC Contract Law (Acquis Group), *Principles of the Existing EC Contract Law. Contract I* (2007).

mann. This book discloses the papers delivered at the Conference and the vigorous debates among the visiting scholars on the contents of the drafts and the drafting process.

In a sense, this volume combines two books. The first one consists of Professors Zimmermann's acceptance speech on legal history and comparative law, and then three laudatios that relate to three of Professor Zimmermann's main fields of interest and research: European private law, Roman contemporary law and Scots law. The second internal book consists of scholarly contributions to debates on the substance of the Study Group drafts. Taken together, the two internal volumes constitute a unit. For the content of each volume illuminates that of the other.

There is still no European civil code, and it is unlikely that such a code will be promulgated in the near term. However, even the fittest athlete could not have imagined the race that European private law has run until now. Two decades ago, one could scarcely have foreseen the intensity and extent of research in European private law. A researcher in this area will be greeted by entire journals and research groups[7] devoted specifically to the new *ius commune europaeum*, books series by every international law publisher, and chairs of European private law. Therefore, the glass is more than half full.

The contributions of Nils Jansen, Pascal Pichonnaz, and Hector MacQueen attest to Reinhard Zimmermann as motivator of the scientific quest that has inspired all of these scholarly developments. The Europeanization of private law is scarcely imaginable without Professor Zimmermann's work. And especially his monumental *The Law of Obligations*. In Nils Jansen's account, this last work has made researchers feel like Saint Paul at Damascus. Zimmermann's chapter highlights results achieved by jurists who have employed the historical and comparative research method that he promoted. Every harmonizing process requires background on similarities and differences among legal systems, and historical and comparative inquiry effectively illuminates this background. As Zimmermann observes, this method can pave the way for rational debate about overcoming differences among European legal systems may be. At least, in my opinion, it can foster the competition between legal systems.[8]

The *academic* CFR is currently envisioned as the cornerstone of the new European private law. Although the CFR is not a civil code law, the best proof that it goes far beyond the initial goal of the European Commission[9] – if there

7 W. Wurmest, "Common Core, Grundreglen, Kodifikationsentwürfe, Acquis-Grundsätze – Ansätze internationaler Wissenschaftlergruppen zur Privatrechtsvereinheitlichung in Europa", (2003) *ZEuP* 714.

8 Cf. J. M. Smits, "European private law: a plea for a spontaneous legal order", in: D. M. Curtin, J.M. Smits, A. Klip, J. A. McCahery, *European Integration and Law; Four Contributions on the Interplay between European Integration and European and National Law to celebrate the 25th Anniversary of Maastricht University's Faculty of Law* (2006), p. 55 ff.

9 The European Commissioner for Consumer Protection M. Kuneva, "The European Contract Law and Review of the Consumer Acquis", (2007) *ZEuP* 955 at 957, has stated that "Once (...) the research-

has ever been *one* purpose[10]– appears in the several drafts analyzed in the second internal book.[11] Contributions of Gerard McCormack and Willem van Boom question respectively the reach of the CFR to credit securities and aspects of tort law, respectively. On unjust enrichment, Jan Smits does not favour of a complete harmonization; in fact, he warns of the risk of "nationalising" European law at a conceptual level when harmonization touches fields that do not need it. For example, the European institutions could scarcely have anticipated a CFR regulation of donation. Further complicating the question, donations are classified as contracts so as to avoid dealing with a mode of acquisition of assets, even though some European legal systems do not follow this classification; Martin Schmidt-Kessel gives us some reasons that justify this option. The classification scheme itself leads to a question: which method was used by the drafting groups. This question then entails whether one opts for the so-called best rule instead of a more comprehensive comparative inquiry. This approach can easily be criticized.[12] How can a rule be deemed the "best rule" if it has not been tested? Assuming that a rule is best in one jurisdiction, it still might not be best in another jurisdiction. Of course, the drafts can be understood as a "model for a harmonized European law" according to Käre Lilleholt, team leader of the SGECC lease of movables group.[13] In this sense, the *academic* CFR draft is only a set of model-rules that some scholars have deemed the best. As such, the CFR is a considerable achievement, judging by the number and prestige of the scholars who have worked on it. If we agree with Hugh Beale, that "for the most part the laws do reach rather similar results; the problem is one of translation between differing terminology and conceptual structures", the CFR can certainly be relevant in providing only aims at presenting the legislators with practical options.[14]

ers have delivered their draft CFR, the Commission will need to select very carefully the parts which correspond to the common legislative objectives. It is already evident that only a part of the research will correspond to these conditions".

10 C. von Bar, "Coverage and Structure of the Academic Common Frame of Reference", (2007) *European Review of Contract Law (ERCL)* 356, has confessed, in relation to the drafting of the CFR, that "It is a unique experience (...) to work under the utmost time pressure generated by one Commission department while at the same time other departments which were not involved in the negotiations here and there leave one with the impression that the worst we can do is to fulfill our contract".

11 This was the option, however, from the very outset: see C. von Bar, "Le group d'études sur un Code civil européen", (2001) *RIDC* 126.

12 Actually, the extent of the comparative research and, especially, the question whether the comparative notes are drafted before or after the black letter rules was vividly debated at the Lleida Conference.

13 According to C. von Bar (n. 10), 350, the academic CFR "is a text serving as a source of inspiration for law making and law teaching at all levels".

14 H. Beale, "The Future of the Common Frame of Reference", (2007) *ERCL* 257, at 268. See also H. Schulte Nölke, "EC Law on the Formation of Contract – from the Common Frame of Reference to the Blue Button", (2007) *ERCL* 332, at 344-348.

Furthermore, for the first time the European legal community, and indeed the global legal community, has a body of authentically European provisions, suitable for adoption as national law or capable of inspiring amendments of national law,[15] or simply an object of scholar debate. Even sharp criticism must be welcome.[16] It has to be borne in mind that the SGECC has tackled intricate matters such as transfer of movable property, a regulation that stands astride contract law and property law. Isabel González and Carlos Díez's contribution illuminates knotty problems arising from transfer of ownership. On the other hand, Anna Veneziano points out the necessity of solving the pending issue of the protection of consumers, especially in relation to sales.

Scholars contemplate the political leaders will embrace the CFR as a valuable *toolbox* for legislation, and not just as a *Professorenrecht* project. But the CFR cannot be the unique way to foster harmonization. Spontaneous harmonization[17] can result from the circulation of ideas and models, broadly applicable comparative research, and successful legal transplants.[18] Gema Tomás's chapter illustrates such spontaneous harmonization in the field of damages for contractual fraud. Necessity may also yield spontaneous harmonization, as the case of trusts. Marius de Waal's contribution makes this last point explicit by demonstrating a longstanding, but maybe seldom noticed basis for a European law of trust. Rosa Miquel's paper reminds us that the efficacy of civil harmonization depends to an extent upon harmonization of procedural law.

The CFR does not question the role of national laws. For, as Willem van Boom and Jan Smits suggest, harmonization should not to be exhaustive across the entire spectrum of regulation of obligations. But national laws are likely to experiment profound amendments *à la européenne*. The CFR offers the most euro-sceptical among the scholars an extra reason to approach the new European private law, while they seek to preserve the indispensable coherence of national legislations, especially their civil codes. Euro-sceptical perspectives

---

15 See M. W. Hesselink, "The Ideal of Codification and the Dynamics of Europeanisation: The Dutch Experience", in Vogenauer/Weatherill (n. 3), p. 39 ff.

16 The first assessments are coming to light: N. Jansen, "Negotiorum gestio und Benevolent Intervention in Another's Affairs: Principles of European Law?", (2007) *ZEuP* 958; R. Zimmermann, N. Jansen, "Grundregeln des bestehenden Gemeinschaftsprivatrechts?", (2007) *Juristenzeitung* 1113; id., "Principles of the Existing EC Contract Law?", (2008) *Modern Law Review* (forthcoming). From another perspective, O. Lando, "The Structure and the Legal Values of the Common Frame of Reference", (2007) *ERCL* 245, at 251 ff, has criticized the too much liberal character of the CFR.

17 Smits (n. 8) 19 f; M. B.M. Loos, "The influence of European consumer law on general contract law and the need for spontaneous harmonisation", Centre for the Study of European Contract Law Working Paper Series No. 2006/02.

18 See A. Watson, *Legal Transplants: An Approach to Comparative Law* (2nd ed., 1993); J. M. Smits, "On Successful Legal Transplants in a Future Ius commune Europaeum", in: A. Harding, E. Örücü (ed.), *Comparative Law in the 21st Century* (2002), 137 ff; A. Vaquer, "Verwirkung *versus* Laches: A Tale of Two Legal Transplants", (2006) *Tulane European & Civil Law Forum (Essays in Honor of Shael Herman)* 53.

are indeed crucial for coherent legal development, because any law – soft law included– requires the ongoing collaboration of the legal profession.

To conclude, I should like to express my gratitude to the University of Lleida, to its Faculty of Law and Economy, to the Government of Catalonia (Department of Innovation & Universities and Department of Justice) and the *Diputació de Lleida* for having generously funded the Conference, to Shael Herman for sharing his wisdom with me, and finally to Andrés Cosialls, Diana Lorenzo and Gerard Castells for their assistance in organizing the Conference.

Antoni Vaquer
Lleida, February 2008

CHAPTER 14 **European Private Law without European Law on Civil Procedure?**

Rosa Miquel Sala

CHAPTER I

Legal History and Comparative Law

Reinhard Zimmermann*

I.

Let me begin these words on an autobiographical note. When I decided to study law, my interests in history and in Latin naturally led me to take whatever courses were available on Roman law. I enjoyed these courses very much. Yet, for me there was something deeply unsatisfactory in all lectures and textbooks on Roman law leading up to Justinian, and all lectures and textbooks on modern German law starting with the BGB or, at best, its *travaux préparatoires* in the late 19th century. Roman law and modern private law appeared to constitute two different intellectual worlds. At the same time, even for a second- or third-year student is was easy to see that there were connections: Latin legal maxims such as *in pari turpitudine, interpretatio contra proferentem, impossibilium nulla obligatio*; basic legal concepts such as delict, *negotiorum gestio, diligentia quam in suis*; systematic subdivisions such as the ones between contract and delict, the law of obligations and property law, or loans for use and loans for consumption: on just about every level from terminology to rules, principles, institutions and legal arguments there was much in modern law that was familiar to the student of Roman law, but also in many ways interestingly different.[1] The same was true when I was made to look beyond the geographical borders of modern Germany: French law, Italian law, or English law were presented as self-contained intellectual constructs and certainly appeared to be different in some respects; but, at the same time, there was also much that was familiar.[2]

I was particularly fortunate in receiving my first "call" (as we express it somewhat oddly in Germany) to a chair of Roman and Comparative Law at the University of Cape Town in 1981. I, therefore, had to teach both subjects that had attracted my attention. Moreover, the application of Roman-Dutch law in South Africa is of particular interest for both the legal historian and the comparative lawyer.[3] For, on the one hand, the tradition of the Roman-Canon *ius commune* is still alive that has prevailed on the European Continent until it was replaced by the great codifications. On the other hand, classical Roman-Dutch law has experienced a reception of concepts, rules and thinking patterns from the English common law. South Africa has thus become a mixed legal system: a synthesis of civil law and common law with its own characteristic identity.[4] At the University of Cape Town in the 1980's Roman law was still an obligatory subject.[5] It was

* Director, Max Planck Institute for Comparative and International Private Law, Hamburg.

1 See R. Zimmermann, "Europa und das römische Recht", (2002) 202 *Archiv für die civilistische Praxis* 243 ff.; *idem*, "Römisches Recht und europäische Kultur", [2007] *Juristenzeitung* 1 ff.

2 For England, see R. Zimmermann, "Der europäische Charakter des englischen Rechts", (1993) 1 *Zeitschrift für Europäisches Privatrecht* 4 ff.

3 For an overview, see R. Zimmermann, *Das römisch-holländische Recht* (1983).

4 R. Zimmermann, D. Visser (eds.), *Southern Cross: Civil Law and Common Law* (1996)

5 For background, see R. Zimmermann, "Roman Law in a Mixed Legal System: The South African Experience", in: R. Evans-Jones (ed.), *The Civil Law Tradition in Scotland* (1995), p. 41 ff.

obvious to me that it should not be taught in an antiquarian spirit but as the foundation of a tradition that has decisively moulded our own legal identity. That was the origin of my book on the Roman foundations of the civilian tradition in the law of obligations.[6] It has been said, occasionally, that the approach adopted in that book is biased in favour of establishing continuity.[7] I do not think that this is true. For the emphasis is as much on change as it is on continuity. In the words of Harold Berman that I have often quoted:[8] "The concept of a ... system of law depended for its vitality on the belief in the ongoing character of law, its capacity for growth over generations and centuries – a belief which is uniquely Western. The body of law only survives because it contains a built-in mechanism for organic change."[9] European private law has been subject to constant adaptation; it has been able to react to changed circumstances and new situations, and it has always displayed an extraordinary capacity for integration. Medieval Roman law was no longer the Roman law of classical antiquity, the *usus modernus pandectarum* no longer corresponded to the *usus medii aevi*, and pandectist legal doctrine was a far cry from the *usus modernus*. At the same time, there were considerable regional variations in the application of Roman law. Thus, in the early modern period, we find Roman-Dutch law existing side by side with Roman-Frisian law,[10] Roman-Scots law, *ius Romanum Saxonicum, Hispanicum* etc. Many individual legal problems were solved differently in different parts of Europe. The texts contained in the *Corpus Juris* were no longer regarded as absolutely binding authority: one could generalize and further develop the ideas contained in them, critically examine them, or even declare them abrogated by disuse.[11] Still, however, they constituted the "legal grammar" for the discussion of private law problems because, in all Universities throughout Europe, they occupied the central place in the study of secular law. The civilian tradition is thus marked by considerable diversity as much as by a fundamental intelletual unity; by change as much as by continuity.

---

6 R. Zimmermann, *The Law of Obligations: Roman Foundations of the Civilian Tradition* (1990); paperback edition (1996).

7 See, most recently, the discussion and the references in R. Manko, "Is the Socialist Legal Tradition 'Dead and Buried'? The Continuity of Certain Elements of Socialist Legal Culture in Polish Civil Procedure", in: T. Wilhelmsson, E. Paunio, A. Pohjolainen (eds.), *Private Law and the Many Cultures of Europe* (2007), p. 85.

8 See, for example, R. Zimmermann, "Das römisch-kanonische ius commune als Grundlage europäischer Rechtseinheit", [1992] *Juristenzeitung* 12; *idem*, "The Law of Obligations – Character and Influence of the Civilian Tradition", (1992) 3 *Stellenbosch Law Review* 6.

9 H.J. Berman, *Law and Revolution*, vol. I (1983), 9; cf. also, e.g., P. Glenn, *Legal Traditions of the World*, 2nd ed. (2004), p. 146 ff.

10 On which see J.H.A. Lokin, F. Brandsma, C. Jansen, *Roman-Frisian Law of the 17th and 18th Century* (2003).

11 Thus, books such as P. Bugnyon, *Tractatus legum abrogatarum et inusitatarum in omnibus curiis, terris, jurisdictionibus, et dominis regni Franciae*, (1563), and S. van Groenewegen van der Made, *Tractatus de legibus abrogatis et inusitatis in Hollandia vicinisque regionibus* (1649), were written.

Today, this fundamental intellectual unity is obscured by the existence of a wide variety of national legal systems and, above all, by the fact that these national legal systems are very widely regarded as comprehensive and autonomous systems of legal rules.[12] Obviously, there are many differences among the modern private law codifications. But, equally obviously, they constitute manifestations of one and the same legal tradition.[13] Contrary to what is sometimes stated, comparative scholarship involves exploring both similarities and differences;[14] and what historical scholarship can contribute is to explain these differences (can they be attributed to differences in cultural environment, social development, or economic basis, to historical accident, misunderstanding, or choice of different sources?) and to recreate an awareness of what the European legal systems have in common.[15] This type of critical inquiry, I think, can pave the way for rational discussions including, if one wants to harmonize the laws prevailing in Europe, a rational discussion as to how the existing differences may be overcome.[16] In what follows I would like to illustrate what can be done by looking at a number of examples. In doing so, I propose, in a way, to turn the tables because my examples are taken from the work of those who have so kindly agreed to take part in the proceedings today.

II.

1) Everywhere in Europe, except for Scandinavia, Ireland and Great Britain, set-off operates in one of two ways. Either both obligations are extinguished, automatically, from the day of their co-existence ("de plein droit par la seule force de la loi, même à l'insu des débiteurs", as Art. 1290 *Code civil* puts it), or the right of set-off has to be exercised by notice to the other party; both obligations are then, however, deemed to have expired at the moment at which, being suitable for set-off, they first confronted each other (this is stated, perhaps most prominently, in § 389 BGB). The French model of set-off (that has

12 For Germany, see R. Zimmermann, "Das Bürgerliche Gesetzbuch und die Entwicklung des Bürgerlichen Rechts", in: M. Schmoeckel, J. Rückert, R. Zimmermann (eds.), *Historisch-kritischer Kommentar zum BGB*, vol. I, (2003), p. 1 ff.

13 The theme is further developed in R. Zimmermann, "The Civil Law in European Codes", in: H.L. MacQueen, A. Vaquer, S. Espiau Espiau (eds.), *Regional Private Laws and Codification in Europe* (2003), p. 18 ff.

14 See the discussion in G. Dannemann, "Comparative Law: Study of Similarities or Differences?", in: M. Reimann, R. Zimmermann (eds.), *The Oxford Handbook of Comparative Law* (2006), p. 383 ff.

15 Cf. also J. Gordley, "Comparative Law and Legal History", in: M. Reimann, R. Zimmermann (eds.), *The Oxford Handbook of Comparative Law* (2006), 753 ff.; and see his work *Foundations of Private Law: Property, Tort, Contract, Unjust Enrichment* (2006).

16 R. Zimmermann, "Savignys Vermächtnis: Rechtsgeschichte, Rechtsvergleichung und die Begründung einer Europäischen Rechtswissenschaft", [1998] *Juristische Blätter* 273 ff.

been adopted, for example, in Belgium, Austria, Spain and Italy) is based on two sources from the *Corpus Juris* which indicate that set-off operates "ipso iure".[17] The draftsmen of the German Civil Code, on the other hand, focused their attention on a phrase used by Justinian which appeared to demonstrate that set-off specifically had to be raised, or pleaded, by the defendant in the course of legal proceedings.[18] Above all, however, they based their decision on the case law of the Supreme Courts in Germany during the second half of the 19th century where it had come to be recognized that even an extrajudicial declaration of the intention to set off two claims against each other had the effect of extinguishing these claims.[19] The German model of set-off subsequently gained acceptance in many European countries.[20] Even in France, courts and legal writers have found it impractical literally to implement the regime envisaged by Art. 1290 *Code civil*. Following the lead provided by pandectist scholarship they have effectively attributed decisive influence to the will of one of the parties to bring about the mutual extinction of the obligation.[21] As a result, there is indeed, as Pascal Pichonnaz has put it, a "convergence avancée" among the European legal systems.[22]

However, even the more modern, i.e. the German, solution suffers from a severe doctrinal flaw: the notion of retrospectivity. Retrospecitvity constituted an attempt, by nineteenth-century German legal doctrine, to reconcile the above-mentioned Roman sources with each other. In the course of time, it has become firmly entrenched, in prevailing legal ideology, as an essential characteristic of a declaration of set-off.[23] Yet, as Pascal Pichonnaz has demonstrated, it is based on a centuries-old misunderstanding.[24] The phrase *ipso iure* was used, in classical Roman law, in the context of the banker's *agere cum compensatione*.[25] But it had merely been intended to indicate that this type of set-off was not effected by the judge. The banker himself was forced, by virtue of the *formula* granted to him by the praetor, to reduce his claim by the amount of the other party's counterclaim. The plaintiff was thus made *ipso iure*, i.e. by the law itself, to effect set-off. It is

---

17 Inst. IV, 6, 30; C. 4, 31, 14 pr.

18 C. 4, 31, 14, 1.

19 On the development in Germany, see R. Zimmermann, in: M. Schmoeckel, J. Rückert, R. Zimmermann (eds.), *Historisch-kritischer Kommentar zum BGB*, vol. II (2007), §§ 387 – 396, nn. 12 ff.

20 It has even been followed in Austrian law, in spite of the fact that § 1438 ABGB appears to endorse the *ipso-iure* effect of set-off; and, in spite of Art. 1242 *Codice civile*, it enjoys widespread support in Italian law.

21 P. Pichonnaz, *La compensation: Analyse historique et comparative des modes de compenser non conventionnels* (2001), p. 505 ff.

22 Pichonnaz (n. 21), p. 601 ff.

23 R. Zimmermann, *Comparative Foundations of a European Law of Set-Off and Prescription* (2002), p. 39 ff.

24 Pichonnaz (n. 21), p. 9 ff. (particularly 127 ff., 295 ff.); cf. also *Historisch-kritischer Kommentar*/Zimmermann (n. 19) §§ 387 – 396, nn. 5 ff.

25 Paul. D. 16, 2, 21; C. 4, 31, 4.

probable that Justinian also still attributed *ex nunc* effect to set-off.[26] The decisive turn came with the Glossators who reinterpreted set-off *ipso iure* as a form of set-off which occurred automatically, *sine facto hominis*. This misunderstanding was to cast its shadow on the discussions concerning set-off in all Continental legal systems, no matter whether they belong to the Romanistic or the Germanic legal families. The Principles of European Contract Law are the first important legal instrument that has made a conscious effort to emerge from this shadow when they state in Art. 13:106: "Set-off discharges the obligations, as far as they are coextensive, as from the time of notice".[27]

What does that teach us? If we look at the Continental European landscape, we observe two different solutions to one and the same legal problem. It is only as the result of an historical inquiry that we start to understand that situation. For, (i) we can now explain the reason for this difference. It lies in the reception of Roman law, with different sources having provided the starting point for different strands of tradition. Moreover (ii) we can trace the development of the problem in the codifications from 1804 to 1992 and in the legal literature relating to these codifications; and we can see a clear convergence towards the model established in the German Civil Code. And finally (iii) we become aware to what extent our thinking is dominated by patterns from the past. The concept of set-off operating retrospectively has been shown to have been based on a misunderstanding of the Roman sources. That misunderstanding was not a productive one,[28] and the modern trend, as evidenced by both the Principles of European Contract Law and the UNIDROIT Principles of International Commercial Contracts is to revert to the solution adopted in Roman law. It appears to be both clearer and more practicable than the *ex-tunc* effect of set-off[29] and conforms to Bernhard Windscheid's observation that retrospectivity is a fiction that should be avoided as far as possible.[30]

2) An historical inquiry is not, of course, bound to reveal that a solution accepted in Roman law may also be suitable today. More often, we find the situation that what worked well in the past has become dysfunctional in modern law. The history of the law of delict provides an example, as Nils Jansen has demon-

---

26 Pichonnaz (n. 21), p. 260 ff.

27 Cf. also Art. 8.5 (3) UNIDROIT *Principles of International Commercial Contracts.*

28 The term "productive misunderstanding" was coined, at least for legal history, by H.R. Hoetink (who, in turn, took it over from theological literature): H.R. Hoetink, *Rechtsgeleerde opstellen* (1982), p. 34 f., p. 266 f.

29 O. Lando, E. Clive, A. Prüm, R. Zimmermann (eds.), *Principles of European Contract Law*, Part III (2003), p. 151 f.

30 B. Windscheid, *Lehrbuch des Pandektenrechts*, vol. II, 7th ed. (1891), 294 (§ 349, 4), n. 12 *in fine*. It is hardly surprising, in view of this, that Windscheid rejected the notion of retrospectivity *de lege ferenda*; see *Historisch-kritischer Kommentar*/Zimmermann (n. 19) §§ 387-396, n. 24.

strated in his great work on the structure of liability law.[31] The law of delict, in the various Continental legal systems, rests on the same historical foundations – in the era of the *ius commune* it constituted an *usus modernus* of Aquilian liability which was reconceptualized under the influence of Natural law theory[32] –, and the ideas prevailing on the Continent have also influenced the development of English law.[33] At the same time, however, in the eighteenth and nineteenth centuries the modernized version of Roman law was no longer really modern. In its basic structure it was still essentially geared towards the sanctioning of private wrongs rather than the reasonable allocation of losses.[34] That was a problem which European legal systems only started to grapple with in the course of the nineteenth century, by which time the first wave of codifications had contributed to a national isolation of the legal discourse. Particularly, therefore, every legal system had to devise its own way of dealing with the problem of strict liability. As a result, the European legal landscape became considerably more patchy in this field than in that of contract law. The development was similar only in so far as it was attempted to supplement, rather than to challenge, the conceptual structure of a law of delict still revolving around the notions of wrongfulness and fault. This has led to a situation which is characterized, at least in some respects, by a lack of fundamental concepts which are both common to the various legal systems and teleologically satisfactory.[35] Thus, we have here the situation that, as a result of a legal institution changing its function, its conceptual infrastructure has become inadequate. The consequence, obviously, cannot be to perpetuate the concepts inherited from Roman law; but we will have to devise a doctrinal structure that is recognizably European and reflects the function of a modern liability law to achieve a reasonable loss-allocation.[36] That is, as Nils Jansen has also pointed out, a constructive task that cannot be tackled by historical or comparative analysis.[37] But it can only be tackled after historical and comparative analysis has cleared the field.

3) The fruitful and productive tension between change and continuity, and unity and diversity, is equally evident in studies tracing the migration of legal doctrines or concepts from one legal system to another.[38] Antoni Vaquer's work

[31] N. Jansen, *Die Struktur des Haftungsrechts: Geschichte, Theorie und Dogmatik außervertraglicher Ansprüche auf Schadensersatz* (2003).

[32] *Law of Obligations* (n. 6), p. 1017 ff.; N. Jansen (n. 31), p. 271 ff.

[33] D. Ibbetson, "Harmonisation of the Law of Tort and Delict: A Comparative and Historical Perspective", in: R. Zimmermann (ed.), *Grundstrukturen des Europäischen Deliktsrechts* (2003), p. 133 ff.

[34] N. Jansen (n. 31), p. 181 ff.

[35] N. Jansen, *Binnenmarkt, Privatrecht und europäische Identität* (2004), p. 33 ff.

[36] See N. Jansen (n. 31), p. 389 ff.

[37] N. Jansen (n. 35), p. 64 ff.; idem, "Dogmatik, Erkenntnis und Theorie im europäischen Privatrecht" (2005) 13 *Zeitschrift für Europäisches Privatrecht* 750 ff.

[38] Generally, see M. Graziadei, "Comparative Law as the Study of Transplants and Receptions", in: M. Reimann, R. Zimmermann (eds.), *The Oxford Handbook of Comparative Law* (2006), p. 441 ff.

provides a number of examples, among them the reception of the German doctrine of *Verwirkung* in Spanish law.[39] The path was paved by the great esteem in which German legal doctrine has traditionally been held in Spain, even if, particularly during the first years of General Franco's dictatorship, influential authors called for the preservation of the Spanishness of Spanish law and for the rejection of extraneous influences.[40] Yet, from 1933 onwards, a Spanish translation of Ludwig Enneccerus, Theodor Kipp, and Martin Wolff, *Lehrbuch des Bürgerlichen Rechts*, was published and thus acquainted Spanish readers in their own language, *inter alia*, with the doctine of *Verwirkung*. In 1959 José Puig Brutau not only translated Gustav Boehmer's book on *Praxis der richterlichen Rechtsschöpfung* (1958) but also specifically drew attention to the desirability of accepting the doctrine of *Verwirkung* in Spanish law. Shortly thereafter one of the most prominent Spanish legal scholars, Luis Díez-Picazo, published a fundamental monograph on the overarching notion of *venire contra factum proprium*.[41] Díez-Picazo clearly drew his inspiration from German law, particularly a work by Erwin Riezler;[42] he analyzed the existing Spanish case law in the light of *venire contra factum proprium* and managed to demonstrate how that notion could beneficially be incorporated into Spanish law. That study marked the break-through of the doctrine of *Verwirkung* on the level of legal scholarship. Judicial acceptance only came in 1992;[43] it followed in the wake of the reform of the *Título preliminar* of the *Código civil*, in the course of which a new Art. 7 was introduced which states that rights have to be exercised in conformity with the requirements of good faith;[44] and it also followed the translation into Spanish of Franz Wieacker's seminal work on how to structure the application of a general good faith provision such as § 242 BGB or Art. 7 *Código civil*.[45] Thus, it can be said today that the doctrine of *retraso desleal* is part of Spanish law; that it is based on the German notion of *Verwirkung*; and that it can be intellectually related to a general good faith provision in Spanish law in a very similar way as in German law. At the same time, *retraso desleal* and *Verwirkung* are not identical: "Verwirkung", as Antoni Vaquer puts it, "has travelled along its own paths

39 A. Vaquer, "Importing Foreign Doctrines: Yet Another Approach to the Unification of European Private Law? Incorporation of the Verwirkung Doctrine into Spanish Case Law" (2000) 8 *Zeitschrift für Europäisches Privatrecht* 301 ff.; cf. also idem, "Verwirkung versus Laches: A Tale of Two Legal Transplants", (2006) 21 *Tulane European and Civil Law Forum* (= Companions and Crossroads: Essays in Honor of Shael Herman) 53 ff.

40 For references for this, and the following statements, see A. Vaquer (2000) 8 *Zeitschrift für Europäisches Privatrecht* 302.

41 L. Díez-Picazo P. de León, *La doctrina de los proprios actos* (1962); on which see also C. Eckl, *Treu und Glauben im spanischen Vertragsrecht* (2007), p. 121 ff.

42 E. Riezler, *Venire contra factum proprium* (1912).

43 For references, see A. Vaquer, (2000) 8 *Zeitschrift für Europäisches Privatrecht* 303 f.; *Eckl* (n. 41), p. 278 ff.

44 For the details, see Eckl (n. 41), p. 139 ff.

45 F. Wieacker, *Zur rechtstheoretischen Präzisierung des § 242 BGB* (1956).

in Spanish law".[46] It tends to be applied more restrictively than in German law, it requires prejudice to the position of the other party, and it has to be distinguished from the established legal doctrine of tacit renunciation of a right.[47] As a result, what appears to be a typical case of *Verwirkung* in German law may appear in an entirely different light in Spain.[48] That makes us realize that law, as a rule, undergoes a transformation when it is transplanted; and we can also see that legal transfers can be successful[49] even if they cut across the boundaries of the established legal families.

4) Transplant, reception, the transfer of legal ideas: these are also key terms for the analysis of mixed legal systems.[50] Scots law was turned into Roman-Scots law with the reception of the tradition of the learned laws in the late Middle Ages and early modern period; and in the course of the 19th and early 20th centuries the influence of English law brought about further changes, both in substance and appearance.[51] A similar story can be told about Roman-Dutch law, first in the Netherlands and subsequently in South Africa.[52] Hector MacQueen has emphasized that modern Scots contract law shares a number of characteristic features with other civilian legal systems:[53] it recognizes contracts in favour of third parties, it accepts an order for specific performance ("specific implement") as the primary right of the creditor, and it does not have a doctrine of consideration. But we also find at least an equal number of rules and legal institutions that Scots law has in common with, i.e. usually borrowed from, English law: an essentially unified concept of breach of contract, breach of contract by repudiation, or the doctrine of the undisclosed principal in the law of agency. Hector MacQueen has also drawn attention to the fact that in all these cases Scots law has anticipated the position eventually adopted by the so-called Lando-Commis-

---

46 21 (2006) *Tulane European and Civil Law Forum* 65.

47 A. Vaquer, (2000) 8 *Zeitschrift für Europäisches Privatrecht* 305 ff.; idem, (2006) 21 *Tulane European and Civil Law Forum* 64 ff.

48 See Case Study 22 (Sitting on one's rights) in: R. Zimmermann, S. Whittaker (eds.), *Good Faith in European Contract Law* (2000), p. 514 ff (515 ff. compared with 522).

49 J. Smits, "On Successful Legal Transplants in a Future Ius Commune Europaeum", in: Andrew Harding, Esin Örücü (eds.), *Comparative Law in the 21st Century* (2002), p. 142.

50 Generally, see V. Valentine Palmer, *Mixed Jurisdictions Worldwide: The Third Legal Family* (2001); J. du Plessis, "Comparative Law and the Study of Mixed Legal Systems", in: M. Reimann, R. Zimmermann (eds.), *The Oxford Handbook of Comparative Law* (2006), p. 477 ff.

51 K. Reid, R. Zimmermann (eds.), *A History of Private Law in Scotland*, 2 vols. (2000).

52 For the Netherlands, see R. Feenstra, R. Zimmermann (eds.), *Das römisch-holländische Recht: Fortschritte des Zivilrechts im 17. und 18. Jahrhundert* (1992); for South Africa, see E. Fagan, "Roman-Dutch Law in its South African Historical Context", in: Zimmermann/Visser (n. 4), p. 33 ff.

53 H.L. MacQueen, *Scots Law and the Road to the New Ius Commune*, Ius Commune Lectures on European Private Law, no. 1 (2000), p. 5 ff.

sion.[54] He has thus emphasized that there are historical experiences in a legal system at the crossroads of common law and civilian jurisprudence which European lawyers in search of a new *ius commune* may be able to draw upon.[55] The same can be said about the development of Roman-Dutch law in South Africa;[56] and in their contribution to "Double Cross", MacQueen and Cockrell have embarked on a detailed comparison not only of Scots and South African law relating to illegality in contract law, but also of chapter 15 of the Principles of European Contract Law, in order to validate that claim.[57] Last year a book was published – it was co-edited by Hector MacQueen – which, *inter alia*, attempted to investigate what criticisms might be made of the Principles of European Contract Law in the light of the experiences gathered in Scotland and South Africa (and also: to what extent Scots and South African law might benefit from a reform along the line proposed by the Principles of European Contract Law).[58] All these projects and studies are predicated upon a close intellectual relationship between the historical and comparative perspectives.[59]

5) So is the work that has recently been done by a scholar who is present tonight and whom I want to mention because I have known him for a longer time than anybody else here in the room and because he had the longest way to travel to Lleida: Marius de Waal. He has embarked on the study of an area of law where both Scots and South African law have found a "third way" between modern civilian systems and the common law: trusts.[60] The development was different in both countries. In Scotland, the *fideicommissum* of Roman law appears to have been an important source. English law gave the Scottish trust its name, but in other respects exercised little influence until the 19th century when the

54 Which has prepared the Principles of European Contract Law; see R. Zimmermann, "The Principles of European Contract Law: Contemporary Manifestations of the Old, and Possible Foundations for a New, European Scholarship of Private Law", in: F. Faust, G. Thüsing (eds.), *Beyond Borders: Perspectives on International and Comparative Law – Symposium in Honour of Hein Kötz* (2006), p. 111 ff.

55 MacQueen (n. 53), p. 1 ff.

56 R. Zimmermann, "Gemeines Recht heute: Das Kreuz des Südens", in: J. Eckert (Hg.), *Der praktische Nutzen der Rechtsgeschichte* (2003), p. 601 ff.; idem, *Roman Law, Contemporary Law, European Law: The Civilian Tradition Today* (2001), p. 126 ff.

57 H. MacQueen, A. Cockrell, "Illegal Contracts", in: R. Zimmermann, D. Visser, K. Reid (eds.), *Mixed Legal Systems in Comparative Perspective: Property and Obligations in Scotland and South Africa* (2004), p. 143 ff.

58 H. MacQueen, R. Zimmermann (eds.), *European Contract Law: Scots and South African Perspectives* (2006).

59 See, concerning Scottish legal history, H.L. MacQueen, "Mixture or Muddle? Teaching and Research in Scottish Legal History" (1997) 5 *Zeitschrift für Europäisches Privatrecht* 369 ff.

60 M.J. de Waal, "Trust Law", in: Jan M. Smits (ed.), *Elgar Encyclopedia of Comparative Law* (2006), p. 755 ff.; idem, "Comparative Succession Law", in: M. Reimann, R. Zimmermann (eds.), *The Oxford Handbook of Comparative Law* (2006), p. 1070 ff. (1087 ff.).

essentials of the Scottish trust had already become well established.[61] In South Africa, on the other hand, it was indeed the English trust that was introduced by British settlers in the course of the 19th century; however, it was soon transformed into a civilian institution.[62] In the end result, therefore, both Scotland and South Africa have produced a civilian form of trust: a proper trust, not just a "so-called" trust, as Marius de Waal has pointed out.[63] It is characterized by four core elements: (i) a trustee who has a fiduciary position; (ii) a separation between the trustee's personal estate and the trust estate; (iii) the operation of real subrogation; and (iv) the construction of trusteeship as an office.[64] The trust, therefore, does not have to be defined, as it traditionally is, in terms of a division of title between the trustee and the beneficiary. That is merely the specifically English manifestation of the trust concept; neither historically, nor rationally can it be said to constitute one of its defining features.[65] That is, obviously, of considerable interest for those countries that wish to introduce the trust into a legal system that has a law of property based on Roman law and also does not recognize the institutional separation of law and equity;[66] and it is hardly surprising that the draftsmen of the Principles of European Trust Law have been inspired by the Roman-Dutch and, particularly, Scots experiences.[67]

III.

It is a great honour and pleasure to be receiving this doctoral degree from the University of Lleida. Under the name of Ilerda, Lleida was a city of considerable importance already in the Roman province of *Hispania*

[61] K.C.G. Reid, "National Report for Scotland", in: D.J. Hayton, S.C.J.J. Kortmann, H.L.E. Verhagen (eds.), *Principles of European Trust Law* (1999), p. 68. For a historical analysis of the development of trust law in Scotland, see George Gretton, "Trusts", in: Reid/Zimmermann I (n. 51), p. 480 ff.

[62] T. Honoré, "Trust", in: Zimmermann/Visser (n. 4), p. 847 ff. – For Louisiana, see A.N. Yiannopoulos, "Trust and the Civil Law: The Louisiana Experience", in: V.V. Palmer (ed.), *Louisiana: Microcosm of a Mixed Jurisdiction* (1999), p. 213 ff.; for Québec, see R. Becker, *Die fiducie von Québec und der Trust* (2007).

[63] M. de Waal, "The Core Elements of the Trust: Aspects of the English, Scottish, and South African Trusts Compared" (2000) 117 *South African Law Journal* 569.

[64] De Waal, (2000) 117 *South African Law Journal* 548 ff.; cf. also *idem*, "In Search of a Model for the Introduction of the Trust into a Civilian Context", (2001) 12 *Stellenbosch Law Review* 63 ff.

[65] See also George Gretton, "Trusts without Equity", (2000) 49 *International and Comparative Law Quarterly* 599 ff.

[66] See for France loi no. 2007-211 du 19 février 2007 instituant la fiducie. That statute introduces the fiducie into art. 2011 ff. Code civil. For comment, see the contributions to a symposium under the title "La fiducie, révolution juridique et pratique des affaires", as printed in (2007) *La Semaine Juridique – Entreprise et affaires* 2050 ff. (6 September 2007) and the Dossier «La fiducie» in (2007) *Recueil Dalloz* 1347 ff. (24 May 2007).

[67] Hayton/Kortmann/Verhagen (n. 61).

Tarraconensis which played a strategic role in the first year of the civil war between Gaius Julius Caesar and his opponents.[68] It produced the only significant Roman law scholar of the period up to 1250 hailing from the Iberian peninsula (Pontius de Ilerda);[69] and, in around 1300, it became the seat of one of the oldest Universities in that part of Europe.[70] Today, the law faculty of the University of Lleida has established itself as a center of learning at the juncture between regional, national and European law. Scholars from the University of Lleida, and Antoni Vaquer in particular, have been active in studying the impact of the process of Europeanization of private law on Catalonia and in bringing to bear, at the same time, the Catalan and the Spanish voices on the discussions about European private law.[71] But it is a particularly pleasant occasion also on account of the fact that so many friends and colleagues are present with whom I have had the privilege of cooperating over a considerable period of time. I have mentioned Antoni Vaquer, Nils Jansen, Hector MacQueen, Pascal Pichonnaz and Marius de Waal because they have spoken here today, or will be speaking tomorrow. They are five scholars from five different jurisdictions. They are all legal historians and comparative lawyers; and they all also regularly contribute to the development of legal doctrine in their respective jurisdictions. Their work reveals interesting differences in approach and outlook. But they would all agree, I think, that while the legal historian must not be the slave of current concerns, his work is of essential importance for enabling us to take stock, and to comprehend, our present legal condition. That knowledge, in itself, will not determine where we have to go. But an understanding of the past is the first and essential prerequisite for devising appropriate solutions for the present day and for the future. If we were just looking at the civilian legal systems as they stand today, we would have to devise a European regime of set-off either on the model of art. 1290 *Code civil* or § 389 BGB. The mere fact that they are both based on a misunderstanding of the Roman sources cannot prompt us to attribute a merely prospective effect to set-off. But it does make us aware of the fact that there is nothing self-evident about the notion of retrospectivity and that we, therefore, have to re-examine the substantive arguments that can be adduced in its favour. If we now know why the conceptual infrastructure of our modern law of delict has become dysfunctional, we still do not know how a modern conceptual infrastructure might look like; but we know from which angle we will have to construct it. A number of European legal systems (among them the Spanish one) have found the notion of *Verwirkung* attractive. That does not mean

[68] See, e.g., Gaius Iulius Caesar, *Commentarii Belli Civilis*, Liber I, 38, 4; Liber I, 48, 5. Cf. also Liber I, 59, 63, 69, 73 and 78, and Liber II, 17.

[69] H. Lange, M. Kriechbaum, *Römisches Recht im Mittelalter*, vol. II (2007), p. 16.

[70] Lange/Kriechbaum (n. 69) 102.

[71] See, e.g., the volumes edited by MacQueen/Vaquer/Espiau Espiau (n. 13) and S. Espiau Espiau, A Vaquer Aloy (eds.), *Bases de un Derecho Contractual Europeo* (2003), and A. Vaquer Aloy (ed.), *La tercera Parte de los Principios de Derecho Contractual Europeo* (2005), all of them based on conferences held at the University of Lleida.

that they all apply it in the same way. But it does indicate that some device for relaxing the *rigor iuris*, revolving around an autonomous notion of good faith,[72] may be required in a set of Principles of European Contract Law. The mere fact that it is perfectly possible to have a civilian trust does not mean that a civilian legal system has to move in that direction. And good or bad experiences with the notion of illegality in one legal system may prompt cognate legal systems to reconsider their own law; but such historical experiences can never have any prescriptive force. I am particularly lucky in having so many friends and colleagues with whom I share a keen interest in the development of European private law as well as the conviction that that development can benefit very much from historical and comparative study. Thank you all for having come to Lleida today.

I have been told that "Ilerdam videas" (may you see Lleida) is a proverbial curse. I cannot confirm that. I have seen Lleida and I have found great kindness, generosity and hospitality in this city. Thank you very much for hosting us all on such an auspicious occasion.

[72] See Art. 1:201 PECL; Art. 1.7 Unidroit Principles of International Commercial Contracts; and see the case studies in Zimmermann/Whittaker (n. 48).

CHAPTER 2

Reinhard Zimmermann and European Private Law

Nils Jansen*

We are very happy today to honour *Reinhard Zimmermann* as one of the leading European private lawyers of our times. Indeed, for me he is probably *the* leading European private lawyer today, because it was *Zimmermann* who opened new perspectives for European private law and at the same time paved the way to explore them. It is the aim of my little speech to justify this rather bold statement. Being a former student of *Zimmermann* I hope to be forgiven for starting of with a more personal remark: Until I read *Zimmermann's Law of Obligations*[1] for the first time, I had been a convinced believer in a theoretical, a-historical perspective on the law. Thus, for me it was a matter of course, that the state was the foundation of every legal system: Legal history, the law's past, was by definition irrelevant to a modern lawyer. It followed as a matter of course that there was no "European private law" – what could that be, apart from some regulations of the European Union? Now, reading *Zimmermann's* book was for me something like the Damascus experience of Saint Paul. I suddenly understood that private law was much more than the provisions of a code or the rules of a state – it is a substantial body of rules, principles, concepts and learned doctrine that develops over time. I realized that a legal system cannot be fully understood if it is cut off its historical roots. And I finally became aware of a European private law beyond the national legal systems.

I think that I am not the only European private lawyer who owes something like this to the *Law of Obligations*, and it is therefore appropriate to focus this *laudatio* on *Zimmermann's opus maximum*. Now, in a formal sense, the *Law of Obligations* is a mere textbook, written for students; and indeed, it is a perfect instrument for the classroom. But such a book would never have achieved its status as a highly authoritative legal text, unless there was more in it, a second dimension, so to speak. And indeed, this book opened new perspectives for European legal thinking. We can conceive of these new dimensions, if we recall three central ideas that already pervade the *Law of Obligations* and also *Zimmermann's* later work.

1. The first central idea consists in the conviction that the law is fully conceivable only if it is understood, from a historical perspective, as the result of a tradition of legal thinking. It is not the occasion here to justify this idea on a more theoretical basis[2] – the *Law of Obligations* is in itself sufficient for proving it. But it might be asked whether this idea was really new in 1989: Were there not chairs for legal history in all faculties in Germany (and, indeed, in Europe)? And is it not true that the idea of a necessary connection between the present and the

* Professor, University of Münster.

1 *The Law of Obligations. Roman Foundations of the Civilian Tradition* (1989); Paperback ed. (1996).

2 N. Jansen, '"Tief ist der Brunnen der Vergangenheit". Funktion, Methode und Ausgangspunkt historischer Fragestellungen in der Privatrechtsdogmatik', (2005) 27 *Zeitschrift für Neuere Rechtsgeschichte* 202-228.

past was part of the romantic philosophy of *Savigny* and the German Historical School?

The correct answer to this question is "yes and no"; and "more no than yes". True, the abstract idea as such was not new. *Zimmermann* himself has pointed this out in his leading programmatic article "Savigny's Legacy".[3] But this idea had never been taken seriously and it had thus not been explored in any doctrinal detail: *Savigny* and the Historical School had discredited most writers and epochs of the *ius commune* as unscientific and too pragmatic. Accordingly, they argued on the basis of Justinian's Roman law and could therefore not see the 19th century law as resulting from developments between the 12th and the 18th centuries. In the 20th century, too, students were only taught Roman law; the connections between the ancient Roman law and the modern European landscape remained obscure. Of course, there had been books about the history of the Roman *ius commune*, most notably *Savigny's* "Geschichte des römischen Rechts im Mittelalter" (The History of Roman Law in Medieval Times),[4] in the 19th and *Franz Wieacker's* "Privatrechtsgeschichte der Neuzeit"[5] in the 20th century. But these works, important as they are, took an external perspective on legal history: they are about legal ideas and schools of thought, about universities and legal writers. These books are not about the substance of the law, about specific legal rules and principles or concrete doctrines. Thus, the idea of modern law being the result of a tradition of legal thinking remained abstract and rather sterile.

Now, there was also some literature on the European *ius commune*: there had been monographs and articles on specific rules or doctrines, exploring e.g. the medieval doctrines on breach of contract,[6] the Natural law contract theory,[7] or on the rules on private punishment and compensation.[8] But there was no comprehensive picture. Thus, the idea of the modern European legal systems emerging from a common legal tradition remained vague. True, there was the first volume of *Coing's* "European Private Law",[9] the result of the first golden years of the Frankfurt *Max Planck Institut für Rechtsgeschichte*. But this work, impressive

---

[3] 'Savigny's Legacy. Legal History, Comparative Law, and the Emergence of a European Legal Science' (1996) 112 *Law Quarterly Review* 576-605; German Translation as *Savignys Vermächtnis. Rechtsgeschichte, Rechtsvergleichung und die Begründung einer Europäischen Rechtswissenschaft* (1998).

[4] F.C. v. Savigny, *Geschichte des römischen Rechts im Mittelalter*, 6 vols. (1815-1831); 2nd ed. in 7 vol. (1834-1851).

[5] F. Wieacker, *Privatrechtsgeschichte der Neuzeit* (1952); 2nd ed. 1967; engl. translation by T. Weir, with a foreword by Zimmermann *A History of Private Law in Europe* (1995).

[6] H. Dilcher, *Die Theorie der Leistungsstörungen bei Glossatoren, Kommentatoren und Kanonisten* (1960).

[7] M. Diesselhorst, *Die Lehre des Hugo Grotius vom Versprechen* (1959).

[8] H. Wieling, *Interesse und Privatstrafe vom Mittelalter bis zum Bürgerlichen Gesetzbuch* (1970); see also H.. Lange, *Schadensersatz und Privatstrafe in der mittelalterlichen Rechtstheorie* (1955).

[9] H. Coing, *Europäisches Privatrecht*, vol. I: *Älteres Gemeines Recht (1500 bis 1800)* (1985). The second volume on the 19th century appeared only in 1989, together with the *Law of Obligations*.

as it is, was written as a handbook, offering an overview of the legal landscape around 1600. It did not tell stories of legal development, and thus it did not lead to a full historical understanding of our modern law. It was only *Zimmermann* who succeeded in painting a full historical picture of European private law.

This new perspective has proved immensely helpful and stimulating – this has not only been shown by the *Law of Obligations* itself but by the subsequent work of *Zimmermann* and young scholars who have followed his path.[10] Now, there was much more than a mere juxtaposition of a Roman rule and its modern successors: the European legal history became much richer: Canon law, Natural law – from the Late Scholastics until the 18th century German theorists –, Europe's different *iura propria*, and the progressive ideas of 17th and 18th centuries Dutch writers[11] became important elements of the European legal heritage. All this can be found in the *Law of Obligations*: Among the principal works, on which this book is based, are not only *Accursius, Bartolus, Donellus* and *Savigny*, but also modern doctrinal writers from the English, German, French, Italian

---

10 See, among others, U. Amelung, *Der Schutz der Privatheit im Zivilrecht* (2002); M. Bauer, Periculum emptoris. *Eine dogmengeschichtliche Untersuchung zur Gefahrtragung beim Kauf* (1998); J.A. Dieckmann, *Der Derivativregreß des Bürgen gegen den Hauptschuldner im englischen und deutschen Recht* (2003); S. Festner, *Interessenkonflikte im deutschen und englischen Vertretungsrecht* (2006); F. Fromholzer, *Consideration. US-amerikanisches Recht im Vergleich zum deutschen* (1997); W. Grobecker, *Implied terms und Treu und Glauben. Vertragsergänzung im englischen Recht in rechtsvergleichender Perspektive* (1999); P. Hellwege, *Die Rückabwicklung gegenseitiger Verträge als einheitliches Problem. deutsches, englisches und schottisches Recht in historisch-vergleichender Perspektive* (2004); N. Jansen, *Die Struktur des Haftungsrechts* (2003); id., *Binnenmarkt, Privatrecht und europäische Identität* (2004); J. Kleinschmidt, *Der Verzicht im Schuldrecht* (2004); S. Meier, *Irrtum und Zweckverfehlung. Die Rolle der Unjust-Gründe bei rechtsgrundlosen Leistungen im englischen Recht* (1999); R. Michaels, *Sachzuordnung durch Kaufvertrag. Traditionsprinzip, Konsensprinzip, ius ad rem in Geschichte, Theorie und geltendem Recht* (2002); P. Pichonnaz, *La Compensation* (2001); A. Richter, *Rechtsfähige Stiftung und Charitable Corporation* (2001); K. Rusch, *Gewinnhaftung bei Verletzung von Treuepflichten* (2003); T. Schindler, *Rechtsgeschäftliche Entscheidungsfreiheit und Drohung. Die englische duress-Lehre in rechtsvergleichender Perspektive* (2005); N. Schneider, Uberrima fides. *Treu und Glauben und vorvertragliche Aufklärungspflichten im englischen Recht* (2004); D.A. Verse, *Verwendungen im Eigentümer-Besitzer-Verhältnis* (1999); S. Vogenauer, *Die Auslegung von Gesetzen in England und auf dem Kontinent. eine vergleichende Untersuchung der Rechtsprechung und ihrer historischen Grundlagen* (2001); H. Walter, Actio Iniuriarum. *Der Schutz der Persönlichkeit im südafrikanischen Privatrecht* (1996); H. Wicke, Respondeat Superior. *Haftung für Verrichtungsgehilfen im römischen, römisch holländischen, englischen und südafrikanischen Recht* (2000). It would be wrong, though, to assume that all these works follow an identical method. Many of them have chosen a rather individual approach – some are written on a more historical, some on a more comparative, and some on a more theoretical basis. Yet, all of them have profited immensely from Zimmermann's inspiring influence.

11 R. Feenstra, R. Zimmermann (eds.), *Das römisch-holländische Recht. Fortschritte des Zivilrechts im 17. und 18. Jahrhundert* (1992); R. Zimmermann, "Das römisch-holländische Recht und seine Bedeutung für Europa" (1990) *Juristenzeitung* 825-838.

and South African legal systems and authorities like *Molina, Lessius* and *Grotius, Domat, Pothier* and *Christian Wolff*, or *Glanvill* and *William Jones, Ulrich Huber* and *Groenewegen*, or *Johann Schilter* and *Augustin Leyser*.

At the same time, Roman law was no longer an abstract ideal. Instead it was regarded as the main "origin" of European legal history. It followed that doctrinal legal history could become, in an important sense, critical: it was evident that fundamental concepts guiding modern legal thinking had become dysfunctional, because they had been conceived by Roman lawyers for purposes different to those inherent in modern law.[12] And it became apparent that modern rules or even fundamental principles of modern law may be the contingent result of earlier doctrinal or conceptual assumptions that are long outdated. *Zimmermann* has shown this for the implausible principle of retroactivity of set-off which had long been founded in an assumed "'essence' of set-off".[13]

2. This leads us to the second central idea of *Zimmermann's* work. It is the observation that the most important historical source of modern European law is not the ancient Roman law as such, but the rich civilian tradition of legal thinking[14] that has never been limited to the European continent but connects the continental legal systems with the English common law. Again, it might be doubted whether this observation was wholly new: is it not true that similar ideas can be found in *Koschaker's Europa und das römische Recht*?[15] Again, the answer is: "yes and no" and "more no than yes". *Zimmermann* does indeed subscribe to large parts of *Koschaker's* historical analysis and legal vision. He has made this explicit in another main programmatic article, for which he even borrowed the title of *Koschaker's* book.[16] But whereas *Koschaker* regarded the history of the common law as separated from the continent and described the English lawyers as "enemies of the reception",[17] *Zimmermann* has early emphasized that the *common law* had always been influenced by civilian ideas and that it must there-

[12] R. Zimmermann, "Wege zu einem europäischen Haftungsrecht", in: id. (ed.), *Grundstrukturen des Europäischen Deliktsrechts* (2003) 19, 29 f.; Jansen, *Haftungsrecht* (n. 10) 185-270.

[13] R. Zimmermann, *Roman Law, Contemporary Law, European Law. The Civilian Tradition Today* (2001) 118 f.; id., "Die Aufrechnung. Eine rechtsvergleichende Skizze zum Europäischen Vertragsrecht", in: *Festschrift für Dieter Medicus* (1999), p. 721 ff. The *ius commune's 'ipso-iure*-conception' of set-off is probably due to a misunderstanding of the Roman sources by the glossators; see P. Pichonnaz, "The Retroactive Effect of Set-Off", (2000) 68 *TR* 541-564.

[14] R. Zimmermann, "Das römisch-kanonische ius commune als Grundlage europäischer Rechtseinheit", (1992) *Juristenzeitung* 8-20; id. "Ius Commune and the Principles of European Contract Law: Contemporary Renewal of an Old Idea", in: MacQueen/Zimmermann, *Eureopan Contract Law* (n. 27) 1-42.

[15] P. Koschaker, *Europa und das römische Recht* (1947; 4th ed. 1966).

[16] R. Zimmermann, "Europa und das römische Recht" (2002) 202 *Archiv für die civilistische Praxis* 243-316; similarly id., *Roman Law, Contemporary Law, European Law* (n. 13), 107 ff.

[17] Koschaker (n. 15) 213 ff., 216 ff.

fore be regarded as a substantial element of our common legal tradition;[18] he has explained this in a couple of pathbreaking articles in more doctrinal detail.[19] Indeed, the close connection between the common law and the civilian legal tradition cannot fully be understood, if the influence of canon law and Natural law ideas on both Roman civilians and common lawyers is not adequately taken into consideration.

What is more, whereas *Koschaker* wrote about "the glossators", "the humanists" and "the reception", about "lawyers' law" as such, "Natural law" and the German Historical School, *Zimmermann* illustrated all this specifically for the law of obligations. Here, the impact of Natural law ideas or of the writers of the *usus modernus* could be seen and really understood. Thus, *Zimmermann* doubted whether the principle of good faith was a civilian peculiarity,[20] or whether the common-law idea of trust was alien to civilian systems[21]; and he described a convergence of different approaches to the law of unjust enrichment.[22] Thus, the historically founded unity of European legal scholarship was again much more than an abstract idea: it could be seen in actual legal practice.

3. The third idea is a constructive and innovative conception of this historical approach to European private law. It would be wrong to see *Zimmermann* as a leading figure of a retrospective "*ius commune*-approach", arguing for a kind of return to a supposedly golden age of the *ius commune*. On the contrary: *Zimmermann* has taken historical observations always as a starting point for arguments about a modernization of private law: his works have never been merely retrospective-contemplative ones. According to *Zimmermann*, the Europeanization of private law means to develop "beyond comparative law" and probably also beyond legal history to constructively devising "adequate conceptual tools which are both common to the national legal systems and teleologically satisfactory".[23]

18 Zimmermann, "Europa und das römische Recht" (n. 16), 255 ff. with further references.

19 R. Zimmermann, "Der europäische Charakter des englischen Rechts", (1993) 1 *Zeitschrift für Europäisches Privatrecht* 4-51; id., "Historische Verbindungen zwischen civil law and common law", in: P.-C. Müller-Graff (ed.), *Gemeinsames Privatrecht in der Europäischen Gemeinschaft* (1993), 47-70; id., "Savigny's Legacy" (n. 3), 587 ff., 582, 606, id., '"Heard melodies are sweet, but those unheard are sweeter ... "', (1993) 193 *Archiv für die civilistiche Praxis* 121, 123 ff., 131 ff.

20 Zimmermann,"Europa und das römische Recht" (n. 16), 271 ff.; see also S. Whittaker, R. Zimmermann (eds.), *Good Faith in European Contract Law* (2000).

21 Zimmermann, "Europa und das römische Recht" (n. 16), 278 ff., 286 ff.; see also R.H. Helmholz, R. Zimmermann (eds.), *Itinera Fiduciae. Trust and Treuhand in Historical Perspective* (1998).

22 Zimmermann, "Europa und das römische Recht" (n. 16), 292 ff.; see also id., "Unjustified Enrichment: The Modern Civilian Approach", (1995) 15 *Oxford Journal of Legal Studies* 403-429; D. Johnston, R. Zimmermann (eds.), *Unjustified Enrichment: Key Issues in Comparative Perspective* (2002); R. Zimmermann, *Grundstrukturen des europäischen Bereicherungsrechts* (2005).

23 R. Zimmermann, "Comparative Law and the Europeanization of Private Law", in: M. Reimann, R. Zimmermann (eds.), *The Oxford Handbook of Comparative Law* (2006), p. 539, 577.

This is obviously a highly innovative, constructive enterprise. It was therefore natural for *Zimmermann* to engage himself in the *Lando*-Project, where his influence can be especially seen in the innovative rules on set-off and prescription.[24] Already before he became a member of this group, *Zimmermann* had promoted these principles actively in a broad series of articles,[25] and later he made the *Principles* the object of thorough academic analyses,[26] most notably in his *European Contract Law*, where the *Lando*-Principles, a mixed legal system in themselves, are analyzed from the perspectives of the mixed legal systems of Scotland and South Africa.[27]

It should be emphasized that *Zimmermann* has never regarded the *Lando-Principles* as a means of legislatively unifying European private law, indeed, he is rather reluctant towards such a step in our days. For *Zimmermann* the *Principles* were an academic enterprise and a means of finding, again, a common legal language or "grammar" – in this respect, and only in this respect, he is indeed favouring ideas which resemble the historical *ius commune*.[28] Thus, it was no

[24] R. Zimmermann was originally not a member of the *Lando*-Commission, but he was the first to write on the Principles in Germany ("Konturen eines europäischen Vertragsrechts" [1995] *Juristenzeitung* 477-491); and he translated them – together with Christian von Bar – into German. Later he became an active, leading member of the commission; cf. O. Lando, E. Clive, A. Prüm, R. Zimmermann (eds.), *Principles of European Contract Law, Part III* (2003).

[25] Zimmermann (n. 24) 477-491; id., "Die 'Principles of European Contract Law', Teil I", (1995) 3 *Zeitschrift für Europäisches Privatrecht* 731-734; id. "Die 'Principles of European Contract Law', Teile II und III", (2000) 8 *Zeitschrift für Europäisches Privatrecht* 391-393; id., "Grundregeln des Europäischen Vertragsrechts und die deutsche Reformdebatte", (2001) 9 *Zeitschrift für Europäisches Privatrecht* 217-222; id., *Die Principles of European Contract Law als Ausdruck und Gegenstand Europäischer Rechtswissenschaft* (2003); id., "Die 'Principles of European Contract Law', Teil III", (2003) 11 *Zeitschrift für Europäisches Privatrecht* 707-713; id. "Die Principles of European Contract Law als Ausdruck und Gegenstand europäischer Rechtswissenschaft", (2005) *Jura* 289-297, 441-447; id. "Comparative Law and the Europeanization of Private Law" (n. 23) 560 ff.

[26] R. Zimmermann, "Remedies for Non-Performance: The revised German law of obligations, viewed against the background of the Principles of European Contract Law", (2002) 6 *Edinburgh Law Review* 271-314; id., "Restitutio in integrum: The Unwinding of Failed Contracts under the Principles of European Contract Law, the UNIDROIT Principles and the Avant-projet d'un Code Européen des Contrats", (2005) *Uniform Law Review / Revue de Droit Uniforme* 719-735; id., "Vertrag und Versprechen. Deutsches Recht und Principles of European Contract Law im Vergleich", in: *Festschrift für Andreas Heldrich* (2005) 467-484; id., "The New German Law of Prescription and Chapter 14 of the PECL", in: A. Vaquer (ed.), *La Tercera Parte de los Pricipios de Derecho Contractual Europeo / The Principles of European Contract Law, Part III* (2005) 451-494.

[27] H. MacQueen, R. Zimmermann (eds.), *European Contract Law. Scots and South African Perspectives* (2006).

[28] R. Zimmermann (n. 23), p. 546-577; cf. N. Jansen, "Das gemeine Recht und der Staat", to appear in: R. Zimmermann (ed.), *Entstaatlichung des Privatrechts*; id., "Dogmatik, Erkenntnis und Theorie im europäischen Privatrecht", (2005) 13 *Zeitschrift für Europäisches Privatrecht* 750-783.

option for *Zimmermann* to engage himself in the *Study Group on a European Civil Code*. However, this does not mean that *Zimmermann* would be disinterested with regard to the current political attempts to unifying the European private law, on the contrary. He is a thorough, critical observer of this process, and I think that the first proposals of the *Study Group* and of the *Acquis Group* may be taken as a confirmation of *Zimmermann's* early scepticism with regard to these codification projects.[29] It is neither possible nor desirable to detach the European private law of our days from Europe's common legal tradition; and it would likewise go astray to separate the European Union's private law artificially from this tradition.

Let me conclude: this short – and inevitably incomplete – overview on *Zimmermann's* main academic achievements with regard to European private law is probably enough for justifying my statement that he should be regarded as a leading father of the modern science of European private law: He has laid the foundations for a historical science of European private law, thus stimulating a highly fruitful academic tradition. At the same time, he has never forgotten that it is anything but obvious that a historical legal science based on the European civilian tradition should today remain limited to the European continent. The mixed legal system of South Africa had been a central focus of his *Law of Obligations*; and in more recent times, *Zimmermann* has started to participate in the work of UNIDROIT. Indeed, if it is true that there is even today no necessary nexus between the science of European private law and the state,[30] perhaps it follows as a natural consequence for our European science of private law to develop beyond the borders of the political Union.[31]

---

29 R. Zimmermann, 'Savigny's Legacy" (n. 3) 577 ff., 582, 60. For a critique of recent proposals of the *Study Group* and the *Acquis Group*, see N. Jansen, R. Zimmermann, "Grundregeln des bestehenden Gemeinschaftsprivatrechts?' (2007) *Juristenzeitung* 1113; N. Jansen, "*Negotiorum Gestio* und *Benevolent Intervention in Another's Affairs: Principles of European Law?*", (2007) 15 *Zeitschrift für Europäisches Privatrecht* 962-995.

30 Cf. N. Jansen, R. Michaels, 'Private Law and the State – Comparative Perceptions and Historical Observations', (2007) 71 *Rabels Zeitschrift für ausländisches und internationales Privatrecht* 345-397.

31 See R. Zimmermann, "Römisches Recht und europäische Kultur", (2007) *Juristenzeitung* 1-12.

CHAPTER 3

Reinhard Zimmermann's Contribution to Contemporary Roman Law

Pascal Pichonnaz*

Dear Reinhard,

The organizers asked me to deliver a talk on "*Reinhard Zimmermann's Contribution to Contemporary Roman Law*". I am of course very much honoured by this invitation and I should thank them for this opportunity. However, I am afraid that I cannot fulfil their expectations since the task given to me is an impossible one.

First of all, the title of my intervention assumes that your contribution, dear Reinhard, may be over, and that it will be possible to make a balance of what you have achieved during your academic life as a specialist of Roman Law. You did – at least indirectly – such an account in 1996 for Savigny, in a beautiful article published in English under the title "Savigny's legacy".[1] Your task was easier of course, Savigny's work is completed. However, with you, dear Reinhard, we do not know whether your most important contribution lies still ahead. It may well be. So my account, of course very subjective, could really be proven wrong in a couple of years' time. The first of eight volumes of Savigny's fundamental work "System of contemporary Roman Law" was published in 1840,[2] when Savigny (born in 1779) was already 61 years old. It appears therefore suddenly very clearly that for you everything is still totally open; you are indeed much younger!

Of course, it would be very easy to save my face by indicating that I will just speak on my personal views on your *actual* contribution to contemporary Roman Law. However, even this would not be easy to do. Indeed, you wrote a seminal article entitled "*Heard melodies are sweet, but those unheard are sweeter*",[3] in which you gave an account of the influence of Continental Law on English Common Law, through the example of the *condicio tacita* and its link to the implied terms doctrine. Should I therefore be "unsweet" to you and play the sweet melody of your contribution to contemporary Roman Law or, what would be of course wiser, to remain silent and let you imagine what I could have said? But of course, then the organizers would complain; after all, they invited me to speak and not to remain silent!

My next problem lies in the second part of the title itself: "*Contemporary* Roman Law". This refers obviously to Savigny's fundamental work ("System des heutigen römischen Rechts"). But I would not dare to speak about you as a

---

* Chair for Private Law and Roman Law, University of Fribourg/Switzerland. I would like to thank my colleague and friend Prof. Stefan Vogenauer, Oxford, who has kindly accepted to check my English text.

1 First published in English as "Savigny's Legacy: Legal History, Comparative Law, and the Emergence of a European Science", *Law Quarterly Review* 1996, p. 576 *et seq.*; and then in German, *Savigny's Vermächtnis: Rechtsgeschichte, Rechtsvergleichung und die Begründung einer Europäischen Rechtswissenschaft*, Tübinger Universitätsreden, Neue Folge, Vol. 23 (1998) [also (1998) *Juristische Blätter* 273; also in P. Caroni/ G. Dilcher (eds.), *Norm und Tradition* (1998), p. 281 ff].

2 *System des heutigen römischen Rechts*, vol. I (1840), published in English as *System of Modern Roman Law*, vol. I (W. Holloway transl.1867).

3 "Heard melodies are sweet, but those unheard are sweeter. – Condicio tacita, implied condition und die Fortbildung des europäischen Vertragsrechts", 193 (1993) *Archiv für die civilistische Praxis* 121.

new Savigny. Not only because this would recall some controversies with Mario Bretone on the idea of "new Savignys", but above all because this would not correspond to your work, truly understood. Indeed, your approach may have some links with the work of Savigny; however, you do not want to impose Classical Roman Law as a solution for the modern legal systems. What you rather achieve is to follow the evolution of some important institutions of European Private Law, in order to lift the veil on some roots of modern difficulties or issues. This is only possible by using a truly historical tool and by following the path of these institutions from Roman Law, through Medieval Law and Natural Law, up to the modern codifications. I would say that your work in such respect has much more nuances and *finesse* than former approaches in legal history.

The title given to me may also imply that there is an outdated or past Roman Law on the one hand and a contemporary Roman Law on the other. First, I am not sure that this is a true account of the reality. Of course, one could say that there is the so-called "Roman Roman Law"[4], which seeks to analyse Roman texts of the Justinian Digest, Codes and other legal and literary texts of Roman times to understand them, put them into context and figure out what the author of the original work said or had envisaged to say. This approach has been in favour since the sixties of the last century, and is still in favour in many places around the world, not the least in Italy or Spain. So, Roman Roman Law could also be recognized as "Contemporary Roman Law", in the sense that it is still a contemporary methodological approach to Roman Law.

Moreover, modern epistemology has shown that a text cannot be interpreted "objectively", without an input from the interpreter. It is sufficient to refer here to Derrida.[5] Thus, any attempt to speak about Roman Law is a contemporary approach to the Roman Law texts. Roman Law is always Roman Law as it is understood at a specific period of the evolution, according to specific needs and to a specific legal and sociological environment. That is exactly what you showed with your piece entitled "*Roman Law, Contemporary Law, European Law: The Civilian Tradition Today*".[6]

There have always been "schools" of ideas, ways to deal with Roman Law sources in each periods. Savigny aimed at using Roman Law to create a System of Law adapted to the German *Volksgeist*, but above all to his understanding of the Law as a System. From 1900 to around 1960, the prevailing approach was to attempt to reconstruct the original wording of Roman Law texts, correcting Justinian's texts, striking down parts of these texts with the mere explanation that they were not authentic. That was the period of the so-called *interpolation hunt*. Later on, the endeavour to understand the Roman Law System of classical times led to important doctrinal works.

---

4 The expression has been used over the years in many of my discussions by my predecessor and maître, Felix Wubbe, Professor emeritus at the Law School of Fribourg (Switzerland).

5 J. Derrida, "Signature événement contexte", in: J. Derrida, *Marges de la philosophie* (1972), p. 371 ff.

6 *Roman Law, Contemporary Law, European Law: The Civilian Tradition Today* (2001).

With your work, dear Reinhard, the idea to use Roman Law for comparative Law purposes and for the affirmation or reaffirmation of a European Private Law rooted in tradition has emerged. After the school of Ludwig Mitteis,[7] your work lets emerge a new school, which might allow me to write an article entitled "In the school of Reinhard Zimmermann" one day in the future – as you did in 2001 for Ludwig Mitteis. I could then of course say that your approach is original in so far as it tries to show the true link between all European Law systems, or to say it with your words, the European Character of the English Common Law. For you, there is a "basic unity of the European Legal tradition",[8] and this does not exclude the Common Law, since, as you wrote in 1990 "throughout the centuries, Roman (civil) law never ceased, through various channels, to exercise a considerable influence on English law and jurisprudence".[9] It is therefore not surprising at all that this understanding let you focus on mixed legal jurisdiction as a kind of evidence of this pervasive influence of Roman Law. Hence, your contribution is really a contribution to "Contemporary Roman Law".

Unfortunately, my task remains still impossible, since I was given only 20 minutes to present your contribution to Roman Law, and it would take me already more time just to evoke all your books and articles in this area, which is only one of your beloved themes, as it appears already through today's list of speakers.

It is true that compared to your *"rather short book"*[10] of 1241 pages entitled "The Law of Obligations: Roman Foundations of the Civilian Tradition", my account will necessarily remain very partial and incomplete.

A fact is however easy to state and clear to me: your "monumental work" as it has been described by Professor Eugen Bucher of Berne University,[11] in his review of your book, your monumental book has changed something in the world. First, in the world of Roman Law professors, who had to imagine that teaching and research in Roman Law should not necessarily stop with Justinian's death. Kaser, as you mentioned in 1997 in your article *"Max Kaser und das moderne Privatrecht"*[12] and Rabel[13] for instance had already an "evolutionary" perspective in some of their articles, but Roman Law professors could ignore these still isolated premonitory signs. With your "big book", ignorance could no longer be a reason; the debate was open and indeed it took place. How should one teach Roman Law? Should Roman Law research be linked to Contemporary

7 "In der Schule von Ludwig Mitteis", *Ernst Rabels rechtshistorische Ursprünge*, (2001)*RabelsZ* 1.

8 R. Zimmermann, *The Law of Obligations* (1996), Preface, p. ix.

9 Ibidem, p. xi.

10 Ibidem, p. vii.

11 E. Bucher, "Gedanken aus Anlass des Erscheinens zweier Monumentalwerke zum Römischen Recht", (1997)*Aktuelle Juristische Praxis* 923-938.

12 "Max Kaser und das moderne Privatrecht", *SZ-RA* 115 (1998), p. 99 *et seq.*

13 B. Huwiler, "Werden und Gestalt. Ernst Rabel und das Römische Recht", *Basler Juristische Mitteilungen* (BJM) 2006, pp. 281-306.

Law? All these questions are still disputed in the very narrow circle of so-called Romanists. Your work has thus brought up a *momentum*, a change in paradigm.

I see many reasons for this:

Firstly, as you mentioned in your preface,[14] you wrote a book that every student would dream of having, easy to read, full of Roman Law excerpts presented in a lively and fascinating way. One can immediately see that the author has been influenced by Thomas Mann's writings. I remember, being a young lecturer at the University of Fribourg in 1991, preparing some exercises on Roman Law, when I discovered your newly published book. I was just fascinated. At last a book which was easy to understand and enabled more lively and interesting lectures and exercices.

Secondly, your book and the underlying method appeared at the right moment. The European Parliament had adopted a resolution in December 1989 asking for a European Civil Code[15], and a couple of months later your book appeared! Congratulations, what a foresight of the evolution!

However, this Copernican revolution was not only visible in some formal aspects. More importantly, your new approach to Roman Law broke down the traditional boundaries between Roman Law and Contemporary Law on the one hand, but also between the Civil Law and the Common Law on the other hand. Thus, you brought a fully new dimension, a kind of "fourth dimension" to the subject-matter. The publication in 2003 of the historical-critical Commentary of the BGB[16] is in some respect the evolution of the method you have introduced with your "Law of Obligations".

What strikes me today, is that we are three speakers to give accounts of your contribution in three various subject-matters, but indeed in your work these aspects were linked together from the beginning and still are. It is not possible to present your method in terms of Roman Law, without referring to your publications on Scots Law or on mixed legal jurisdiction. It is really an account of "Roman Law and European Culture", as you put it recently.[17] The relative weight of these different elements may evolve from time to time, from article to article, but your fundamental idea and conviction to link together these perspectives remains. For the time being, this is certainly one of your major contributions. You have used it not only in Contract Law, but really in all major aspects of Private Law, such as restitution, and the Law of Delict (Larva Legis Aquiliae,[18] or "effusum vel deiectum"[19]).

---

14 Zimmermann (n. 8), Preface, p. xi.

15 JO C 158 du 26.6.1989, p. 400; JO C 205 du 25.7.1994, p. 518, JO C 140 E du 13.6.2002, p. 538; JO C 76 E du 25.3.2004, p. 95.

16 M. Schmoeckel, J. Rückert, R. Zimmermann (eds.), *Historisch-kritischer Kommentar zum BGB*, Vol. I: Allgemeiner Teil, §§ 1-240 (2003).

17 "Römisches Recht und europäische Kultur", (2007) *Juristenzeitung* 1.

18 M. Hewett, R. Zimmermann, *Larva Legis Aquiliae* (2000).

19 "Effusum vel deiectum", *Festschrift für Hermann Lange* (1992), p. 301 ff.

This methodology has now been endorsed by a large number of scholars and, of course, by a large number of your PhD students. By doing so, you certainly went further than Ernst Rabel, who had some comparable ideas, but the subject-matter you covered is much wider and the walls into which Roman Law was confined have not just been shaken, but have really fallen apart. In a way, your "Law of Obligations" could be compared to the Trumpets of Jericho!

Your message was of course also sent to modern Lawyers. Like Pascal Mercier in his book "Night train to Lisbon", you could say: "We commit a mistake, an absurd act of violence, when we concentrate ourselves on here and now, in the conviction to be able to grasp what is essential".[20]

Your contribution to Contemporary Roman Law can also be measured by the scale of individual achievement which you facilitated. Your ability to identify, to support and to promote researchers in Roman Law had a tremendous impact. You have not only already supervised a great number of PhD theses in the field of Contemporary Roman Law and Comparative Law, but several of the researchers you motivated are now Law Professors around Europe (Stefan Vogenauer in Oxford, Nils Jansen in Münster, Dirk Verse in Osnabrück, myself in Fribourg/Switzerland and certainly more others). They mostly teach Roman Law and/or Comparative Law, in a way or another. I would say that this achievement is even greater than your mere scientific production, since it will have and has already had an exponential effect of the number of young researchers interested in and convinced by the usefulness of a historical and comparative perspective on contemporary law.

In a time in which we aim at a European Private Law, rooted in tradition, but seeking to answer actual problems, this contribution is essential.

Your methodology brought excellent results in the Lando Commission, with regard to set-off and periods of limitation among other issues,[21] and of course will continue to be amongst the leading contributions in these areas.

Dear Reinhard, as you can hear, I finally composed a panegyric. It felt that, even incomplete, my account should help the audience realize the main aspects of your contribution. Of course, most people present tonight are aware and probably convinced by the importance of your contribution to legal science. My contribution may therefore have been superfluous.

I could therefore have chosen to follow another trail, a wittier mode. Unfortunately – or should I say fortunately? – this has already been done by a wonderful writer, Alexander McCall Smith, author of a bestseller called "Portuguese Irregular Verbs". The book is dedicated to Reinhard Zimmermann. And in some way, the main character, Prof. Dr. Igelfeld has some common features with *our* Reinhard Zimmermann, as it appears from the following excerpts:

---

20 P. Mercier, *Train de nuit pour Lisbonne* (2006), p. 282 (original German version : *Nachtzug nach Lissabon* (2004).

21 *See* R. Zimmermann, *Comparative Foundations of a European Law of Set-Off and Prescription* (2002).

"Of the three professors, von Igelfeld was undoubtedly the most distinguished. He was the author of a seminal work on Romance philology, Portuguese Irregular Verbs, a work of such majesty that it dwarfed all other books in the field".

The author continues then:

"It was a lengthy book of almost twelve hundred pages, and was the result of years of research into the etymology and vagaries of Portuguese verbs. It had been well-received – not that there had ever been the slightest doubt about that – and indeed one reviewer has simply written, 'There is nothing more to be said on this subject. Nothing.'"[22]

So, I will say nothing more.

My dear Reinhard, it is time to conclude my incomplete, very subjective and impossible account on your contribution to Contemporary Roman Law. I do not know whether you already achieved your greatest contribution to contemporary Roman Law, even at an earlier age than the great Savigny himself, or if something even more exceptional is still to come, which could well be the impact of your Historical Critical Commentary on the German Civil Code. Let posterity decide!

In any case, I would say that you can be really proud of what you brought to the Roman Law Community of researchers and to students. So let us appreciate this precious moment of recognition: the award of a Doctor *honoris causa* you fully deserve. And may my impossible account on your achievement have at least reached one result: Make you happy!

---

[22] A. McCall Smith, *Portuguese Irregular Verbs* (2003), p. 10 *et seq.*; see now also in a German edition, A. McCall Smith, *Die verschmähten Schriften des Professor von Igelfeld* (2007), p. 10 ff.

CHAPTER 4

Reinhard Zimmermann and Scots Law

Hector L. MacQueen*

I first met Reinhard Zimmermann at a seminar in Edinburgh in 1990, just a month or two after the publication of his great work on the law of obligations. It was his first visit to Scotland since his childhood,[1] but he already had good friends based in the country, such as my Edinburgh colleague Sandy McCall Smith and David Carey Miller of Aberdeen.[2] Both of these gentlemen had strong connections with the University of Cape Town where Professor Zimmermann had held a chair until not long before that Edinburgh visit in 1990. But Regensburg had called, Scotland was much closer than it had been, and the book on obligations had already not only sealed an international reputation for its author, but also caught the attention of Scottish academic lawyers.

The reasons for this attention are not to be found in the book's investigation or consideration of Scots private law, for it takes only the most fleeting of glances in that direction.[3] Attention was aroused because of the nature of Scots private law, which is a mixed legal system – classically, the only such system in Europe.[4] The structure, concepts and much of the content of private law lie in the Continental or Roman Civil Law – the result of the many centuries before 1750 when most leading Scots lawyers spent their intellectually formative years in the study of Canon and Civil Law at Continental universities. Yet Scots law had also from the medieval centuries on a close relationship with the Common Law of England, a relationship which intensified after the two countries formed the union which is marking its tercentenary in this year of 2007, and gave the two systems a common legislature and final court of appeal. To many commentators in the second half of the twentieth century, this ever closer relationship appeared to be demolishing the Civilian aspects of Scots law, and making the system simply the poor and dependent relation of its bigger neighbour. Academics like T B Smith argued however that this trend could and should be reversed, and that the re-Civilianisation of Scots law would make it a more just as well

* Professor of Private Law, University of Edinburgh.

1 Information from Professor Zimmermann.

2 The Aberdeen and Edinburgh connections explain why Reinhard Zimmermann has also received LLDs from these universities, in June 2002 and June 2007 respectively. He is also a Fellow of the Royal Society of Edinburgh (elected 2001).

3 There is no index reference to Scotland or Scots law in *Obligations*. A few Scottish cases appear in the table of cases, mostly well-known delict decisions of the House of Lords cited in their English form – *Donoghue v Stevenson* [1932] AC 652 (cited at pp. 11, 22, 911, 1038, 1039), *Muir v Glasgow Corporation* [1943] AC 448 (cited at p 1009), *Junior Books v The Veitchi Co* [1983] 1 AC 520 (cited at p. 1039). Note also *Mackay v Dick & Stevenson* (1881) 6 AC 251 (cited at p. 746, a decision on conditions in a Scots appeal). Some cases are however footnoted with their Scottish citation: i.e. *Sloan's Dairies v Glasgow Corporation* 1977 SC 223 (cited at p. 292); *Christison v McBride* (1881) 9 R 34 and *Graham v Pollok* (1848) 10 D 646 (both cited at p. 8).

4 See generally on mixed legal systems V.V. Palmer, *Mixed Jurisdictions Worldwide: The Third Legal Family* (2001).

as a more principled and coherent system.[5] But the difficulty in doing this was that Scots lawyers in general had lost touch with the Civilian tradition, in both its historical and contemporary contexts, and the arguments of Smith and his supporters made little headway.

Professor Zimmermann's great book offered a way past this dilemma. Its scale and comprehensiveness meant that on virtually any topic in the law of obligations there was now a detailed treatment of the Civilian tradition on it, written in lucid English and vouched by a detailed apparatus. While the book was avowedly historical, it placed that history in relation to contemporary law by showing how it had led up to the German codification in 1900 and subsequent developments. Even more importantly for Scots lawyers, however, it showed how the tradition had played out in the uncodified Roman-Dutch tradition of South African private law. Like Scots law, but for different reasons, South African law had been heavily influenced by English law, making it a mixed legal system; the Civilian tradition had inter-acted with the Common Law, but, crucially, without the diminishment that had been the fate of its Scottish counterpart. In the 1950s T B Smith argued that Scots private law had much to learn from its South African equivalent, but had rarely pursued the question in depth. With Zimmermann's book in hand, however, the Scots lawyer could begin to test in detail the claim made by Smith. The death of apartheid (in which Zimmermann played an academic role[6]) also meant that politically it began to be possible to look at South Africa in a comparative and open spirit.

Although, as I have said, Zimmermann's *Obligations* says almost nothing directly about Scots law, its impact began to be apparent in Scotland by the mid-1990s. At that time, the subject of unjustified enrichment was the "hot" topic for private lawyers in the United Kingdom. England, inspired by the work of Professor Zimmermann's friend Peter Birks (once a Professor of Civil Law at Edinburgh), had begun to grope towards a general enrichment principle, and Scots lawyers had in consequence been forced to recognise, not least by Birks, that their enrichment law, undoubtedly of Civilian origin, had lost all contact with principle and coherence.[7] In some shape or form, the modern Civilian tradition, and in particular German and South African law, offered ways forward. In 1994 the Scottish Law Commission and Edinburgh Law School organised a seminar on the subject and, in the knowledge that a potentially crucial case would shortly be before the Court of Session, invited the participation of, not only the judges of the Court and the lawyers appearing in the case, but also Professors Zimmer-

5 See e.g. Smith's most famous works: *A Short Commentary on the Law of Scotland* (1962); *Studies Critical and Comparative* (1962). His contribution to Scots law is discussed in depth in E. Reid, D.L. Carey Miller (eds), *A Mixed Legal System in Transition: T B Smith and the Progress of Scots Law* (2005).

6 See D. Cowen, D. Visser, *The University of Cape Town Law Faculty: A History 1859-2004* (2004) p. 101-2, 105-6.

7 See further H.L. MacQueen, "Peter Birks and Scots enrichment law", in A. Burrows, Lord Rodger of Earlsferry (eds), *Mapping the Law: Essays in Memory of Peter Birks* (2006), p. 401-417.

mann and Birks. (Incidentally, one of my happy memories of that occasion is the expression on Reinhard Zimmermann's face as Peter Birks launched with characteristic energy and panache into an extended comparison of approaching questions of enrichment law with peeling an orange.) Professor Zimmermann's powerful analysis of the German approach to enrichment on that occasion was also memorable and, I think, influential;[8] certainly when the case of *Morgan Guaranty of New York Co Ltd v Lothian Regional Council*[9] was decided shortly afterwards, it reset Scots law on a basically Germanic path. The case was also notable for its respectful citation of living academic authors, not always a trait of Scottish courts in the past; and prominent amongst those so named was Reinhard Zimmermann.[10]

There is at least one other Scottish case in which Professor Zimmermann's book on obligations has been cited to and by a Scottish court. The subject on this occasion was the law of individual privacy, another "hot" topic in the United Kingdom since the Human Rights Act 1998 domesticated the European Convention on Human Rights in both Scots and English law.[11] The discussion cited was on the *actio iniuriarum*,[12] undoubtedly received in Scots law in the seventeenth or earlier centuries, but very much neglected since at latest the mid-nineteenth. T B Smith had argued as far back as the 1960s that Scots law should follow the example of South Africa and redevelop the *actio* to protect privacy;[13] but until *Martin v McGuiness*[14] this argument had gone nowhere. Now it was thoughtfully received by the judge and although in the end he did not require to decide the point, he left open the route to further discussion in the future, saying of an argument that Scots law has never recognised a specific right to privacy, "[o]f course it does not follow that, because a specific right to privacy has not so far been recognised, such a right does not fall within existing principles of the law"[15] – a very Civilian approach.

These cases show that where a question of fundamental principle arises in modern Scots law Professor Zimmermann's work is referred to, because it is likely to demonstrate the bases on which the law rests as well as giving some indication, through its consideration of German and South African law, of the contemporary development of that law. Very few writers have achieved such

8 Later published as "Unjustified enrichment: the modern civilian approach" (1995) 15 *Oxford Journal of Legal Studies* 403.

9 1995 SC 151.

10 See the report at p. 155, where Lord Hope cites *Obligations* p. 843 on the *condictio causa data causa non secuta*.

11 See further H.L. MacQueen, "Searching for privacy in a mixed jurisdiction", (2006) 21 *Tulane European and Civil Law Forum* 73-97.

12 *Obligations*, p. 1053-1059.

13 Smith (n. 5), p. 653-656.

14 2003 SLT 1424. The reference is to *Obligations*, p. 1053-1059.

15 At para 28.

a position in Scots law; fewer still have been from Germany; and nearly all of them are no longer alive! If not unique, Professor Zimmermann is certainly a remarkable figure in Scots law.

However, nearly twenty years after the publication of *Obligations*, it can no longer be said that Professor Zimmermann's contribution to the development of Scots law is solely confined to that work. I have counted seven books on Scots law of which he has been a co-editor and to which he has generally been a contributor as well: their subject-matter has ranged from general considerations of the history of private law and the Civilian tradition in Scotland to discussions of more specific topics in contract law, the law of delict, the law of succession and personality rights.[16] There are also numerous discussions of Scots law in other books and articles of a more general comparative and historical nature.[17] Mixed legal systems engage him: as he wrote in his Clarendon Lectures of 1999 in Oxford, "[t]hey present the particularly fascinating picture of courts and legal writers still having to grapple with the historical sources of the *ius commune* and of the English common law and thus being faced with the specific problems and challenges arising from a living inter-action between civil law and common law."[18] Intellectually and in other highly practical ways he has fostered major collaborations between Scots and South African lawyers, investigating the historical and contemporary operation of *mixité*, with highly beneficial effects for the former in particular.

But mixed legal systems are not simply interesting in their own right. Professor Zimmermann is not just a legal historian and comparative lawyer. He looks

---

16 *The Civilian Tradition and Scots Law: Aberdeen Quincentenary Essays* (1997; co-edited with David Carey Miller and contributed a chapter on the Civil Law in European codes); *History of Private Law in Scotland* (2 vols, 2000; co-edited with Kenneth Reid and contributed chapters on "Strict Liability" and on "Liability among Neighbours", both co-authored with Philip Simpson); *Unjustified Enrichment: Key Issues in Comparative Perspective* (2002; co-edited with David Johnston, and having four Scottish contributors [James Wolffe, Hector MacQueen, George Gretton, Niall Whitty]); *Mixed Legal Systems in Comparative Perspective: Property and Obligations in Scotland and South Africa* (2004; co-edited with Daniel Visser and Kenneth Reid and provided the Introduction); *European Contract Law: Scots and South African Perspectives* (2006; co-edited with Hector MacQueen and contributed first chapter on European Contract Law as a new ius commune); *Exploring the Law of Succession: Studies National, Historical and Comparative* (2007), co-edited with Kenneth Reid and Marius de Waal; *Rights of Personality in Scots Law* (forthcoming 2008; co-edited with Niall Whitty).

17 See e.g. R. Zimmermann, P. Hellwege, "Belohnungsversprechen: 'pollicitatio', 'promise' oder 'offer'", (1998) 39 *Zeitschrift für Rechtsvergleichung* 133; R. Zimmermann, *Comparative Foundations of a European Law of Set-Off and Prescription* (2002), index references for "Scotland"; R. Zimmermann, J.E. du Plessis, "The relevance of reverence: undue influence Civilian style", (2003) 10 *Maastricht Journal of European and Comparative Law* 345.

18 R. Zimmermann, *Roman Law, Contemporary Law, European Law: The Civilian Tradition Today* (2001), p. 127 f.

into the future as well as the past and the present, and takes seriously a remark first made by Zweigert and Kötz in 1971:

> Scots law deserves particular attention ... as a special instance of the symbiosis of the English and Continental legal traditions; this may be of some assistance to those who embark on the great project of the future, namely to procure a gradual approximation of Civil Law and Common Law.[19]

For Zimmermann the study of mixed systems like Scots law tests the extent to which problems on which Civil Law and Common Law traditionally take a different view can be solved in a coherent and rational way, and thus also helps to probe the possibilities and solutions proferred in projects towards a European private law. It is a matter of deep gratification for Scots lawyers such as myself that Reinhard Zimmermann's reaction to what he has found in our system has been positive, if never uncritical. But the criticism is that of a good friend who has our best interests close to his heart; and his contribution has done very much to bring our law to the attention of others, and to give us the confidence and means to go forward in step with our past, our comparative traditions, and the genuine possibilities of the future.

---

19 See now K. Zweigert, H. Kötz, trans T. Weir, *Introduction to Comparative Law* (3rd edn, 1998), p. 204.

CHAPTER 5

A Common European Law on Sales?

Anna Veneziano*

I Introduction

In certain key areas of European law one is stricken by the fact that despite their economic importance, there appears to be very few uniform or common rules. The question is therefore whether or not the European legislator should fill in a conspicuous gap, be it the case by looking also at international instruments which themselves are quite recent. A good example is represented, among others, by the law on secured transactions.

On the other hand, it may well be said that in the field of sales law there is already too much legislation. First of all, this is one of the first areas of contract law where long-standing efforts at drafting uniform rules at an international level were successful. Universally known is the 1980 UN Convention on International Sales (hereinafter CISG),[1] which is the end result of decades of work on this topic and was itself one of the main models, not only for recent domestic law reforms and even European legislation (in particular, the 1999 Consumer Sales Directive), but also for soft law instruments on general contract law such as the Principles on European Contract Law[2] (hereinafter, PECL) and the UNIDROIT Principles on International Commercial Contracts.[3] These achievements may lead to question the very need of drafting specific European rules on sales, especially with regard to commercial contracts.

On the other hand, recent years have seen an unprecedented development of Community law in the realm of contracts through the means of directives, dealing in particular, though not exclusively, with some aspects of consumer sales.

Certainly, the risk of any new project relating to European sales law is either to 'reinvent the wheel', by failing to treasure what has already been achieved, or to create contradictory instruments in the same field of law. Thus, instead of achieving simplification and clarification, a new project may end up adding to the existing confusion. The above-mentioned risks are in fact not so peregrine. Some caution is necessary, especially if we look at the most recent communications issued by the European Commission on contract law in general and

---

* Professor of Private Comparative Law at the University of Teramo (Italy). The opinion expressed in this paper are purely personal and do not necessarily reflect those of other members of the Study Group on a European Civil Code nor of the Compilation and Redaction Team for the Common Frame of Reference.

1 1980 UN Convention on International Sales of Goods. Unless otherwise specified, the source for case law applying CISG is the database UNILEX, at www.unilex.info. Of the numerous commentaries on CISG, I would like to refer in particular to the one issued by the late Prof. Schlechtriem: P. Schlechtriem (Ed.), *Commentary on the UN Convention on the International Sale of Goods (CISG)*, English Transl. of the 2nd Edition (1998).

2 O. Lando, H. Beale (Eds), *European Principles of Contract Law, Parts I and II* (2000); O. Lando, E. Clive, A. Prüm, R. Zimmermann (Eds), *European Principles of Contract Law, Part III* (2003).

3 *UNIDROIT Principles of International Commercial Contracts*, Rome 1994, 2nd Ed. (2004); M.J. Bonell, *An International Restatement of Contract Law*, 3rd Ed. (2005).

sales law in particular, and specifically at the Green Paper on the Review of the Consumer Acquis (hereinafter Green Paper).[4]

There is no doubt, however, that it is necessary to take into account the growing acquis communautaire dealing with the protection of the consumer, which has had a great impact, especially on sales contracts. As it is well known, both CISG and the UNIDROIT Principles expressly exclude consumer transactions.[5] Even the PECL, though formally open to all kinds of contracts and also applicable to domestic transactions,[6] do not contain much in terms of acquis.[7] It leaps to the eye that existing community law in this area is excessively fragmented, incomplete and sometimes even contradictory. Action is therefore called for in order to facilitate its interpretation and application.

In attaining the result of taking consumer protection seriously, different approaches may be followed, which will lead to different results. On the one hand, the recent wave of European legislation may appear to justify the position that European contract law should shift its focus on the protection of the weaker party, which means that even the general rules (for general contract law and for the specific contracts) should be created (or re-created) to the perspective of this protection. Another, certainly more traditional, approach envisages the insertion (or addition) of a number of special protective rules for business-to-consumer transactions only. For all the rest, the provision of a general good faith principle or of specific manifestations of that principle within general contract law, or the

---

4 Reference is to the latest green paper of the Commission on the *Review of the Consumer Acquis*, 8 February 2007, COM (2006) 744 final. See below, para. 2, for further treatment of the approach followed by the Green Paper regarding sales law.

5 Article 2(a) CISG: [The Convention does not apply to sales] 'of goods bought for personal, family or household use, unless the seller, at any time before or at the conclusion of the contract, neither knew nor ought to have known that the goods were bought for any such use'; Preamble, first sentence, UNIDROIT Principles: 'These Principles set forth general rules for international commercial contracts' and Official Comment, at 2, according to which the reference to 'commercial contracts' aims at 'excluding from the scope of the Principles so-called "consumer transactions" which are within the various legal systems being increasingly subjected to special rules, mostly of a mandatory character, aimed at protecting the consumer, i.e. a party who enters into the contract otherwise than in the course of its trade or profession'.

6 "The Commission has made an effort to deal with those issues in contract law which face business life of today and which may advance trade, especially international trade. However, the Principles are not intended to apply exclusively to international transactions": O. Lando, "Why does Europe Need a European Civil Code?", in: S. Grundmann, J. Stuyck (Eds), *An Academic Green Paper on European Contract Law* (2002), 207, at 213.

7 Most of the work on the PECL was in fact accomplished before the completion of many EU Directives in this field. See R. Zimmermann, "The Principles of European Contract Law. Contemporary Manifestation of the Old, and Possible Foundation for a New, European Scholarship of Private Law", in *Beyond Borders: Perspectives on International and Comparative Law, Symposium in Honour of Hein Kötz* (2006), 111 ff., at 115.

use of a standard of reasonableness by courts in various circumstances, may well be considered sufficient to produce good results also for consumers; certainly to adapt the general rules to the specificities of the parties' bargaining power in any given circumstance.

I tend to prefer the latter position for a number of reasons which I will discuss below.[8] On its part, the European Green Paper on the Consumer Acquis, while it represents a commendable step in the direction of a much-awaited community action in the field of contract law, may lead to an uncritical application of the former approach, if taken too literally. A summary reference to the content of the Commission Green Paper is useful in order to substantiate this point.

II The General Approach to Sales Law Taken in the Green Paper on Consumer Aquis

With regard to the specific topic of the present paper, the Commission envisages that if the (preferred) "horizontal approach" is followed,[9] the ensuing horizontal instrument would be divided into two parts. In the first one, topics relating to contract law in general, "extracted from the existing directives",[10] would be systematically presented. A second part of the horizontal instrument on consumer law would be devoted to the contract of sale ("by far the predominant consumer contract").[11] The bulk of this second part would be represented by the consumer sales directive. The Commission, however, recognizes that the Consumer Sales Directive is far from complete. The need for a broader regulatory framework on contracts is in fact the basis for the proposal of the horizontal, more systematic instrument. Specifically mentioned are not only certain topics relating to general contract law,[12] but also some issues which might be addressed in a specific part on sales as opposed to a general part on consumer

8 Some of the following is based on A. Veneziano, "How to ensure mutual consistency between the Common Frame of Reference and the Review of the Consumer Acquis in the field of sales law", Background note for the European Parliament, 8 July 2007, available at: http://www.europarl.europa.eu/comparl/juri/ hearings/20070626/veneziano_en.pdf.

9 It is worth recalling that the Green Paper offers, among different ways to achieve more coherence within European contract law, the individual review of each directive (so called "vertical approach"), as well as the creation of a framework instrument on general issues of consumer contract law applicable to all directives (so called "horizontal approach"). The two approaches may be combined and pursued at the same time: Green Paper, above fn 4, at para. 4.2.

10 Ibidem, para. 4.2. (third sentence).

11 Green Paper (n. 4) at para. 4.6.

12 Such as the right to withdrawal; the regulation of unfair terms; the possible introduction of a general duty of good faith; the general remedies for breach (in particular as regards damages, but also lack, late or partial performance).

contracts. Among the latter, the definition of the concept of delivery, the regulation of the passing of risk as well as the extension of the rules to contracts for the sale of intangibles (such as software and data) are specifically mentioned.[13] Moreover, given the fact that a "full harmonization" approach is suggested, the inclusion of rules deriving from the Consumer Sales Directive would entail the elimination of the options which are now available to Member States. In turn, this would generate the need to develop uniform provisions on those topics. As an example we may cite the buyer's duty to notify the seller within a specified time period of any non-conformity of the goods.[14]

Finally, the Green Paper points out that the practical application of some provisions of the Consumer Sales Directive has created difficulties. This is why further questions are asked concerning not so much "where", but "how" to regulate consumer sales. Expressly mentioned are *inter alia* the burden of proof regarding non-conformity of the goods; the impact of the exercise of specific remedies for the seller's breach, such as repair or substitution of the goods, on the two-year cut-off period of guarantee; the right of the consumer to be free to choose any of the available remedies, provided that the conditions for their application are fulfilled (repeal of the "hierarchy of remedies" rule); the introduction of a direct liability of the producer; the introduction of default rules for the content of commercial guarantees.[15]

I would like to draw attention to the fact that those general rules of consumer contract law should be drafted by "extracting them from the existing directives" and generalizing their core principles in a systematic fashion. This marks a difference with the approach of previous communications of the same Commission, launching the project of a Common Frame of Reference in European Contract Law. As it is well known, the latter had referred not only to the existing Community acquis and domestic law of the Member States, but also, explicitly, to relevant international instruments such as CISG as well as to the PECL.

There might be, however, certain problems with this approach. It could be perceived as feasible for some of the issues mentioned in the Green Paper (just to mention a couple of them: the right to withdrawal and the treatment of unfair terms, whether in standard or in individually negotiated terms). These topics are typically connected with the protection of consumer in a strict sense. Other rules, however, such as a "general right to damages" or other general contractual remedies would not be so easily extracted from existing directives. This is especially true because, as already mentioned, the Green Paper avoids referring to other sources such as CISG or the PECL.

This is where the risk of "reinventing the wheel" might be encountered. Certainly, there would be a very important practical value in envisaging an optional European instrument putting together all rules applying to consumer

13 Green Paper (n. 4) para. 4.6.

14 Id. (n. 4) para. 5.8.

15 Id paras 5.6 ff.

sales (or to other consumer transactions). The suggestion of a European "blue button" decorated with stars to be placed on the home-page of vendors and triggering the application of European sales law has been favourably commented upon.[16] It has been convincingly argued that such an instrument would be useful not only (or even, not necessarily) to consumers themselves but especially to businesses (and in particular to small to medium ones) wishing to sell to consumers in other Member States but worried about the possible pitfalls of the application of an unknown foreign contract law.[17] The political impact and the incentive for the European market of such a device should not be underestimated.

My concerns relate to the *process* of developing such common rules. I strongly believe that they have to be discussed in the wider context of general contract law and therefore, that the Common Frame of Reference on a European Contract Law has to play an important role in this respect.

A potential problem lies in the temptation to extend typically protective rules to other contractual parties, which may be considered to be in the same position as the consumer in a strict sense as far as their access to information and bargaining power is concerned. This is especially the case if the position is taken that protective rules should be extended to European SMEs, at least when they deal with non-SMEs professionals.[18]

Leaving all other issues aside (just to mention a few: the difficulties in defining an SME for the said purposes; the need to provide transparent rules for the end user), there is a very concrete risk, in business to business transactions, of making European enterprises less competitive in a wider economic context. Even if the European legislation has to be adapted to the specific needs of its market and to the underlying domestic laws of its member States, we cannot forget the wider economic and legal context represented by the rest of the world. The development of a "European lex mercatoria", that will significantly be more paternalistic than the rules emerging at a world level, could entail the risk of putting European enterprises in a disadvantageous position.

---

16 For this suggestion see now H. Schulte-Nölke, "EC Law on the Formation of Contract – From the Common Frame of Reference to the 'Blue Button", *European Review of Contract Law* 332, at 348 ff; H. Beale, "The Future of the Common Frame of Reference", (2007) *European Review of Contract Law* 257, at 270. For a favourable comment see among others M.J. Bonell, "European Contract Law and the Development of Contract Law Worldwide", paper presented at the 4th European Jurists' Forum, forthcoming (cited here with the kind permission of the Author).

17 See Beale (n. 16) at 270-271.

18 For a well argued suggestion in this sense see M.W. Hesselink, "SMEs in European Contract Law", Background note for the European Parliament, 5 July 2007, available at http://www.europarl.europa.eu/comparl/juri/hearings/20070626/hesselink_en.pdf.

Moreover, it is undeniable that CISG now represents the law of international commercial sales for most European States,[19] and that with its 70 ratifications around the world by now, it is abstractly applicable to a great number of contracts. To this we have to add the strict approach taken by the great majority of international case law on the question of the exclusion of CISG in the contract.[20] Even the constant practice in some countries (notably the US and the Scandinavian countries) to expressly exclude CISG in standard terms was recently questioned and seems to be in decline.[21] Finally, a body of case-law and scholarship developing the interpretation of many rules in CISG has helped to clarify many rules and render them even more settled.

Certainly, CISG is far from perfect. It has been criticized both for its ambiguities and for its gaps. Most of the latter pertain to questions of general contract law as well as general law of obligations, which were taken up in more ample instruments such as the PECL and the UNIDROIT Principles (for instance, just to mention a few: standard terms; pre-contractual liability; specific performance; set-off and limitation period (prescription)). As to the unclear or bad rules, suffice it to mention the right to cure and its relationship with the duty to cure as a remedy in favour of the buyer, as well as the ambiguous provisions on the determination of price. We have to admit, however, that numerous CISG provisions (also through analogous or ameliorated provisions in the mentioned soft-law instruments) have exercised a great influence on the most recent reforms of the law of obligations in Europe (suffice it to mention the German *Schuldrechtsreform* or the rules on sales in the Dutch Civil Code) as well as on the Consumer Sales Directive itself.

In fact, a review of the case law published so far shows that CISG tends to apply in particular to contracts concluded by small-to-medium enterprises and not so much to fully negotiated, high profile, "self-executing" contracts. Adopting a different standard for SME's in Europe would de facto amount to repealing the Convention despite its direct and indirect wide acceptance.

---

19 Admittedly with the exception of UK, Ireland and Portugal. It must be recalled, however, that Article 1(1)(b) CISG makes it possible for a party situated in a non-contracting State to be faced with the application of CISG when the relevant conflict of law rules refer to the law of a contracting State. Just to mention an example, CISG is in principle automatically applicable when a party with place of business in UK is the buyer of goods sold by a seller with place of business in a contracting State. See as an example *Landgericht Saarbrücken*, 25 November 2002, at http://www.unilex.info/case.cfm?pid=1&id=917&do=case.

20 Among the numerous decisions on this point see *US District Court, New Jersey, Valero Marketing v. Greeny Oy*, 15 June 2005; *Hof van Beroep Antwerpen*, 24 April 2006; *Bundesgerichtshof*, 25 November 1998, French *Cour de Cassation*, 17 December 1996, all available with an abstract in English at: http://unilex.info.

21 For more details see Bonell (n. 16).

III The General Approach to Sales Law in the Draft Common Frame of Reference

The considerations expressed above are useful to understand the rules on sales law in the Draft Common Frame of Reference (DCFR). In fact, the provisions on the contract of sale try to find a compromise between the two mentioned approaches (building a general contract law from the viewpoint of the protection of the weaker party on the one hand, and keeping a "commercially oriented" general part and adding consumer protection rules when necessary, on the other hand). I am not advocating that all solutions offered in the DCFR on sales should be accepted (in fact, many of them were the subject of ample and long-standing debates) but they can be seen as a good starting point for a future European law on sales. The need for 'new', specific European rules on this subject-matter, as it was forcefully argued, lies at the very least in their role as a "translation tool",[22] offering useful common terms of reference and enabling and enhancing the dialogue of scholarship.[23] Were this common language endorsed by the Commission, it would certainly bear much more influence in developing a fruitful dialogue within the different European legal systems.

The provisions on sales, originally drafted by a team established by Ewoud Hondius of the University of Utrecht,[24] were discussed during the plenary sessions of the Study Group on a European Civil Code and were subject to further scrutiny during the preparation of the Common Frame of Reference. They are contained in Book IV of the DCFR, "Specific Contracts and Their Effects", as part A. As far as the relationship between general rules and consumer protection rules is concerned, part A did not follow the example of other specific contracts (such as personal security);[25] thus, the rules protecting consumers are not included in a separate Chapter at the end of the regulation but are interspersed within the text.

It is not my intention to give a detailed description of the draft CFR text on sales.[26] In connection to the issues treated in the preceding paragraphs of this

[22] See on this point Beale (n. 16), esp. at 276.

[23] The importance of enhancing the development of a common European legal scholarship has often been put forward in the debate concerning the future of European contractual law. See in particular Zimmermann (n. 6), at 111 et seq. There are certainly more sceptical opinions regarding the practical effectiveness of an academic European law, not leading to legislation: see Lando (n. 6), at 213.

[24] The black letter rules, comments and national notes approved by the Study Group will be separately published: E. Hondius, V. Heutger, C. Jeloschek, *Sales Contract. Principles of European Law* (forthcoming 2008). The text benefited also by considerable input on the part of Hanna Sivesand.

[25] The black letter rules, comments and national notes referring to personal security are published within the Study Group series: U. Drobnig, *Personal Security. Principles of European Law* (2007).

[26] A general overview of the European Principles on Sales Contracts is offered by H. Sivesand, "Principles on European Law on Sales", presentation at the ERA Conference "Towards a Common Frame of Reference", Trier 19-21 September 2007, available at: http://www.era.int/web/en/resources/5_1095_6259_

paper, I would specifically like to briefly focus on three points. First of all, the CFR has incorporated a number of settled rules (we could even say European and international "common core rules"), relating to contracts in general and applicable also to sales, already contained in previously drafted texts. Secondly, another set of rules may be considered to have been positively influenced by the very width of the CFR project, which not only enabled a discussion on the relationship between general vis-à-vis specific contract law, but also with regard to other specific contracts and even other areas not usually classified within contract law. Having said this, a number of important questions are certainly still open, among which the extent of mandatory rules in view of protecting the weaker party and in particular the consumer.

Most of the rules that we referred to as "settled" were previously contained in CISG and had already been shifted to general contract law and completed by the PECL and the UNIDROIT Principles at the same time. As an example we may mention some of the "classic" rules on formation of the contract (meaning of "offer" and "acceptance";[27] modalities and time of conclusion of the contract;[28] revocation of offer;[29] modified acceptance;[30] letters of confirmation;[31] importance of usages[32]). These are mostly CISG-based provisions, ameliorated and clarified by the above mentioned soft law instruments. Another example of provisions which were moved to general contract law and at the same time greatly clarified by the PECL and the UNIDROIT Principles is represented by the rules on determination of price.[33] Further instances of "settled rules" (taking into account not only CISG but also the PECL and the UNIDROIT Principles) are to be found in the general approach to remedies for non-performance (withholding of perform-

---

file_en.8990.pdf. The DCFR is now published as *Principles, Definitions and Model Rules of European Private Law. DCFR Interim Outline Edition* (2008).

27 Arts 14 and 18 CISG; Arts 2:201 and 2:204 PECL; Arts 2.1.2, 2.1.6 and 2.1.7 UNIDROIT Principles. DCFR Book II, Arts. II-4:201, II-4:204.

28 Article 23 CISG; Arts 2:101-2:103 and 2:205 PECL; Article 2.1.1. UNIDROIT Principles; DCFR Book II, Arts II-4:101 to II-4:103, II-4:205.

29 Article 16 CISG; Article 2:202 PECL; Article 2.1.4 UNIDROIT Principles; DCFR Book II, Article II-4:202.

30 Article 19 CISG; Article 2:208 PECL; Article 2.1.11 UNIDROIT Principles; DCFR Book II, Article II-4:208.

31 This question is not treated in CISG (but for the decisions applying Article 9 on usages see with different results *Oberlandesgericht Dresden*, 9 July 1998, available at: http://www.unilex.info/case.cfm?pid=1&do=case&id =502&step=Abstract; *Zivilgericht Kanton Basel-Stadt*, 21 December 1992, available at http://www.unilex.infocase. cfm?pid=1&do=case&id=104&step=Abstract); Article 2:210 PECL; Article 2.1.12 UNIDROIT Principles; DCFR Book II, Article II-4:210.

32 Article 9 CISG; Article 1:105 PECL; Article 1.9 UNIDROIT Principles; CFR Book II, Article II-1:104.

33 On the difficulties in interpreting Arts 14 and 55 CISG as regards this point see Schlechtriem (n. 1), at 108-110; see Article 6:104 PECL; Article 5.1.7 UNIDROIT Principles; DCFR Book II, Article II-9:104.

ance;[34] inclusion of specific performance;[35] limitations to the right to terminate the contract[36] as well as generalization of termination by notice;[37] damages[38]). Still within remedies, noteworthy is the generalization of price reduction (traditionally still limited to sales in some domestic laws but already treated as autonomous, general remedy for non-performance in PECL).[39] Finally, with specific reference to sales, the definition of non-conformity[40] and the inclusion of non-conformity in the general notion of non-performance should be mentioned.

However, in order to take consumer protection into account, different rules are envisaged in some instances for the case in which the contract is concluded with a consumer (as an example, see the different language used to limit termination of the contract – which tracks down the Consumer Sales Directive).[41]

On the other hand, some provisions were changed or added, taking into account the fact that sales law is included in the wider framework of other specific contracts. As an example the issue of "mixed contracts" may be cited. The approach to mixed contracts was developed taking into account that the CFR contains specific parts on services, leases and donations. Thus, while a simple generalization of the rather inclusive rule in CISG was not acceptable in the drafting of a general rule on mixed contracts,[42] the specificities of sales had to be considered in carving an exception to the general rule.[43] Furthermore, the CFR deals with some areas of the law which are outside contracts, but are closely

---

34 Article 71 CISG; Article 9:201 PECL; Article 7.1.2 UNIDROIT Principles; DCFR Book III, Article III-401.

35 While Article 28 CISG leaves the matter to the otherwise applicable law, both PECL and the UNIDROIT Principles admit a general right to performance under certain conditions: see Arts 9:101 and 9:102 PECL; Arts 7.2.1 and 7.2.2 UNIDROIT Principles; DCFR Book III, Article III-3:301 and 3:302.

36 Arts 49 and 64, in conjunction with Article 25 CISG; Article 9:301(1) in conjunction with Article 8:103 PECL; Article 7.3.1 UNIDROIT Principles; DCFR Book III, Article III-502.

37 Article 26 CISG; 9:303 PECL; Article 7.3.2 UNIDROIT Principles; DCFR Book III, Article III-507.

38 Arts 74 et seq. CISG; Arts 9:501 et seq. PECL; Arts 7.4.1 et seq. UNIDROIT Principles; DCFR Book III, Arts 3:701 et seq.

39 The starting point is Article 50 CISG; see Article 9:401 PECL; DCFR Book III, Article III-3:601.

40 See Article 35 CISG; the DCFR takes into account also the Consumer Sales Directive in this respect: see Arts IV.A.-2:301 to 2:303.

41 DCFR, Book IV A , Article IV A. – 4:202.

42 Article 3 CISG solves the relationship with service contracts by considering that when the sales element is prevailing, the submission of the entire contract to sales law is justified. See for all R. Herber in: P. Schlechtriem (n 1), at 38 et seq.

43 The general rule is contained in DCFR, Book II, Article II-108 (2): "Where a contract is a mixed contract then, unless this is contrary to the nature and purpose of the contract, the rules applicable to each relevant category apply, with any appropriate adaptations, to the corresponding part of the contract and the rights and obligations arising from it". The exception for sales (permitted by Article III 108 (3)(a)) is to be found in Book IV, Article IV-1:102 on goods to be manufactured or produced: 'A contract under which one party undertakes, for a price, to manufacture or produce goods for the other party and to

related to certain issues pertaining to contracts. As an example, the consequences of termination of the contract – which are dealt with in the general part of contract law – have benefited by the existence of a separate part on restitutionary rules (unjustified enrichment rules). This interaction is also present in specific sales issues, such as product liability and the relationship between the liability of the seller and that of the producer.

Finally, the work pursued within the Study Group on a European Civil Code has put sales in the wider context of further fields of law (included in the original mandate of the research contract with the Commission). This was fruitful in particular with reference to the law of secured transactions and to the treatment of reservation of title in sales contracts. Retention of title represents in practice a security device for the protection of the vendor when the latter, as it is often the case, has to sell on credit, but the buyer is allowed to take delivery of the goods before payment. While this clause – and others deriving from it – are widely used in many Member States, the great differences in the domestic rules applying to such clauses, coupled with the application of the *lex situs* conflict-of-law rule, make recognition of foreign retention of title clauses very difficult, if not impossible, within the European market. This hinders cross-European commerce as well as the granting of credit to buyers coming from different jurisdictions. Thus, there might be a well-founded interest on the part of the Commission or other European institutions to foster (minimum) common provisions.[44] If, however, discussions on this topic take place within the limited framework of (consumer) sales contracts, the retention of title clause is isolated from other devices ensuring an analogous protection to providers of loans specifically aimed at enabling the use of assets on credit (such as for example finance leases). Furthermore, it would not be connected to the general topic of security devices over movable goods (personal property). This could lead to rules which are unbalanced and unsound either from an economic or from an equitable point of view. The "wider" CFR has the merit of putting the mentioned clauses into their proper context.

As it was already mentioned, some questions regarding the European law on sales were particularly difficult to address within the CFR.[45] One of the

---

transfer their ownership to the other party is to be considered as primarily a contract for the sale of the goods'.

44 We may recall that the extent to which a retention of title clause should be regulated was discussed within the framework of the 35/2000/EC Directive on combating late payments in commercial transactions (*OJ* L 200, August 8, 2000, at 35 et seq.). The result was, however, disappointing. See the recent ECJ Case C-302/05, *Commission v. Italy*, Oct. 26, 2006, where the Court confirmed the view held by scholars that the Directive applies only to the relationship between seller and buyer and does not deal with opposability to third parties. In particular, E.-M. Kieninger, in: J. Basedow et al (Eds), *Aufbruch nach Europa* (2001), 151 et seq., at 160 et seq.

45 Just to mention some of the most debated provisions: the need for the buyer to give notice of non-conformity of the goods within a certain period in order to be able to exercise the remedies against the

crucial points is certainly to what extent the protection of the consumer (or the weaker party in general) may be enhanced by a greater use of protective mandatory provisions, compared to what we now find in the CFR. In fact, the failure to address this question was indicated as one of the main open issues of the PECL.[46] Some commentators have criticized the PECL for not considering the importance of mandatory rules and, more generally, for begging the question of the underlying politics of contract law.[47] The CFR on sales emphasizes the default character of its rule,[48] but it does contain some specific mandatory rules in favour of consumers.[49] While the issue is still open, it must be pointed out that mandatory rules are just one of the possible ways to reach the goal of protecting the weaker party,[50] and that an excessive recourse to them may sometimes result in detriment to the weaker party (see as an example the rigid "hierarchy of remedies" in the Consumer Sales Directive), or in the abandoning of protective measures by enterprises (as could be the case for an excessive rigidity of the provisions on the optional consumer guarantee).

---

seller; the extent of the information duties imposed on the parties, especially before conclusion of the contract; the extent of the principle of good faith and fair dealing.

46 "The Lando-Commission has never addressed the difficult question, to what extent and in which way the mandatory rules on consumer protection can be integrated into a set of principles of general contract law": see Zimmermann (n 6), at 115.

47 See most recently M.W. Hesselink, "European Contract Law. A Matter of Consumer Protection, Citizenship or Justice?", (2007) *European Review of Private Law*, at 323 et seq.; M. Loos, "The influence of European Consumer Law on General Contract Law and the Need for Spontaneous Harmonisation", (2007) *European Review of Contract Law* 515, at 528 et seq.

48 See DCFR Book IV, Arts IV.A.-1:301, according to which the rules are to be understood as default rules except when otherwise provided.

49 Some of the mandatory rules are in the form of limits to derogation from certain rights recognised in favour of the consumer (see Article IV.A.-2:309 and IV.A.-4:104 relating to conformity and remedies for non-conformity); other rules expressly state their mandatory character (see Article IV.A.-5:103 on the passing of risk in consumer contracts as well as many rules in Ch. 6 dealing with consumer guarantees). All mandatory rules do not exclude a modification to the benefit of the consumer.

50 On the wide range of forms to protect the weaker party in a contract see for all G. Howells, S. Weatherhill, *Consumer Protection Law*, 2nd ed. (2005).

CHAPTER 6

A European Law of Lease?

Kåre Lilleholt*

I Introduction

In Reinhard Zimmermann's *The Law of Obligations*, lines are drawn from the Roman *locatio conductio* to the present-day rules in Europe on contracts for temporary use of things in exchange for payment.[1] The roots may be common, but a study of modern lease law reveals quite significant differences from country to country, not only differences between English law and Irish law on the one hand, and the continental systems on the other, but also within the continental systems. If the title of this intervention should be read as a question of whether or not there is a European law of lease today, the answer must be: it depends. It depends on the degree of coherence and common solutions that should be required in order to speak of "European law" in a specific area. If one asks for a set of lease rules that could possibly meet practical needs, the answer must probably be no, there is no such European law of lease.

The title can also be read as a question concerning the possibility of a model for a European law of lease. A proposal for such a model will be presented in a few weeks in the form of a new volume in the series *Principles of European Law* from the Study Group on a European Code,[2] and some comments will be given here on the preparation and contents of this book. The subtitle of the volume is *Lease of Goods*, and it contains, like the other volumes of the series, a set of black letter rules, accompanied by comments and comparative notes. For the sake of convenience, the term 'lease principles' will be used both for the proposed black letter rules and for the entire volume, including comments and notes.

The lease principles were prepared by a Working Team, with advice from an Advisory Council, consisting of senior researchers from several European countries, and with the approval of the Co-ordinating Group within the Study Group on a European Civil Code. It may be of interest to note that the lease principles were prepared by a Working Team based in Bergen, Norway – the only team with a base outside the European Union, reminding us that Europe is a little wider than the Union.

II The Lease Principles and the Draft Common Frame of Reference

A contract for the lease of goods is defined in the lease principles as "a contract under which one party, the lessor, undertakes to provide the other party, the lessee, with a temporary right of use of goods in exchange for rent" (IV.B – 1:101). The elements of this definition are well known to all European legal systems: we talk about a "contract", the contract concerns a "right of

* Professor, University of Oslo.

1 R. Zimmermann, *The law of obligations. Roman foundations of the civilian tradition* (1996), 338-383.

2 K. Lilleholt et al., *Principles of European law on lease of goods (PEL LG)*, (2008).

use", the right of use is "temporary", and this temporary right of use is provided "in exchange for rent".

The lease principles deal only with movable property, as already indicated by the word "goods". This is a result of the Study Group's general demarcation against the law concerning immovable property. Proposing general principles of lease of immovable property would have been a most challenging task, not only because of the intriguing varieties of national legal traditions in field of immovable property, but also due to the social and political aspects that are embedded in particular in housing law.

Even if the elements of such contracts are known in all systems, the categorization within the system differs. In common law, we find ourselves within the wider category of "bailment", including other legal relationships of voluntary possession of goods belonging to another,[3] while on the continent a contract for the use of movable property is regarded as part of a wider category including rights of use of immovable property as well. However, this difference in systematic approach has not caused much difficulty in the preparation of the lease principles.

The term "lease" was no obvious choice. In English there are other candidates, like "hire" and "rent". The Co-ordinating Group settled for "lease". One reason is that "lease" corresponds to convenient terms for the parties to the contract, "lessor" and "lessee". The word "rent" could consequently be reserved for the remuneration. As usual, the native English speakers generously accepted a word that probably may sound strange to them in some contexts. It seems easier to find the appropriate terminology in most continental systems, although a choice sometimes has to be made, like *location* instead of *bail* or *louage* in the French translation (the volume contains eleven language versions of the black letter rules).

For some time, the Study Group on a European Civil Code has participated in the wider Joint Network on European Private Law, preparing an academic Draft Common Frame of Reference on the background of the European Commission's initiatives on European contract law.[4] The Commission has carefully insisted that the Common Frame of Reference is not meant to become a European Civil Code,[5] and so the academic draft is not a draft Civil Code, either. However, the texts prepared by the Study Group and the Draft Common Frame of Reference have the *formal outline* of a civil code, with books, parts and chapters, and – more important – they seek the coherence and systematization typical of a civil code. Thus, the lease principles cannot be a stand-alone proposal for a European lease law. The principles form an integrated "Part B of Book IV" of a much wider text.

---

[3] P. Birks (ed.), *English private law*, II, (2000), 357-358 (Norman Palmer).

[4] See for further information, www.copecl.org.

[5] The most recent statements are found in COM(2007) 447 final. Second progress report on the common frame of reference, see in particular pages 10-11.

The previous publications from the Study Group[6] have references to the Principles of European Contract Law when it comes to general contract law. Not so anymore: the lease principles refer to the updated and expanded general parts found in the Draft Common Frame of Reference as well as to other parts of that text. The first publication of the black letter rules of the Draft Common Frame of Reference will be early in 2008, and in the meantime the reader of the lease principles has to put up with some references that seem to go up in thin air.

This integration into a wider project has consequences for the material rules proposed. First of all, rules of a general character are not repeated in the lease principles; the general parts of the Draft Common Frame of Reference apply. The purpose of the lease principles is to make supplements and adjustments to the general parts where this is needed because of the particular constellations of a lease contract. Secondly, the lease rules are harmonized with the general parts of the Draft Common Frame of Reference, concerning both results and the model of regulation. The idea has been that there should not be unnecessary deviations from the general rules. Thirdly, there has been a harmonization with the rules on other specific contracts, mostly the sale principles, for example regarding rules on the conformity of the goods with the contract.

In addition to this harmonization with the general parts of the Draft Common Frame of Reference and with the rules of specific contracts other than lease, the lease principles are of course inspired also by national law on lease contracts. It follows, however, from what is said, that the principles are not some sort of restatement of European lease law. Neither is it a proposal for a possible common legislation for a stand-alone European lease law. The principles only have a meaning in the light of the entire Draft Common Frame of Reference.[7]

From a Nordic point of view, this has been an interesting process. As the there are no civil codes in the Nordic countries, general rules on contracts, or the general law of obligations, are seen as the extract or generalization of rules on specific contracts, rules that have often been laid down in legislation. Formulating general contract law is regarded as a process from the bottom up; sometimes the term "induction" is used to describe the process. The work on lease principles within the Study Group has been much more of a process from the top down, as the general rules were mostly given. Of course, to some extent there has been influence the other way round as well. General rules of the Draft

6 C. v. Bar, *Principles of European law on benevolent intervention in another's affairs (PEL Ben. Int.)*, (2006); M.W. Hesselink et al., *Principles of European law on commercial agency, franchise and distribution contracts (PEL CAFDC)*, (2006); M. Barendrecht et al., *Principles of European law on service contracts (PEL SC)* (2007); *U. Drobnig, Principles of European law on personal security (PEL Pers. Sec.)* (2007).

7 For a statement concerning the present state of work of the Study Group, see C. v. Bar's Foreword in Lilleholt et al., VII-IX. There is already a rich literature concerning the methodology aspects of European law projects. See for a recent and open-minded contribution, E. Örücü, "What next in the convergence process in Europe", in M. Bussani, U. Mattei (eds.), *Opening up European law* (2007),175-194.

Common Frame of Reference have sometimes been adjusted when the need for refinement was found in the process of drafting rules on specific contracts.

III Rules Specific to Lease Contracts – An Overview

One of the characteristics of the lease contract that makes special regulation necessary is the time aspect. The lease contract is performed over a period of time. The lease principles contain rules on the start of the lease period, the duration of the lease period and on the expiry of the lease period. Rules on tacit prolongation are also found, implying that the lease period is prolonged in some cases where the lessee, with the lessor's knowledge, continues to use the goods after the expiry of the agreed lease period (IV.B – 2:103). Tacit prolongation is well known in many jurisdictions, but controversial on a European level. In short, the solution chosen in the lease principles may be characterised as a rebuttable presumption for prolongation in certain situations.

Furthermore, the lease contract implies that goods are made available to the lessee and should remain so throughout the lease period. This element of the contract requires rules concerning the conformity of the goods with the contract. The rules on conformity at the start of the lease period are mainly similar to the corresponding rules found in the sale principles. The time aspect of the lease contract calls for additional rules on conformity of the goods during the lease period, and these are rules without clear parallels with other contracts. There is even a dynamic element in the lease rules, in that not only maintenance and repair but also modifications to the goods may be necessary if they are to remain fit for the agreed purpose (IV.B – 3:104).

In a lease, goods belonging to one party are left in the hands of another party who has a right to use the goods but also an obligation to take care of the goods (IV.B – 5:104). Partly, the rules on care overlap the rules concerning maintenance and repair, but there are more independent rules as well, e.g. rules on obligations to inform the lessor and even to intervene in some cases to prevent damage or danger to the goods (IV.B – 5:105, IV.B – 5:107).

As for remedies against non-performance, the lease principles mainly refer to the general parts of the Draft Common Frame of Reference. Supplements are required just at few places. One example is rent reduction, a remedy that is applicable not only in cases of lack of conformity, like it is in a sale, but also for situations of delay (IV.B – 4:104). Another example is the lessee's right to "self-help", i.e. to have a lack of conformity remedied by doing the work himself or having a third party doing it (IV.B – 4:103). Unlike the corresponding situation in a sale, where the buyer may do as he likes with his purchase, the lessee is performing work on goods belonging to another person, and the limits must then be the same as the limits to a claim for specific performance.

The Draft Common Frame of Reference will include – in the same ways as the Principles of European Contract Law – rules on assignment of rights under a contract and also on substitution as a debtor under a contract. For lease contracts, the rule is that the lessee cannot assign his rights without the lessor's consent (IV.B – 7:102). This has been chosen as a starting point, even if the solutions vary throughout Europe. Also for subleasing, the lessor's consent is required, but the lease principles include a rule that is found in several jurisdictions, allowing the lessee to terminate the lease period by giving notice if consent to sublease is withheld without good reason (IV.B – 7:103).

Change in ownership of the goods raises some difficult questions. Must the lessee accept that the new owner is substituted as a party to the lease contract? And must the new owner respect the lease contract? At least for a Nordic lawyer, raising such questions seemed like entering into a continental conceptual minefield where one had to avoid stepping on strange explosives like proprietary rights and a variety of forms of possession and detention. The solution chosen in the lease principles may be called an *ex lege* transfer model. The new owner is automatically substituted as a party to the lease contract if the lessee has possession of the goods at the time ownership passes. The lessee must accept this, but the former owner remains subsidiarily liable for the non-performance of the contract as a personal security provider. The lessee must also respect a reversal of the passing of ownership IV.B – 7:101). The lease team was happy to leave the question on what happens to the lease when the lessee is *not* yet in possession of the goods to the team working with rules on transfer of ownership.

IV Do We Need Rules on Specific Contracts?

We have just seen that the regulation of lease contracts must be coordinated with general contract rules as well as rules concerning specific contracts other than lease. The next question is: do we really need rules on specific contracts?[8] Would it be possible to refine the general rules of contract law to the extent that rules on specific contracts were superfluous? The black letter rules of the lease principles are already rather few and brief. Would the ultimate success of the lease team have been to deliver a book with blank pages only?

The team found that some special rules on leases were needed. There were aspects more or less of exclusive interest to lease contracts, for example the rules on maintenance and repairs. But the lease principles also contain rules on contractual elements that are at least to some extent common with several types of contracts. Performance over a period of time is found in several service contracts, in distribution contracts, in loan contracts, etc. Taking care of another person's goods is relevant not only to leases but also to storage contracts and

[8] On the development of general contract law, see R. Zimmermann (n. 1), 337–343 and *passim*. See also K.-P. Nanz, *Die Entstehung des allgemeinen Vertragsbegriffs im 16. bis 18. Jahrhundert* (1985).

some other service contracts. Rules on conformity of the goods are important also in sale contracts.

An intriguing idea is to include in a body of general contract law specific rules on certain *elements* – or functions – of a contract, for example the element of making goods available to another person, the element of a contract period, including start, duration and expiry, the element of taking care of another person's goods, etc. In order to avoid the much-used term "functional", we could call this an "element-based" approach to contract law. A successful element-based regulation could make rules on specific contracts unnecessary.

Such thoughts are not new, in particular not in systems without codifications of the law of contracts,[9] but the idea has hardly ever been set into life. An element-based approach to contract law has not been part of the plan of the Study Group on a European Civil Code, and neither is it part of the Common Frame of Reference project. The idea would perhaps also have been too radical from a political point of view. However, the work on the Draft Common Frame of Reference has shown that a lot of co-ordination is possible across the borders of specific contracts, and it may be possible to go further on this road of systematizing and generalizing contract law in the future.

Regulating contract elements rather than specific contracts could solve some of the problems we have with what is often called "mixed" contracts, "combined" contracts, or "new" contracts. Elements of different specific contract are often combined in practical life, and these contracts do not always easily fit into traditional categories. In many cases, we are not content by just saying that such contracts are regulated by general contract rules. Instead, we try to classify according to the traditional system of specific contracts. Now and then we resign and just label contract models with some permanency as "new" contract types.[10]

There is hardly a generally accepted approach to handling contracts with elements of different specific contracts. For the so-called mixed contracts, it is sometimes held that a preponderant element is decisive; and sometimes it is held that the rules on different specific contracts should be applied in combination, with necessary adaptations. Probably, there is not one single answer; different approaches must apply according to the circumstances. Some guidelines will be given in the general part of the Draft Common Frame of Reference. Here, only one example will be dealt with, the so-called "finance leases" or "financial leasing".

9 For a Norwegian contribution to the discussion, see K. Krüger, *Norsk kontraktsrett*, (1989), in particular 129-145. More generally, one could mention the discussion on "a law of contract or contracts" found in several English books on contract law, see for example M. Furmston, *Chesire, Fifoot and Furmston's Law of contract*, Fifteenth edition (2007), 29.

10 For a comprehensive discussion, see R. Sacco and G. de Nova, *Il contratto*, II, 3rd ed. (2004), 439-469. See also J. Oechsler, "Vertragstypen", in *Eckpfleiler des Zivilrechts*, ed. Michael Martinek (2005), 493-512.

V The Example of "Finance Leases"

A lease contract normally includes an element of credit or deferred payment compared with a sale: the lessee obtains the use of goods without paying the full price at once. Further, to the extent that the lessor's right in the goods is protected against the lessee's general creditors, this right in real terms secures the lessor's claim for payment under the contract: the goods will be returned to the lessor if the lessee ceases to pay. These basic characteristics of a lease contract are often used for financing purposes; that is, one party provides capital for another party's acquisition of goods from a third party. The goods are bought from the supplier of the goods by the financing party, who, taking the role of a lessor, will then lease the goods to the party who is going to use them, the lessee. The lessee may have a right to become owner of the goods later on or he may not. Often, such contracts are made for a period corresponding to the expected economic life span of the goods, and if that is the case, the question of ownership after the expiry of this period is of very little interest from an economic point of view. It should be noted, however, that the lease contracts under these financing transactions may be entered into for much shorter periods, often including a stipulation of a "residual value" at the end of the lease period.[11]

Under the UNIDROIT convention on international financial leasing (Ottawa, 28 May 1988), an essential characteristic of the contracts to which the convention applies, is the role of the lessor as a financing party, acquiring the goods in connection with the lease contract, at the lessee's specification and from a supplier selected by the lessee. It is, however, obvious that other lease contracts, not meeting this specific criterion, will serve the same purposes and have the same effects as the contracts described as "financial leasing" or "finance leases". For example, the lessor may have the role of a financing party by obtaining the goods and the rights under the lease contract from the original lessor. And the element of credit is the same in two-party transactions as it is in three-party transactions. The functional similarity with a sale depends on the lease period and on possible agreements concerning passing of ownership, not on the three-party relationship. And so on.

Should "finance leases", according to one definition or the other, be regarded as a contract type of its own kind, a specific contract *sui generis*, falling outside the scope of the lease principles? Or should "finance leases" be re-characterised as sale contracts, loan contracts, contracts on security rights, or perhaps as a combination of two or more of these contracts? This question turned out to be controversial during the preparation of the lease principles, and this was to be expected, there being so many opinions as to what a "finance lease" really is.

The solution chosen in the lease principles is rather simple and may be summed up in four points.

The first point is that the lease principles do not apply where the parties have agreed that ownership will be transferred after a period with right of use, even if the parties have described the contract as a lease (IV.B – 1:101(3)). These are

11 For an overview of national law, see Lilleholt et al. (n. 2), 118-121.

contracts that fall under the definition of a contract for sale. To what extent the lease principles can be applied with appropriate adaptations during the period prior to the passing of ownership, may partly depend on the general provision on mixed contracts in the Draft Common Frame of Reference.

The second point is that the application of the lease principles is not excluded by the fact that the contract has a financing purpose, that the lessor has the role as a financing party, or that the lessee has an option to become owner of the goods (IV.B – 1:101(4)). This does not prevent the application of rules from other parts of the Draft Common Frame of Reference, for example, rules on loan contracts concerning pre-contractual information duties. Also here, the application with appropriate adaptations of rules on specific contracts other than lease contracts, for example rules on sale in a situation where an option to buy is exercised, may partly depend on the general provision on mixed contracts.

Third point is that the lease principles apply only to the contractual relationship between lessor and lessee (IV.B – 1:101(5)). This is rather obvious, but it implies that it is left to other parts of the Draft Common Frame of Reference to decide whether or not the lessor's ownership should be regarded as a security right, perhaps entailing extra requirements for the protection against the lessee's general creditors.

The fourth point is that the lease principles contain some special rules inspired by the regulations of the UNIDROIT convention on international financial leasing. The idea has been, not to implement all the rules of the convention, but to find out which elements of a contract can serve as a justification of each special rule. Only the two most important rules will be mentioned here. The first special rule is that the lessee, and only the lessee, bears all obligations of repairs and maintenance where the rent is calculated so as to take into account the amortization of the cost of the goods by the lessee (IV.B – 3:104(2), IV.B – 5:104(2)). This rule applies whether there is a three-party transaction or a two-party transaction. In such cases the entire economic interest in the goods, apart from the lessor's security for payment, is in real terms transferred to the lessee. The second special rule to be mentioned here is that most of the lessee's remedies for non-performance may be channelled towards the supplier, past the lessor, where the goods are acquired for the lease contract, at the specification of the lessee, from a supplier selected by the lessee (IV.B – 4:107). The justification for this rule is that the lessor has the role only of a financing party: when you have received non-conforming goods you normally turn to the supplier, not to the lender. In this case, there is no requirement concerning the amortisation of the cost, and the rule will apply also to leases with a residual value.

The rules just mentioned may be regarded as examples of an element-based approach to regulation, albeit within the frames of the rules on a specific contract.

CHAPTER 7

Damages for Fraud in Case of not Avoiding the Contract

Gema Tomás*

I Introduction: Focus of the Issue

This paper focuses on the question of claiming damages in cases of fraud when the deceived party is not interested in avoiding the contract. Beyond any doubt, fraud or *dolus* in the formation of the contract entitles the aggrieved party to avoid the contract and to claim liability for damage as well, if there is such damage. But it has been discussed in Spanish Law whether or not it is possible to claim damages without avoiding the contract. That is to say, it is a question of knowing whether the action to claim *id quod interest* works notwithstanding the action for avoidance of the contract. A recent decision of the Spanish Supreme Court of 18 January 2007 tackles this subject for the first time in Spanish judicial history. The findings of the court are very interesting and cover a gap in Spanish law. Besides, it is interesting to see the correspondence between this decision and the Principles of European Contract Law (PECL) in relation with this issue. As we will see in this paper, the Spanish judicial decision fits in with the harmonizing principles in European contract law and also with the UNIDROIT principles related with fraud, which makes it interesting also in the field of the European Common Frame of Reference.[1]

The regulation of fraud in Spanish Civil Code (CC), published in 1889, leaves some questions to be solved. Fraud is considered a vice in agreement which affects the validity of the contract (Article 1.265). There is fraud, when a party is led to conclude a contract whether by mischievous words or conduct of the other party (Article 1.269).[2] The deceived party is entitled to avoid the contract within a four years term since the moment of consummation of the contract (Article 1.301.3°) as long as the fraud is serious or important and has been only used by one of the parties (Article 1.270.1°).

This sort of fraud is known as *dolus causam dans*, in the sense that one party has been led to conclude the contract by those words or conduct. But if the fraud is not serious or important (the CC calls it specifically in this case "dolo incidental", *dolus incidens*), it does not entitle the deceived party to avoiding the contract, but only leads to liability for damage.[3] The difference between the two sorts of

* University of Deusto.

1 C. Von Bar, "Working together toward a Common Frame of Reference", X (2005) *Juridica International* 17 26.

2 Article 1.265 CC: "Es nulo el consentimiento prestado por error, violencia, intimidación o dolo". And fraud is defined in the article 1.269: "Hay dolo cuando, con palabras o maquinaciones insidiosas de parte de uno de los contratantes, es inducido el otro a celebrar un contrato que, sin ellas, no hubiera hecho". See Y. Atard, R. González, *El dolo en el Derecho civil* (s.d.); A. Cossío y Corral, *El dolo en el Derecho civil*, (1955); L. Díez-Picazo, *Fundamentos del Derecho civil Patrimonial*, vol.I (Introducción. Teoría del contrato), 6th ed., (2007), 198 ff; F. De Castro, *El negocio jurídico* (1971) (reprint1991), 147-156; L. Rojo Ajuria , *El dolo en los contratos* (1994)

3 Article 1270.1 CC: "Para que el dolo produzca la nulidad de los contratos, deberá ser grave y no haber sido empleado por las dos partes contratantes. 2. El dolo incidental sólo obliga al que lo empleó a indem-

fraud was elaborated by the Glossators from Roman sources and it is still alive in many legal European systems, also in the Spanish system.[4] It is difficult to make the distinction in real practice, and only the *dolus causam dans*, because of its importance, entitles to avoid the contract.

But as far as we concerned, nothing is said in the CC about claiming damages in case of serious fraud. Hence, two questions arise:

1) is it possible to claim damages in cases of serious fraud, even if nothing is stated in the law? It seems easy to give a positive answer for two reasons: On the one hand, because it would be absurd being able to claim damages for less serious fraud and to be denied it in cases of important fraud which actually leads a party to the agreement and to the conclusion of the contract. And on the other hand, because avoiding a contract does not mean to delete all the possible consequences from the contract (*id quod interest*);
2) is the aggrieved party entitled to claim damages, even if it is not interested in avoiding the contract, or does it not have this right?

Notwithstanding the silence of the Civil Code, Spanish scholars have stated the compatibility between avoiding the contract and claiming liability for fraudulent behaviour since the fifties. They are different actions, they give rise to different effects and also, they work in independent ways. In consequence, the aggrieved party can choose whichever it prefers or even claim both.[5] From then on, the Supreme Court has decided on some occasions on claims of liability joined to the avoidance of the contract, but it had never pronounced itself about damages for fraud without avoiding the contract. Besides, there has been a certain amount of confusion about the notion of avoidance as a remedy to get damages.[6]

---

nizar daños y perjuicios".

4 See R. Zimmermann, *The law of obligations. Roman Foundations of the Civilian Tradition* (1990), p. 670 ff. Also H Kotz,. and A. Flessner, *European contract law*, vol.I (1997), p. 196 ff.

5 The first scholar to raise the question was Cossío (n. 2) 365-372; later M. Alonso Pérez., "La responsabilidad precontractual", (1971) *Revista Crítica de Derecho Inmobiliario* 916; Rojo Ajuria (n. 2), p. 124 ff, and A. Cabanillas Sánchez, "El ámbito de la responsabilidad precontractual o la culpa *in contrahendo*", (1995) *Revista Crítica de Derecho Inmobiliario* 747-788.

6 Rojo Ajuria (n. 2) 124 ff, explains that confusion by pointing at the influence of the French scholarship after codification, which was very close to the Roman tradition of the *actio doli*, and conceived the action to avoid the contract by fraud as an action to claim liability.

II Decision of the Spanish Supreme Court of 18 January 2007 on Damages for Fraud

The Spanish Supreme Court has decided on this question for the first time in its recent decision of 18 January 2007.[7] The case concerns a claim for damages by a leasing company (Infoleasing S.A.) against three linked companies and the five brothers and sisters in charge of the management of these companies, on the ground that all of them had acted fraudulently.

The decision declares that three options are available in Spanish law:

a) to avoid the contract and claim damages (that is to say, two actions);
b) to avoid the contract without claiming damages (one action);
c) to claim damages without avoiding the contract (one action). This last one is the most controversial question, as has been mentioned above.

The first option raises no doubts, neither for Spanish scholarship[8] nor in court practice.[9] Nevertheless, what is stated now is the independence of the two actions. They pursue different goals and can work separately. Hence, it is admitted to claim damages while maintaining the validity of the contract.

The court's decision is based on two reasons: firstly, because legal provision prevents such a result, and secondly, by analogy with what is regulated in case of non-performance. According to article 1.124 CC, the parties have the right to terminate a contract and also to claim damages. Both intentions can be combined or asked separately, one without the other. The Supreme Court seems to fill a legal gap concerning this issue. Moreover, the Supreme Court overturns the decision of the lower court (Audiencia Provincial),, which had avoided the contract even notwithstanding the fact that the plaintiff had not claimed it.

Now we can study the subject from two other points of view: first, the approach of the issue from what it is called *culpa in contrahendo* and second, the PECL's regulation on this point.

III Fraud and Liability for Damage in *Contrahendo*

Fraud in formation of the contract may be analysed as a phenomenon closely related with *culpa in contrahendo*. The Spanish Civil Code does not contain this concept wrought by Ihering in 1861 to refer to liability in the pre-contractual period. His theory is based on Roman sources related with sales of *res extra commercium* or an inexistent inheritance whenever the seller knows

---

7 LA LEY 66/2007

8 Cfr. J.R Verda y Beamonte, "El dolo *in contrahendo*", 16 (2006) *Revista de Derecho Patrimonial* 65.

9 Several Spanish Supreme Court decisions have stated the compatibility between damages and avoidance: for example Decisions of 18 July 1988, LA LEY JURIS: 107-1/1988 and 26 October 1981, LA LEY JURIS: 12819- JF/0000).

this point and does not inform the buyer. This behaviour can be defined as dolus *in contrahendo* or rather *culpa in contrahendo*, as Ihering calls it. In these cases, a *bona fide* buyer has a contractual action to obtain *id quod interest* apart from the action to avoid the contract.[10]

Spanish scholars have studied the so-called *culpa in contrahendo*[11] and they allow, without any doubt, claiming damages in pre-contractual liability. Delving into the expression "pre-contractual liability", this one is focused rather on acting against good faith in preliminary negotiations,[12] than on calling for liability in cases of contractual avoidance – in this sense, it appears to come closer to Ihering's concept of *culpa in contrahendo*.[13] Among these last ones we find fraud or *dolus in contrahendo*[14] and the Spanish scholars do not object to

---

10 R. von Ihering, "Culpa *in contrahendo* oder Schadenerzartz bei nichtigen oder nicht zur Perfection gelangten Verträgen", 4 (1861) *Jahrbücher für die Dogmatik des heutigen römischen und deutschen Privatrechts* 1-113.

11 Vid. about culpa *in contrahendo* in Spanish law: M. Alonso Pérez.(n. 5) 859-922; C.I. Asúa González, *La culpa in contrahendo (Tratamiento en el Derecho alemán y presencia en otros ordenamientos)* (1989); C.I. Asúa González, J.J. Hualde Sánchez, "Codificación de la culpa *in contrahendo* en el Derecho alemán", in: *Estudios en Homenaje al Profesor Luis Díez-Picazo*, t.II (2003), 1415-1433; F. de P. Blasco Gascó, "El contrato antes del contrato (Reflexiones sobre la responsabilidad contractual)", in: *Contratación y Consumo* (1998); Cabanillas Sánchez (n. 5) 747-788; A. Carrasco Perera, "Cartas de intenciones, precontratos, responsabilidad *in contrahendo* y obligatoriedad de los tratos en la jurisprudencia española", (2006) 21 *Aranzadi Civil* 15-38; J.L. De Los Mozos, "Responsabilidad en los tratos preparatorios del contrato", in: *Estudios sobre Derecho de contratos, Integración europea y codificación* (2005), 77-99; Díez-Picazo (n. 2) 314-326; Mª. Paz García Rubio, *La responsabilidad precontractual en el derecho español* (1991); A. Manzanares, (1984) "La responsabilidad precontractual en la hipótesis de ruptura injustificada de las negociaciones preliminares", *Anuario de Derecho civil* 687-748; and *Id*, "La naturaleza de la responsabilidad precontractual o culpa *in contrahendo*", (1985) *Anuario de Derecho Civil* 979-1009; E. Vázquez De Castro, *Ilicitud contractual. Supuestos y efectos* (2003), 529 ss; Verda (n. 8) 25-69.

12 Situations as we can mention here: a) To negotiate or breaking off a preliminary negotiation contrary to good faith; b) To enter or continue a negotiation without non real intention to reach an agreement; c) Disclose the confidential information given in the course of negotiations or use it for its own purposes against good faith. Vid decision of the Supreme Court (First. Section) 16 December 1999, LA LEY JURIS: 2642/2000. It is no included situations like *Linoleumfall* (a leading case of German Law related with the accident suffered by a client in a shop at the moment of the purchase and that was caused by an employee). They can be included in wide article 1.902 CC which is inspired in the principle *alterum non laedere*. That would rather be a non-contractual liability than a pre-contractual liability.

13 Vázquez De Castro (n. 11) 538; García Rubio (n. 11) 64 ff.

14 The following situations are usually included: a) Non disclosure that one party has an impediment to perform the contract beyond its control or that its performance would be illegal or immoral; b) Non disclosure the lack of capacity to enter into a contract; c) Causes to avoid a contract as: mistake, fraud, threats o violence; d) To ask for liability for damage in cases of sales without conformity (Article 1.486.2° CC) or in contract of depot or *comodatus* (ad ex. Article 1.752); e) Cases of *falsus procurator*, whenever the third party acts according with good faith.

claiming damages in these situations, given that avoidance does not always put the aggrieved party into the same position as if the agreement had not been concluded.

So, if the facts of this case had been seen to be in the realm of *culpa* or rather *dolus in contrahendo,* it would have led to the same solution: to award damages, either if the party had claimed avoidance, or not. The Spanish Supreme Court decision mentioned above goes further, because it establishes, for the first time, the independence of both actions. Until now, the court only had recognised damages if the contract was declared void at the same time.[15]

IV Damages For Fraud and Principles of European Contract Law

Last but not least, it may be interesting to compare how the subject is dealt with in the Principles of European Contract Law. These principles establish good faith and fair dealing as general duties in Article 1:201 (1)[16] and they are applied to both the pre-contractual period and the contractual relationship. Hence, on the one hand, it regulates liability for negotiations contrary to good faith and breach of confidentiality (Article 2:301 y 2:302).[17] On the other hand, fraud is regulated in Chapter 4 ("Validity" of the contract) and is related to good faith and fair dealing as well.

[15] Cfr. Decisions 26 October 1981, LA LEY JURIS: 12819-JF/0000; 18 July 1988, LA LEY JURIS: 107-1/1988; 30 June 2000, LA LEY JURIS:178049/2000, in a "dolus incidens"'situation. In any case, Spanish courts seldom speak of *dolus* or *culpa in contrahendo.*

[16] Article 1:201 (1) PECL: "Each party must act in accordance with good faith and fair dealing". See: R. Zimmermann, S. Whittaker (ed.), *Good faith in European Contract Law* (2000); H. Kötz, "Towards a European Civil code: the duty of good faith", in: P. Cane, J. Stapleton (ed.), *The Law of obligations. Essays in celebration of John Fleming* (1998), p. 243-259. From a Spanish perspective see F. Martínez Sanz, "Buena fe", in S. Cámara Lapuente (coord.), *Derecho privado europeo* (2003), p. 481-498; and in similar terms: "Good faith of the Parties", in R. Schulze, H. Schulte-Nölke, (dirs.), *European Contract Law in Comnunity Law* (2002), p. 127 ff.

[17] Article 2:301 PECL: Negotiations Contrary to Good Faith: "(1) A party is free to negotiate and is not liable for failure to reach an agreement. (2) However, a party who has negotiated or broken off negotiations contrary to good faith and fair dealing is liable for the losses caused to the other party. (3) It is contrary to good faith and fair dealing, in particular, for a party to enter into or continue negotiations with no real intention of reaching an agreement with the other party". Article 2:302: "Breach of Confidentiality": If confidential information is given by one party in the course of negotiations, the other party is under a duty not to disclose that information or use it for its own purposes whether or not a contract is subsequently concluded. The remedy for breach of this duty may include compensation for loss suffered and restitution of the benefit received by the other party". On this subject: Y. Zahn, J. Machteld, S. Rook, A.S. Poissonnet, "Withdrawing from Pre-contractual negotiations and the Duty of Good Faith-Harmonising European Views", (2007) *Ars Aequi* 487-494.

Fraud implies that a party has been led to conclude a contract by the other party's fraudulent representation, whether by words or conduct, or fraudulent non-disclosure of any information which in accordance with good faith and fair dealing it should have disclosed (Article 4:107).[18] There is no distinction between *dolus causam dans* and *dolus incidens.*

That party may avoid the contract with the logical effect of avoidance, which will be, as article 4:115 says, to claim restitution of whatever it has been supplied under the contract.[19] But moreover, article 4:117 (1) entitles the avoiding party to recover damages in order "to put the avoiding party as nearly as possible into the same position as if it had not concluded the contract".[20] More precisely, this measure of damages is usually called "negative interest" or "reliance interest", and it is generally accepted with regard to culpa *in contrahendo.* It was the measure proposed by Ihering because it is a question of awarding damages for the loss suffered through reliance in the other party's good faith. The "negative interest" deals with putting the avoiding party as nearly as possible into the same position as if it had not concluded the contract.[21] This measure is also adopted in article 2:301 PECL concerning liability for preliminary negotiations.[22]

So far, so good; but the first and foremost issue is what is added in the second paragraph of article 4:117. According to this rule, if a party who has the

---

18 The regulation on fraud belongs to First and Second Part of PECL, revised in 1998. It is regulated in article 4:107 (1) PECL: Fraud: A party may avoid a contract when it has been led to conclude it by the other party's fraudulent representation, whether by words or conduct, or fraudulent non-disclosure of any information which in accordance with good faith and fair dealing it should have disclosed". (2) A party's representation or non-disclosure is fraudulent if it was intended to deceive. Cf. M. Fabre-Magnan, R. Sefton-Green, "Defects of Consent in Contract Law", in A. Hartkamp, M. Hesselink, et alii, *Towards a European Civil Code*, 3ª ed., (2004), p. 399-413. From a Spanish point of view, see: A.M. Morales Moreno, "Validez del contrato", in S. Cámara Lapuente (n. 16), p. 371-397.

19 Article 4:115 PECL: "On avoidance either party may claim restitution of whatever it has supplied under the contract, provided it makes concurrent restitution of whatever it has received. If restitution cannot be made in kind for any reason, a reasonable sum must be paid for what has been received".

20 Article 4:117 PECL: Damages: "(1) A party who avoids a contract under this Chapter may recover from the other party damages so as to put the avoiding party as nearly as possible into the same position as if it had not concluded the contract, provided that the other party knew or ought to have known of the mistake, fraud, threat or taking of excessive benefit or unfair advantage".

21 According to Díez-Picazo (n. 2), p. 325, the "negative interest" is also the traditional measure in these cases, as in general it is considered.

22 Article 2:301 PECL (Negotiations Contrary to Good Faith), paragraph (2): "A party who has negotiated or broken off negotiations contrary to good faith and fair dealing is liable for the losses caused to the other party" and the article 2:302 PECL (Breach of Confidentiality): "If confidential information is given by one party in the course of negotiations, the other party is under a duty not to disclose that information or use it for its own purposes whether or not a contract is subsequently concluded. The remedy for breach of this duty may include compensation for loss suffered and restitution of the benefit received by the other party".

right to avoid the contract, but does not exercise its right or has lost it (for example, for "time limits" to avoid the contract, or "confirmation" of contract), it may recover damage as well.[23] This means that, whether it avoids the contract or not, it may claim damages. However, there is an important difference in this case: damages are limited to the loss caused by the fraud to the party which avoided the contract.

Hence, we can draw some important conclusions:

a) liability for damages may be claimed whether or not the deceived party claims the nullity of the contract;
b) the measure of damages is the negative interest if the avoidance is claimed as well;
c) PECL limit the measure of damages in case of claiming damages while maintaining the validity of the contract. In this case the limit is the loss suffered by the aggrieved party.

And we can also add another one: if there is contractual liability along with pre-contractual liability, it will be possible to claim the positive interest or performance interest. For instance, when there is not only fraud leading a party to conclude the deal, but there is also fraud in order not to perform the contract. The final words of article 4:117 must be understood in this sense : "In other respects, the damages shall be in accordance with the relevant provisions of Chapter 9, Section 5, with appropriate adaptations" (that means: with the remedies for non – performance). And the general measure of damages in this case is such a sum that it will put the aggrieved party as nearly as possible into the position in which it would have been, had the contract been duly performed. (Article 9:502).[24]

---

[23] Article 4:117 PECL: Damages: 2) If a party has the right to avoid a contract under this Chapter, but does not exercise its right or has lost its right under the provisions of Articles 4:113 or 4:114, it may recover, subject to paragraph (1), damages limited to the loss caused to it by the mistake, fraud, threat or taking of excessive benefit or unfair advantage. The same measure of damages applies when the party was misled by incorrect information in the sense of article 4:106 PECL. The article 4:113 (1) PECL refers to "time limits": Notice of avoidance must be given within a reasonable time, with due regard to the circumstances, after the avoiding party knew or ought to have known of the relevant facts or became capable of acting freely. Article 4:114 PECL refers to "confirmation": If the party who is entitled to avoid a contract confirms it, expressly or impliedly, after knowing of the ground for avoidance, or becomes capable of acting freely, avoidance of the contract is excluded.

[24] Article 9: 501 states: "The aggrieved party is entitled to damages for loss caused by the other party's non-performance which is not excused article 8:108. The measure for which damages are recoverable includes:(a) non-pecuniary loss; and (b) future loss which is reasonably likely to occur". And the article 9:502: "General measure of damages: The general measure of damages is such sum as will put the aggrieved party as nearly as possible into the position in which it would have been if the contract had been duly performed. Such damages cover the loss which the aggrieved party has suffered and the gain of which it has been deprived".

To be precise, in the above decision of the Spanish Supreme Court, the defendant is condemned to pay the sum that the plaintiff could have received if fraud had not occurred. That is because in this case there was fraud (liability *in contrahendo*) and also negligent non-performance (contractual liability). So, the best measure of damage in this case is the positive interest.

Besides PECL, attention must also be paid to UNIDROIT Principles of International Contracts (edition 2004). Both instruments, PECL and UNIDROIT, show a clear proximity.[25] Thus, the principles of good faith and fair dealing bind the parties in the international code as well.[26] Fraud, related with fair dealing, is defined in similar terms to PECL: it may entitle avoiding the contract (Article 3.8)[27] with the typical effect of restitution of whatever has been supplied (Article 3.17)[28] and it will be possible to claim damages, whether or not the contract has been avoided (Article 3.18).[29]

Therefore, the final result is very similar to PECL, since both principles award the right to claim damages with independence of the contract is avoided or not.[30]

---

25 O. Lando, "CISG and its Followers: A Proposal to Adopt Some International Principles of Contract Law", *American Journal of Comparative Law* (Spring 2005) 379-401. PECL and UNIDROIT Principles show similarity about the time and the members of the different commissions were working on them. But the UNIDROIT Principles are focused on international trade contracts and PECL on European contracts, beyond commercial nature. Also, from a methodological point of view, PECL are closer to American Restatements than UNIDROIT. Cfr. J.C. Fernández Rozas, "Alternativa conflictual o material en la búsqueda de un derecho contractual europeo más coherente", (2005) 6199 *La Ley* 1-9.

26 Article 1.7 UNIDROIT states that "each party must act in accordance with good faith and fair dealing in international trade".

27 Article 3.8 UNIDROIT: "A party may avoid the contract when it has been led to conclude the contract by the other party's fraudulent representation, including language or practices, or fraudulent non-disclosure of circumstances which, according to reasonable commercial standards of fair dealing, the latter party should have disclosed". See on the relationship between good faith and vices of consent: E.A. Kramer, "Fair dealing in International Trade et vices du consentement", in M.J. Bonell, F. Bonelli, (eds.), *Contratti commerciali internazionali e Principi UNIDROIT* (1997), 161-169.

28 Article 3.17 (2) UNIDROIT: "On avoidance either party may claim restitution of whatever it has supplied under the contract or the part of it avoided, provided that it concurrently makes restitution of whatever it has received under the contract or the part of it avoided or, if it cannot make restitution in kind, it makes an allowance for what it has received".

29 Article 3.18 UNIDROIT: "Damages: Irrespective of whether or not the contract has been avoided, the party who knew or ought to have known of the ground for avoidance is liable for damages so as to put the other party in the same position in which it would have been if it had not concluded the contract". See L. Alvarado Herrera, "Validez", in *Comentario a los Principios de UNIDROT para los Contratos del Comercio Internacional* (1999), 161-223 (on fraud see: 189-191 and 217-219).

30 There is an enormous closeness between PECL and the UNIDROIT principles. As M.J. Bonell, "UNIDROIT Principles 2004. The new edition of the Principles of International Commercial Contracts adopted by the International Institute for the Unification of Private Law", (2004) 1 *Uniform Law Review*

V Concluding Remarks

We can draw the following conclusions in view of the Common Frame of Reference:

1) the party deceived or aggrieved by fraud is entitled to claim damages, irrespective of the claim to avoid the contact. Liability for damage works independent of the action to leave the contract without any effect. This issue has been clarified in Spanish law in recent times, thanks to a decision of the Supreme Court which sheds a first light on it. Modern legal systems distinguish the rule of avoidance and rule of liability, each of which has its own requirements and effects;[31]
2) however, the measure of damages is different depending on possible situations. It may be the negative interest if the contract is avoided, or only the loss caused by fraud if it is not avoided. If non-performance occurs, the sum of damages may even reach the positive interest;
3) athough the Spanish judicial decision does not quote the Principles of European Contract law,[32] the comparative exercise we have carried out in this paper shows a closer approach to them and to other principles of legal harmonisation.[33] If we take an optimistic view, the Spanish decision may show that harmonization of contract law is already taking shape.

5-40, puts it: "about two thirds ot the 185 articles contained in the UNIDROIT principles 2004 have almost literally correspondence in the articles of PECL".

31 See Kötz (n. 16), p. 207 ff ("Claims for damages").

32 On the reception of PECL and the UNIDROIT principles in the Spanish case law, Mª.P. Perales Viscasillas, "La aplicación jurisprudencial en España de la Convención de Viena de 1980 sobre compraventa internacional, los principios de Unidroit y los principios del Derecho contractual europeo: de la mera referencia a la integración de lagunas", (2007) 6725 *La Ley* 1-7. See also the decision of de Supreme Court of 4 June 2006, which contains references to both instruments in a case of non-performance of a commercial contract and the remedies available in this case.

33 On the concept of damage in European law: A. Vaquer Aloy, "Hacia un concepto de daño en el Derecho comunitario", 263 (2006) *Noticias de la Unión europea* 81-92.

CHAPTER 8

At the Frontiers of Contract Law: Donation in European Private Law

Martin Schmidt-Kessel*

I Introduction

What is a donation? The answer to this question is by no means clear in European Private Law. Definitions and ideas of donation in the several national legal systems diverge significantly. As is well known from a comparative law analysis, such divergences often do not follow from conscious policy decisions but ensue primarily owing to historical coincidence. Apart from popular explanations based on the dualism of Common Law and Civil Law legal orders, the main reason for the different conceptual understanding of donation lies in continental legal history: the classical Roman Law did not develop a uniform concept of donation similar to other types of contract. In particular, there was no *actio donati* invented by the *praetor* and donation was not accorded a systematical place of its own in the system proposed by Gaius. The pronounced influence of medieval Canon Law did not help to reduce the complexity of the whole field. The Napoleonic *police des libéralités* by attempting to downgrade the attractiveness of donations[1] encumbered this area of the law with additional policy considerations.

Any short outline of the topic of donation in European Contract Law has, therefore, to begin with some structural questions and notions. As our project is part of the work prepared by the Study Group on a European Civil Code, these questions are closely connected with the other texts produced by the group. Compared to (general) contract law, there are then three further points to discuss. The first one concerns the prerequisites of making a binding donation. The second point concerns obligations and remedies of the parties to a donation. Finally, the binding force of the juridical acts concerned is, in many legal orders, reduced on the one hand *inter partes* by so-called rights to revoke and as against third parties, on the other hand by several mechanisms including the so-called *actio pauliana*.

From a practical point of view most cases of donation are closely connected to questions of inheritance or family law. The core issue pertaining to these connections is the conflict with the mandatory rules of inheritance or family law which donors try to circumvent by way of donation. The most well-known example is the idea of reserved portion in many continental legal systems which preserve a significant part of the patrimony of the deceased for the deceased's wife and children and other relatives. Other rules protect the distribution of patrimony between husband and wife. The solutions adopted by the respective legal orders in order to deal with these conflicts diverge considerably. These mechanisms, however, are not dealt with in the following parts of my paper

* Professor of Civil Law, Comparative Law, European and International Private Law, University of Osnabrück. I am very grateful to Susan Singleton for bringing my English in a readable form; all remaining errors, however, are mine.

1 See R. Barbaix, "Hoe anders is de overeenkomst schenking, en waarom?", Proefschrift Antwerpen 2007, No 1229 ff.

because they are not of decisive importance in order to understand how the juridical act "donation" works in the several jurisdictions of Europe and in our draft.[2]

Please allow me one more technical remark on the draft that I have distributed. Therein you will find a bifurcation of sorts: The Osnabrück Working Team is advised by a Group of seven colleagues, the so-called Advisory Council, which meets twice a year. At these Advisory Council meetings the articles of the draft were agreed upon; consequently, these are marked by the simple margin line. During several meetings of the Coordinating Committee of the Study Group some of these articles were approved by that committee. All of the respective articles and paragraphs are marked by the double margin line in the draft distributed. The drafting was in many respects revised by *Eric Clive* to whom we owe many thanks.

II Working on Gratuitous Contracts: Donation First

The Osnabrück Working Team on Gratuitous Contracts decided not to start by drafting universal rules on gratuitous contracts.[3] The more or less established types of contracts (or – depending on the respective legal tradition – juridical acts) under which only one of two or more parties renders or is obliged to render performance gratuitously comprise of the donation or gift, the gratuitous loan (or – as we call it – contract for gratuitous use) and the gratuitous service in its several manifestations (eg. custody, the gratuitous *mandatum*). In addition to these types of contracts, there are in the legal orders of the Member States several legal concepts which should come under consideration as well, for example, waiver, estoppel, or different forms of binding unilateral promises.

It is, obviously, impossible to consider each of these topics simultaneously. Our approach was, therefore, to start with donation, which is the one type of gratuitous juridical act, which is basically known to all of the Member States' legal orders and where there is, under a functional approach at least, a core of common understanding. There is, however, no common conception as to gratuitous services, which are referred to in Article 1:101(6) PEL Service Contracts. There may be such a common core in the field of the gratuitous loan, but the number of court decisions and other materials at hand seems to be significantly insubstantial. Nevertheless we have – in the meantime – started to draft rules

[2] The draft distributed in Lleida was work in progress of an earlier phase of our work and is therefore not published in this book. The actual draft can be found at: http://www.schenkung.uos.de/.

[3] In the meantime we prepared a first draft of general rules, which is based on our drafts for contracts for donation and contracts for gratuitous use. This draft raises methodological questions, because general rules for contracts where one party undertakes to render his performance without any reward, are unknown to most legal orders in Europe.

on Contracts of Gratuitous Use. Donation may, on the other hand, serve as a kind of *pars pro toto* representing all types of gratuitous performances and serving as an indicator as to the major problems in this area, e.g. the minefield of the exact components of "gratuitousness" and the applicable standards of liability in this context. Our comparative analysis which prepared and accompanied the drafting process started, therefore, with donation[4] and so did our drafting work.

Concentrating our work on donation leads to the consequence that this type of contract or juridical act will be – most probably – the only gratuitous one to be dealt with in the DCFR. The only universal rule the working team could provide so far is a more general definition of gratuitousness; which in my view sounds rather trivial by now. The definition in Article 1:301 of our draft is set to become a more general definition later on. It is used in the draft for the Principles of European Law on Trust prepared by the Study Group.

III "Predispositions" in the Work of the Study Group

The work of the Study Group is in rather an advanced phase. When starting a new subject under the auspices of the project of the Study Group, the Working Team and the Advisors had to accept the parts of the project which had been completed before as a reference point to the substantial policy issues, to the concepts used and furthermore to terminology. To give account of these "predispositions" at the same time demonstrates, how far the rules of donation are ensnarled in the respective Private Law System.

The common structure for the whole work of the Study Group is built on the Principles of European Contract Law, which, thus, have to act as a basis for a Book on Donation as well. According to these principles a contract does not presuppose any consideration for a performance promised. Articles 1:107 and 2:107 PECL show, that the Principles even apply "with appropriate modifications" to unilateral promises. PECL therefore apply to the obligatory part of every agreement under which one party gratuitously undertakes to render a performance or gratuitously renders it.

While some Principles of European Law drafted by the Study Group's Working Teams do not deal with the gratuitous mutations of the respective type of contract, the Principles of European Law on Services Contracts do consider gratuitous services: Article 1:101(6) states that the Service Principles apply "with appropriate modifications to contracts whereby the service provider is to supply a service to the client otherwise than for remuneration". Taking into account Article 1:107(4)(c) and (d) of the Service Principles those modifications will, at least, affect the standard of care the service provider has to exercise. Similarly the Principles of European Law on Commercial Agency, Franchise and Distribu-

[4] Parts of the materials will be published in 2008 in a Book called "Donation in Europe" which contains contributions of many advisors and working team members.

tion Contracts apply to contracts by way of analogy where one party promises such a service gratuitously. This follows from Article 1:101 PEL CAFDC[5] and is supported by Comment A to Article 2:201 PEL CAFDC.

At least two aspects in the Principles of European Law on Benevolent Intervention in Another's Affairs are closely connected to principles on gratuitous contracts. The reason for acting of the person who renders the characteristic performance, in both cases is, basically at least, a benevolent one. In the case of benevolent intervention the "intention of benefiting" is therefore part of the definition in Article 1:101 PEL Ben.Int. However, this intention of benefiting has its own special function under these Principles because it provides an indispensable element of the intervener's justification to intervene in the principal's affairs. Further on, Article 3:104(1) PEL Ben.Int.[6] contains a concept which is extensively referred to in the Comments as *animus donandi*. This formula denotes that the intervener "did not want to demand indemnification, reimbursement, remuneration or reparation, as the case may be". The broad meaning of the Latin word *donare* as it is used in that context of benevolent intervention covers all kinds of gratuitous performances (but probably not all cases of gratuitousness). It could therefore have been regarded as an impediment to employ the word "donation" to designate only one type of gratuitous contract; fortunately, however, it is only used in the Comments and is therefore not exhausted for our purposes.

The Principles of European Law of Unjustified Enrichment – in their last version – no longer deal expressly with questions of gratuitousness. Former versions dealt with "gratuitous dispositions" namely in Article 2:101 PEL Unj. Enr. and the Comments thereto. Today it is replaced by the wider formula of "contract or other juridical act", which at least includes donations if not every gratuitous performance. Essentially, a donation is therefore sufficient justification (in our technical sense) for an enrichment conferred by the donor on the donee. The Principles of European Law of Unjustified Enrichment, however, bring about a significant weakening of the binding force of an executed donation. This results from the application of articles 4:104, 6:102, 6:101(3) PEL Unj. Enr. If the debtor of an unjustified enrichment claim for restitution of a specified asset *bone fide* disposes gratuitously of that asset, this transaction leads to a disenrichment of that debtor (Article 6:101 (1) und (2) PEL Unj.Enr.) and is to be understood as an innocent onward transfer in the sense of Article 4:104 PEL Unj.Enr. The consequence of this understanding is a direct unjustified enrichment claim of the disenriched person against the tranferee (cf. Article 6:101(3) PEL Unj.Enr.). The transferee has no defence under the agreement with the transferor, which only takes effect between its parties (see Article 2:101(1)(a) PEL

5 "This Chapter applies to commercial agency, franchise and distribution contracts *and to other contracts* where one party, engaged in business independently uses its skills and efforts to bring another party's products on to the market." (emphasis added).

6 "The intervener's rights are reduced or excluded in so far as the intervener at the time of acting did not want to demand indemnification, reimbursement, remuneration or reparation, as the case may be."

Unj.Enr.), nor may he invoke a good faith acquisition, because that defence does not operate in the case of a gratuitous acquisition (see Article 6:102(b) PEL Unj. Enr.).

Bearing in mind that, in some European legal orders, donation is primarily understood as a way of transferring property,[7] the importance of the different rules for the transfer of assets, namely the Principles of European Law on Transfer of Movables and the rules on assignment in Articles 11:101 – 11:401 PECL, should not be underestimated. Article 2:103(2) PEL Tr.Mov. shows that these Principles apply to gratuitous transfers, which means that there is no room for a separate set of principles for the gratuitous transfer of ownership. The paragraph states, that the obligation to transfer (which, as a rule, is necessary for the transfer, see Article 2:101(1)(c) PEL Tr.Mov.) in the case of a (immediate) gratuitous transfer of ownership is "implied" in that transfer, in other words the obligation is to be assumed, at the very least. Additionally the transfer of property in movables under the Principles of European Law on Transfer of Movables basically requires a delivery or an equivalent to delivery (Articles 2:101(1)(b), 2:104 – 2:110 PEL Tr.Mov.). The Principles, therefore, presuppose the possibility that an agreement to gratuitously transfer movables may create obligations and does create them in cases of a delivery or the equivalent thereto under Articles 2:101(1)(b), 2:104 – 2:110 PEL Tr.Mov. after the parties have reached an agreement.[8] The same conclusion is to be drawn from the fact that the assignment of a claim under Article 11:202 PECL does not depend on the underlying obligation. Therefore, the agreement, under which one party promises to gratuitously assign a claim, does not include necessarily the assignment itself.

IV Terminology and Definitions

1. Donation, Gift, Contract of/for Donation

As regards terminology, we preferred the broader meaning of "donation" to the less restricted meaning of "gift". The reasons for this decision not only derive from the necessity of a later translation, which to us seemed to be less difficult. The decision on terminology was in fact taken in view of the examination of the question regarding the exact connotations of the concept we opted for, namely the contract itself and not its fulfilment.

We originally had argued for the adoption, not of a "contract *for* donation" but a "contract of donation" for the following reason, namely the donation itself is not owed by the donor but is the subject matter of the contract. We were convinced by our native speakers that the risk of misunderstandings is not that significant and we agreed to use "contract for the donation of goods".

[7] Cf. Barbaix (n. 1), No 321, for a reminiscence.

[8] As to further connections to the Principles of European Law on Transfer of Movables cf. Articles 2:203, 2:204 PEL Tr.Mov.

2. Definition of the Contract for the Donation of Goods

Article 1:101 defines donation in para (2) as "a contract under which one party, the donor, gratuitously undertakes to transfer the ownership of goods to another party, the donee, and does so with an intention to benefit the donee." Donation is thereby essentially defined as a contract (with the undecided cases of Article 1:102), thereby a decision was made to opt for the general application of contract law.

Article 1:102(b) intentionally leaves undecided the question of whether the simple straightforward gift is a contract or not by determining the most important question, namely, that contract law applies to such a donation.

By a clear majority, the Advisory Council decided not to include unilateral promises in the chapter of donation, and thereby implicitly makes clear that such a promise is not binding without acceptance.[9] This point will have to be decided by the Coordinating Committee, see Article 1:102(a). Bearing in mind Articles 1:107 and 2:107 PECL the draft would need to be amended if unilateral promises are to be excluded from its scope of application.

Our rules do not only apply to goods, but apply to other assets as well, see Article 1:203. Therefore, we follow the line proposed by the PEL Sales; we were convinced that replicating their list here complies better with the standards of good drafting then inserting a cross-reference. In any case our principles do not apply to the donation of immovable property.

3. "Intention to Benefit" in particular

The Working Team originally proposed to qualify the gratuitousness of the undertaking to transfer or the transfer by utilising a subjective test ("intention to benefit"). Some of our advisors would have preferred a more objective yardstick. After some considerations, following a proposal for the definition of gratuitousness by the Advisory Council on trusts, we now propose not to add this subjective qualification here, but propose adding it to the definition of donation.

The crucial problem of any objective test is the necessary valuation of the asset to be transferred on the one hand, and of the relevant conduct of the donee on the other: there is no absolute value or *iustum pretium* of an asset to be transferred to the donee. A subjective test similar to the one proposed in this instance can be found in Article 1:101 PEL Ben.Int. The benefit is not equivalent to enrichment under the Principles of Unjustified Enrichment; even the conclusion of a court that the asset is without any economic value does not prevent the contract from qualifying as a donation.

In examining this subjective qualification, one has to bear in mind that the "intention to benefit" is not necessarily congruent to each of the various notions of the term "animus donandi"[10] (which obviously cannot define donation, because the definition would then be circular). The concept of donation is, there-

[9] As to the background in the Napoleonic system see Barbaix (n. 1), No 236 ff.

[10] Cf. Barbaix (n. 1), No 189 ff.

fore, wider than in several national legal systems. Article 1:303 makes clear that a promotional purpose and not even the fulfilment of a moral obligation would exclude a contract from the scope of our principles.

4. Definition of Gratuitousness

After shifting the subjective qualification to the definition of donation, gratuitousness is defined in very simple terms, Article 1:301. We do not propose to include in the definition the cases of a trivial counter-performance, which should be dealt with under the heading of mixed contracts. The reason for this is that there is a – very small – non-gratuitous element in the contract, which makes the contract only primarily gratuitous and leads to the need to deal with that non-gratuitous element.

5. Transactions which are not entirely gratuitous

Many continental legal orders are familiar with concepts such as the *negotium mixtum cum donatione* i.e. cases in which the transaction resembles a donation, but is not entirely gratuitous. These concepts usually fulfil their functions in the field of inheritance and family law where testators or relatives try to circumvent restrictions on their autonomy and freedom of contract e.g. the reserved portion or the *Pflichtteil*.[11] Our draft does not deal with restrictions of this kind nor does our rule pertaining transactions which are not entirely gratuitous.

The function of Article 1:302 is confined instead to the separation of types of contract, in order to circumscribe the scope of application of our Principles. In cases where the donee pays some reward, a mixture of several types of contract can be observed. This mixture often consists of a donation element and a sales element, but other combinations can be also be envisaged, e.g. a minor service of the donee which is far from being equivalent to the performance of the donor. The Draft Common Frame of Reference will contain a general rule for mixed contracts in II.-1:108 which focuses on mixtures on one side of the contract, e.g. the delivery of goods and the transfer of property combined with some permanent maintenance service. One could come to reasonable results by applying this general rule to the situation which we envisage; however, we were of the opinion that it was necessary to establish additional concrete criteria.

The first step is to deal with the case of a trivial reward, Article 1:302(3). In such a case, the contract is regarded primarily as a contract for the donation of goods. This, along the lines of II.-1:108 DCFR, leads, on the one hand, to the application of our principles and, on the other, to the possibility of applying the rules of general contract law (or rules for the relevant specific contract).

The second step is drawing a line of demarcation, beyond which our rules no longer apply. This line is fixed by reference to a subjective criterion, namely,

11 See the comparative material presented by P. Schlechtriem, *Restitution und Bereicherungsausgleich in Europa*, Vol. I (2000), p. 794 ff.

that the values to be conferred by the performances are regarded by the parties as not substantially equivalent, Article 1:302(4). If this requirement is not met, the whole contract lies outside the scope of application of our Principles. In the opposing case, the contract is primarily treated as a non-gratuitous contract, which, normally, would connote a sales contract, while our rules apply only to those elements of the contract which are gratuitous. We intentionally use the word "elements" here, so as not to give the impression that divisibility is a prerequisite for the applicability of the whole paragraph: In the case of mixed contracts one could speak of a partially gratuitous transfer and this, in the view of the working team, would be a very useful approach, in the event that it is possible to split up the contract in several parts. However, it is not always possible to split up a mixed contract e.g. where a significantly low price is paid for a building. In such circumstances, the term "partially gratuitous" would have added nothing in substance but would have emphasised the special mixed nature of the contract.

Paragraphs (5) to (7) deal with a number of consequences of the applicability of our rules to the gratuitous elements of the contract in certain situations where the bifurcated regime leads to some difficulties. The first of these situations concerns the voidness or avoidance of the contract, which might be possible in relation to the gratuitous elements but not possible in respect of the rest of the contract, paragraph (5). We propose to apply then the general rule of change of circumstances, Article 6:111 PECL, paragraph (5). When the donor revokes the gratuitous elements under Chapter 4 of our rules the solution is similar, but is in the hands of the donee: The revocation captures the whole contract i.e. the non-gratuitous elements as well. However, the donee has been provided with a right of preventing the effects of the revocation by offering a reasonable reward within a reasonable time after notice of revocation, paragraph (6).

The most difficult questions arise, where different standards of liability and different rules on the measure of damages apply to such a mixed contract, paragraph (7). As we propose special rules for the contract for the donation of goods for both questions, this may come up in situations covered by paragraph (4), where the donor breaches his obligations. We formulated two alternatives for this event, the pro rata solution on the one hand, and the exclusion of the special rules of the Principles of Donation on the other. The question will be decided by the Coordinating Committee of the Study Group in summer.

6. Donation with Charge

The Working Team had severe difficulties with the donation with charge, the *donatio sub modo*, well known to many continental jurisdictions.[12] The core problem was the definition of charge and the ensuing delineation from the mixed contracts situation. This was problematical, owing to the fact that we did not find a convincing criterion which would have the effect of separating a charge

[12] See Schlechtriem (n. 11), p. 820 ff.

from a reward. In our opinion, everything the donee is obliged to do (or refrain from doing) could be analysed as a reward. This being the case, therefore, each donation with charge could be seen as a mixed contract. As we were unable to develop a convincing criterion for the borderline between charge and reward, we thus decided to abstain from formulating special rules.

V The *Cantus Firmus*: Restricting Donations and Their Effects

The overwhelming majority of European legal systems restrict the effect of donations when compared to contracts (in general). The techniques used to effect these restrictions may be categorised in the following manner:

1) restrictions as to formation and validity e.g. the doctrine of consideration, form requirements, the proscription on some kinds of donations (e.g. between spouses, in favour of guardians, see Article 779 Ital.C.c. etc.);
2) restrictions on the obligations of the donor under a valid contract of donation, e.g. the exclusion or restriction of duties regarding the conformity of the assets transferred or promised (e.g. only defects known by the donor but concealed);
3) limitations of remedies available to the donee, e.g. the exclusion or restriction of the right to specific performance, or of claims for interest or damages;
4) constraints as to the binding nature of a contract (or promise) for donation as illustrated, e.g. by the different rights of revoking a contract.

As PECL (and the DCFR) apply to donations, the policy question arises as to how far it is necessary to restrict liabilities under PECL in the case of a donation. There is no doctrine of consideration under PECL but the Coordinating Committee did vote in favour of a form requirement for donations.

The original idea of the Working Team was to propose restrictions under all four categories but we were convinced that it would be wise to reduce the number of restrictions to three of the four. We, therefore, propose to establish a nearly complete set of obligations (Arts. 3:101-3:104, 3:301 Draft) and to confine the restrictions to the fields of formation, remedies and revocation. The advantage of such an approach lies in the field of technical clarity of the draft, the disadvantage in the tremendous difference between the broad set of obligations and the rather severe restrictions in the field of remedies.

VI Form Requirement and Reduction of the Binding Force

1. Form Requirement

Most European legal orders are familiar with a form requirement for the validity of the promise of the donor. Freedom of form is the exception. The usual continental form of a deed produced by a notary is, however, not open to us because the *notariat latin* does not exist in each Member State. We therefore favour a more flexible approach, favouring a document in writing as a starting point (cf. Article 243(1) Swiss Code of Obligations) and providing the Member States with a right to opt for a higher standard of form.

A further question is the scope of the form requirement. Should it encompass, as for example under the Napoleonic system, the whole contract or should it be merely restricted to the promise of the donor? The majority of our group was in favour of confining the requirement to the promise of the donor. The accepted purpose of the requirement, namely the protection of the donor, would not support the broadening of the requirement.

2. Exceptions to the Form Requirement

The most important exception to the form requirement is the case of the immediate transfer of property, Article 2:102(a). In this case of a *don manuel,* no form is needed. We had major discussions with our advisors on the question as to whether the transfer of the property should have a retroactive effect and therefore would cure a donation lacking the necessary form.[13] This point is open to be decided by the Coordinating Committee of the Study Group.

The second exception depends on how donations by businesses, especially promotional gifts, are treated. If they are included in our principles, a proposition which the Working Team and Advisors are in favour of, the form requirement will not apply, Article 2:102(b). Still open to debate, however, is the question as to whether the undertaking of the donor, which is declared in a statement broadcast in the radio or television or published in print and which is not excessive in the circumstances should be valid without form.

Even where a contract for the donation of goods is invalid for lack of form, the donee may be protected at least in some respect: The donor is, under Article 2:104, obliged to compensate the donee for loss suffered by the donee acting in the mistaken belief that the contract was binding if it was reasonable for the donee to believe that the contract was binding, the donor knew or could reasonably be expected to have known that the donee relied on the contract, and the donor knew or could reasonably be expected to have known that the donee believed that the contract was binding.

[13] Cf. for the French idea of the *nullité absolue* which prevents the solution of the void donation cured by transfer of the property Barbaix (n. 1), No 303 ff.

3. Additional Cases of Avoidance

Two further articles alleviate the avoidance of a contract for the donation of goods, and thereby weaken the binding force of the latter. Article 2:105 broadens the possibility of avoiding the contract on the grounds of fundamental mistake. While Article 4:103(1)(a) PECL prescribes rather high hurdles for avoidance, the only remaining prerequisite would be the fundamental nature of the mistake. In this case, not only the specific performance of the donor's promise but the claim for damages would also be excluded, provided that the right to avoid the contract is not excluded because the mistake was inexcusable or the party in error was assumed to bear the risk of an error of this kind (see Article 3:103(2) PECL).

Many legal orders prohibit donations to certain persons like the treating medic or the legal guardian, who might exercise undue influence over the donee. We decided not to take over that enumerative approach, but to work with a general tool: The general right to avoid the contract for unfair exploitation under Article 4:109 PECL has been assimilated as part of the Draft namely Article 2:106 of our draft: A donor who was dependent on, or was the more vulnerable party in a relationship of trust with, the donee may exercise his right to avoid for unfair exploitation unless the donee proves that the donee did not exploit the donor's situation by taking an excessive benefit or grossly unfair advantage.

VII Obligations and Remedies

1. General Structure

Article 3:101 provides for obligations of the donor to deliver goods which conform to the contract and to transfer ownership in them. Fruits acquired from the goods after the time, when the delivery of the goods becomes due, must be transferred as well and the whole chapter applies to other assets with appropriate modifications. In our view, it is necessary to spell out these obligations, because the formation of the contract is neither necessarily associated with an immediate delivery, nor with a transfer of title. The standards of conformity are dealt with in Article 3:102 and deviate in several respects from a typical sales standard, while, on the other hand, the responsibility of the donor is not confined to cases of fraud. Freedom of third party rights is, in general, an implied term of every contract for the donation of goods.

As regards the remedies generally, the rules of PECL apply. By means of Article 3:201 we propose, therefore, to refrain from establishing completely new rules on remedies. However, the usual remedies are restricted in several respects. Article 3:202 excludes the right to enforce performance in two cases. Article 3:203 changes the standard of liability of the donor into what, from a functional approach, may be analysed as a modified negligence standard and Article 3:204 reduces the measure of damages. The modified standard of liability also applies to the right to interest under Article 9:508 PECL. Other remedies remain untouched: price reduction does not apply in any event. There may be a right to withhold performance on the part of the donee (e.g. taking delivery in cases of non-conformity) but there is, in our view, no reason to restrict that right. Moreover, there is now reason to modify the rules on termination.

2. Obligations of the Donor

It was necessary to establish an obligation to transfer ownership along the lines of the approach of the Principles of Transfer of Movables, which is based on earlier decisions taken by the Study Group. The obligation to deliver, on the other hand, is inevitable if the principles are not restricted to the cases of *don manuel*, which is evidently not the case. Even for the *don manuel* the obligation is useful under a system similar to that erected by Article 2:101 PEL Unj.Enr. and Arts. 2:101, 2:103 PEL Tr.Mov. Neither transfer of title nor delivery are defined explicitly in our rules. In respect of the former, a cross reference to the Principles on Transfer of Movables is implied and for the latter, we use the general definition which will be contained in the DCFR.

The article on conformity of the goods, Article 3:102, starts by referring to the objective standard regarding the reasonable expectations of the donee; this rather broad responsibility of the seller would lead to a strict liability under PECL, but under the Principles of Donation we – as aforementioned – propose to restrict not the obligations but the remedies of the donee. However, we propose to modify the usual objective standard by a set of criteria which incorporate at the very least, the gratuitous nature of the contract and an examination of whether the transfer or delivery of the goods was immediate. Other factors like the purpose of the contract of donation known by the donee or obvious to him, the value of the goods, and whether the donor was a business remain still to be discussed. The objective standard constitutes the only basis for implied terms as to the quality. While the goods do not conform to the contract if they are not of a quantity, quality or description provided for by the express terms of the contract, Article 1:102(3), the donor does not owe a duty to ensure the fitness of the goods for a particular purpose. Contrary to the contract for the sale of goods, it is not evident, that the donor must take positive steps and warn the donee that the purpose envisaged by the donor or agreed upon by the parties may not be attained.

Freedom of third party rights is, in general, an implied term of every contract for donation, Article 1:103. We do not propose a separate article on intellectual property rights of third parties as can be found in the CISG. The draft deviates from the rules of many national legal orders, which exclude any responsibility of the donor for defective goods or restrict it to cases of fraudulent concealment. Again, this rather broad standard is mitigated by the restriction of the remedies of the donee.

3. Remedies of the Donee

The starting point of our draft here is the applicability of PECL to all cases of non-performance under our draft. In our view, there is no need to establish a complete new set of rules. The Working Team and, at least some of our advisors, find it useful to have an explicit remainder pointing to the PECL-provisions on remedies.

3.1. Right to enforce Performance

We propose to provide the donee with a right to performance along the lines of Article 9:101, 9:102 PECL. There was some dispute at the advisory meeting on this question; the counter argument was that, absent bargain, specific performance should not be granted. The current framework of PECL provides the creditor with a right to performance, which is independent of consideration provided by the debtor. In our view the right to performance under PECL as amended by our proposals in Article 2:105, 3:202 Draft, is restrictive enough to establish an agreeable line of compromise.

We propose restrictions on the right to performance under Article 9:102 PECL only in the case of replacement or repair where the goods are defective, as in the case of a contractual undertaking to transfer goods to be acquired (Article 3:202). By contrast, no restrictions on claims of money under Article 9:101 PECL are proposed at all. To balance this – in the view of some legal orders especially the common law world – rather generous approach to specific performance, we propose to broaden the possibility of avoiding the contract for mistake of fact or law (Article 2:105).

The first restriction, primarily, has in mind the case of a *don manuel* under which defective goods are transferred, Article 3:202(1). In this case, no form requirement is applicable to protect the donor who nonetheless accomplishes a valid donation. Bearing this in mind, in our view, there are good grounds for giving the donor protection in so far as the right to performance is concerned.

Article 3:202(2) deals with a situation, which cannot occur in some legal orders, namely, where the transfer of goods or assets is promised by the donor and, at the time of the conclusion of the contract, the goods or assets are not in the hands of the donor: in some legal orders there would be no valid contract of donation even if the respective form requirements are fulfilled. We propose to include this case of goods to be acquired; however, we see the need to restrict the risks which could accrue to the donor in such a case as far as specific performance is concerned. This result would, in many cases, follow from Article 9:102(2)(d) PECL but there remain some cases of specific goods, which should be dealt with additionally.

3.2. Damages

The most difficult rules we agreed on are the articles on damages, Article 3:203, 3:204. Compared to PECL, we propose to restrict the possibility to claim damages for non-performance. The policy reason for this is, again, the gratuitous nature of the contract. In essence we propose two restrictions: first, the proposed standard of liability is less strict than the standard anchored in PECL, in particular under Article 8:108 PECL. Second, we propose not to provide for full compensation.[14] Both restrictions should, in our view, not apply to tort law claims. Owing to the fact that Article 1:103(a) PEL Liab.Dam. opens up the possibility of restricting tortious liability by applying legal rules of contract law, therefore it is necessary to have an explicit rule here, see Article 3:203(4), 3:204(5).

As to the standard of liability, the starting point is Article 3:203(1), which, in fact, establishes liability for negligence without explicitly adopting the term negligence. The standard is attained by adding to the general force majeure defence under Article 8:108 PECL a separate defence, which is not confined to impediments *beyond control*. By giving the donor a defence in case of internal impediments (such as error, illness, strike etc.), the standard functionally corresponds to the standard of negligence. As many legal systems restrict the general standard of liability under a contract of donation, the standard of liability, in some legal orders, even restricted to proof of gross negligence, we propose to modify the normal standard of negligence, having regard to the gratuitous nature of the contract. In determining what impediment or consequences the donor could reasonably be expected to have avoided or overcome under Article 3:203(1), regard is to be had to the gratuitous nature of the contract. The reason for this restriction is that we see no basis for some kind of guarantee or warranty of the donor.

In our view, not all possible interests of the donee are worthy of legal protection when it comes to the question of the amount of damages. The decision is very difficult here because the policies accepted in the Member States diverge significantly: In our view the default rule should be that a claim for damages for non-performance should not cover a gain of which the donee has been deprived, Article 3:204(1). The donor is, therefore, usually obliged only to compensate the donee for loss suffered by him acting in the reasonable belief that the donor would fulfil the obligations. However, this is not the end of the story: A supplementary sum of damages, up to the full expectation interest, may be awarded by the court if it is seen as just and reasonable in the circumstances, Article 3:204(2), (4). In determining what is just and reasonable under paragraph (2), the court will consider not only the gratuitousness of the contract but other factors as well, to which our draft makes explicit reference, namely, the declarations and acts of the parties, the donor's purpose in making donation, and the reasonable expectations of the donee.

3.3. *Interest*

Several legal orders restrict or exclude claims for interest on a sum of money promised by way of donation. In our view, it would be contradictory not to give

[14] On an earlier stage of the draft Barbaix (n. 1), No 734.

the donor in this case at least the same defences that he has under the general damages claim. We therefore agreed on applying the defences under Article 8:108 PECL and Article 3:203 of our principles also to a claim for interest under Article 9:508 PECL.

4. Obligations of the Donee and Remedies of the Donor

As a default rule the donee should be merely obliged to take delivery and to accept transfer, Article 3:301. There may be other obligations in mixed contracts but they should be organised in a different way by applying the rules on mixed contracts.

As regards the remedies we propose simply to advert explicitly to the fact that PECL rules apply. There were some discussions on excluding the right to performance of the donor, i.e. not to enforce taking delivery and accepting transfer against the donee. In our view, which was challenged by some advisors, the interest of the donor is not worthy of protection, because if there were a real interest of the donor in getting rid of the goods the contract should not be qualified as a contract of donation. There is jurisprudence emanating from Germany relating to cases where an element of waste disposal was included in a contract of donation.[15] In such a case it should be clear that the rules which restrict the liability of the donor do not apply. If there is a donation at all, there is no legally protected interest of the donor in a right to performance. Finally we left that point to the comments.

VIII Revocation by the Donor

1. Overview

Contracts for donation are binding. Many legal systems nevertheless restrict the binding character by introducing rights of the donor to revoke "the donation" for some specified circumstances, which change after the contract was concluded. In some countries, the list of those rights is closed, while in others, only certain special cases of the possibility to rescind the contract are regulated in a list, which is amended by applying general rules which point to the change of circumstances.

The main ideas of the rules we propose here are the freedom of parties to agree on rights to revoke (Article 4:101(a)),[16] the protection of reasonable reliance of the donee by giving him the defence of disenrichment (Article 4:103) and the implementation of a general clause (Article 4:203) amended by rules on two specific cases (Article 4:201, 4:202).

---

15 See the famous "Kartoffelpülpe" decision of the German Supreme Court, BGHZ 93, 23.

16 The French tradition points strongly against contractual freedom in this field: Barbaix (n. 1), No 651 ff; Schlechtriem (n. 11), Vol. I, p. 761 ff.

2. The General Clause

Article 4:203 amends Article 6:111 PECL, which is restricted to cases where performance of the duties of the debtor has become too burdensome. We propose to establish such a general rule because the several special rules in national codifications show the need to imply several rights to revoke. The most well-known examples are the *donation en vue de marriage,* where the assets may be claimed back where the marriage fails[17] and the case of an unforeseen child-birth.[18] In our view, the Principles on Donation should not deal with all of these cases explicitly, but contain a general clause which covers them.

On the other hand, there is a strong need to have this general clause formulated in a rather restrictive way. These restrictions are to be found first in paragraph (1), which clarifies that a *material change* of *essential circumstances* upon which the donation was *based* must have occurred. This change must lead to a manifest conflict with principles of justice either because the benefit of the donee seems to be "manifestly inappropriate or excessive" or because it is "manifestly unjust to hold the donor to the donation". Additionally, paragraph (2) excludes the right to revoke in cases of foreseeability and assumption of risk.

3. Ingratitude

From a functional point of view, revocation for ingratitude is a simple case of breach of contract by the donee.[19] However, when one comes to the issue of formulating the respective duty of the donee to be grateful, this turns out to be quite a difficult task, reaching too far into the realm of social graces and etiquette. Many legal orders, therefore, define a case of ingratitude, in which the donor may revoke the donation. Sometimes a – more or less – closed list of cases is used, while other countries use again a general clause.

As our Principles cannot simply point to the interlinked rules of criminal law, we propose a general clause, Article 4:201(1). Gross ingratitude is required and is defined by a serious wrong against the donor which was committed intentionally by the donee. The main cases are murder of the donor and serious bodily injury. The donor (and only the donor) may waive the right to revoke by way of forgiveness, Article 4:201(2). As the article deals with a case, which from a functional point of view is to be seen as a breach of contract, the defence of disenrichment does not apply, Article 4:201(4).

4. Impoverishment

Rights to revoke in case of impoverishment may be seen under two policy aspects, the first is one of ingratitude of the donee in not maintaining the donor, and the other is of a more general nature by distributing the risk of maintenance obligations under a "donee pays first" rule. We opted for the second approach

---

17 Cf. Schlechtriem (n. 11), Vol. I, p. 830 ff.

18 See the comparative material presented by Schlechtriem (n. 11), Vol. I, p. 812 ff.

19 In this direction the analysis of Barbaix (n. 1), No 900 ff.

in Article 4:202. Additionally, paragraph (4) establishes a right to withhold performance, in the event the donor has not yet fulfilled his obligation when the impoverishment arises.

Paragraph (1) states the basic rule that the donor may revoke the donation if he is not in a position to maintain himself. By the words "out of his own patrimony or income", the "donee pays first" rule is established; the fact that the donor is maintained by another person does not bar the right to revoke. Paragraphs (5) and (6) amend this rule by determining the order of several rights to revoke. Paragraph (3) provides the donee with the possibility of preventing revocation by maintaining the donor along the lines established in paragraph (2). If the donor has not performed all of his obligations he may prevent the situation under paragraphs (1) and (7) by withholding performance under paragraph (4), in which case the donee may terminate the contract.

The Working Team was advised by the advisors to explain in paragraph (2) what is meant by not being in the position to maintain oneself. The main yardstick for this is the applicable maintenance law, which is complemented by the rules of social assistance for those cases where no hypothetical maintenance obligation exists. Paragraph (7) adds the further policy question of whether the inability to meet maintenance obligations of the donor against third persons should be seen as equivalent to the donor's own impoverishment. Finally, we propose to declare the whole article mandatory by paragraph (8). An exception to paragraph (6) is conceivable.

5. *Notice of Revocation and its Consequences*

The right to revoke should be exercised in a similar manner to a right to terminate the contract, Article 4:102(1). We do not propose a form requirement for giving notice to the donee. In terms of flexibility, a partial revocation should be possible as long as it is not unreasonable to uphold the remaining contract, Article 4:102(2).

The revocation brings the unfulfilled obligations of both parties to an end. As far as one or both parties have performed, the performances are to be reversed. We propose to apply the rules on unjustified enrichment to this reversal. In our view the rules dealing with the consequences of termination do not fit with the purpose of protecting the reliance of the donee.[20]

The Working Team proposes to set a time limit for the revocation. The donor must revoke within a reasonable time after his knowledge or "constructive" knowledge of the right to revoke arose. The rules on the extension of a prescription period should apply by analogy. This would result in a maximum period of ten years plus a reasonable time which is to be calculated as if the donor had knowledge of his right to revoke.

[20] See the positive comments on this proposal in Barbaix (n. 1), No 667.

IX Conclusion

As the "contract for the donation of goods" is not an accepted mechanism throughout Europe and the policy considerations connected to the rules diverge significantly, the formulation of European rules on donation based on the Principles of European Contract Law is a difficult task. The main purpose of our work, therefore, can only be to provide possible future discussions on our topic with a structured list of policy questions and a set of – as we hope – acceptable terminological proposals. These two more strategic objectives are shared by the whole project of the Common Frame of Reference, which is about to build up new dogmatical precepts of European Private Law.

CHAPTER 9

The CFR and Credit Securities – A Suitable Case for Treatment?

Gerard McCormack*

I Introduction

This paper looks at the possible content of a Common Frame of Reference (more provocatively called a European Civil Code) in the realm of credit securities.[1] In particular it asks whether the most comprehensive international standard – the United Nations Commission on International Trade Law (UNCITRAL) Legislative Guide on Secured Transactions – is suitable for adoption at the European level to form the basis of the Common Frame of Reference (CFR). The UNCITRAL Legislative Guide has not yet gone through all the UN approval stages but its present content is likely to reflect its final form.[2] The paper begins by adding to the growing literature examining the need for a CFR/European Civil Code but focuses the debate on the possible application of the CFR to credit securities.[3] At the time of writing the draft academic CFR has been published. This draft does not include rules on credit securities, but such rules are intended to be included in the revised academic CFR.

II The Need for a CFR Applying To Credit Securities?

In the UK I suspect that the proposal that one should have a CFR/European Civil Code is likely to meet with the same level of public acceptance as the proposal that one should have a European Constitution – practically zilch.[4] The objections are constitutional, economic and cultural though these

---

* Professor of International Business Law, University of Leeds.

1 For background see the three primary European Commission documents – "Communcation from the Commission to the Council and the European Parliament on European Contract Law COM (2001) 398 final; "A More Coherent European Contract Law, An Action Plan" COM (2003) 68 Final; "European contract law and the revision of the acquis: the way forward" COM (2004) 651 Final. For more detail see the "European Contract Law" website of the Directorate General for Health and Consumer Protection accessible via the Europa website at http: www.ec.europa.eu/. See also the von Bar Study Group on the European Civil Code – www.sgecc.net/ and the Acquis Group on European Private Law – www.acquis-group.org/ and see also the Joint Network on European Private Law – www.copecl.org. There is a vast academic literature and for a taster see A. Hartkamp et al (ed.) *Towards a European Civil Code* (3rd ed 2004); M. Van Hoecke, F. Ost (eds.), *The Harmonisation of European Private Law* (2000). See also M. Kenny "The 2004 Communication on European Contact Law: Those Magnificent Men in Their Unifying Machines", (2005) 30 *European Law Review* 724; "Constructing a European Civil Code: Quis Custodiet Ipsos Custodes?" (2006) 12 *Columbia Journal of European Law* 775; "Standing Surety in Europe: Common Core or Tower of Babel?", (2007) 70 *Modern Law Review* 175.

2 Up-to-date information on the progress of the work may be found on the UNCITRAL website – www.uncitral.org/ and see generally S. Bazinas "UNCITRAL's Work in the Field of Secured Transactions", in: J. Norton, M. Andenas (eds.), *Emerging Financial Markets and Secured Transactions* (1998).

3 A team headed by Professor Ulrich Drobnig (Hamburg) is producing a draft dealing with aspects of the proposed Common Frame of Reference concerned with credit securities – see www.sgecc.net.

4 The difference in nomenclature may mean that there is slightly less hostility engendered towards the idea of a Common Frame of Reference. One may ask why any hostility if the CFR is merely a toolbox

objections are inextricably interlinked.[5] Firstly, the enactment of a European Civil Code trenches upon national sovereignty and involves the European Union arrogating to itself powers which it does not possess and ought not to possess.[6] To paraphrase the views of a lot of critics, cooperation between nation states is fine but what is invidious are creeping encroachments on the sovereignty of nation states. More invidious still are frontal assaults on such sovereignty which the proposal for a European Civil Code invariably entails.[7] A European Civil Code involves the suppression of national differences for the sake of uniformity.[8] All for one, and one for all, with no opportunity for national autonomy and divergence. The creation of uniformity may also lead to economic sterility.[9] The end of jurisdictional diversity also means the elimination of opportunities for

for improving the Community Acquis and a standard set of terms that contracting parties are free to adopt or not, as they please, as the latest iterations from Brussels would suggest? But it may be unwise to assume that the desire of Euro Code enthusiasts for a binding instrument has dimmed.

5 See generally S. Weatherill, "Why Object to Harmonization of Private Law by the EC", [2004] *European Review of Private Law* 633.

6 On the legal basis for a European Civil Code see generally W. van Gerven, "Coherence and National Laws: Is there a Legal Basis for a European Civil Code", [1997] *European Review of Private Law* 465; "Codifying European Private Law? Yes, If", [2002] *European Law Review* 156.

7 In the Tobacco Advertising Case *Germany v Parliament and Council* Case C-376/98 [2000] ECR I-8419 the ECJ held that a "mere finding of disparities between national rules and of the abstract risk of obstacles to the exercise of fundamental (economic) freedoms or of distortions of competition liable to result therefrom" was not sufficient to justify the vesting of legislative competences in the European Community institutions. On the other hand, in *Netherlands v Parliament and Council* Case C-377/98 [2001] ECR I-7079 it was held that the institutions had legislative competence "if the aim is to prevent the emergence of future obstacles to trade resulting from multifarious development of national laws provided that the emergence of such obstacles is likely, and the measure in question is designed to prevent them".

8 See, for example, P. Legrand, "European Legal Systems are Not Converging", (1997) 45 *International & Comparative Law Quarterly* 52; "Against a European Civil Code", (1997) 60 *Modern Law Review* 44; "On the Unbearable Localness of the Law: Academic Fallacies and Unseasonable Observations", [2002] *European Review of Private Law* 61; "The Impossibility of Legal Transplants", (2003) 4 *Maastricht Journal* 111; "Antivonbar", (2006) 1 *Journal of Comparative Law* 1 and for a slightly different perspective that such a Code may be an impossibility see G. Teubner, "Legal Irritants: Good Faith in British Law or How Unifying Law Ends Up in New Divergences", (1998) 61 *Modern Law Review* 11. See also B. Markesinis "Why a Code is Not the Best Way to Advance the Cause of European Unity", [1997] *European Review of Private Law* 519.

9 See generally A. Ogus, "Competition Between National Legal Systems: A Contribution of Economic Analysis to Comparative Law", (1999) 48 *International & Comparative Law Quarterly* 405 and see also U. Mattei, "A Transaction Costs Approach to the European Civil Code", [1997] *European Review of Private Law* 537.

competition between national legal orders.[10] There is no scope for innovation at the local level. This means that there is less chance for initially unpromising but ultimately beneficial ideas to win through and gain general acceptance. At the moment, these seeds of ingenuity can be tested and put into play at the local national level and then reproduced across national frontiers if they turn out to be generally beneficial. The submergence of national legal systems in a Pan-European legal Order would destroy these potentially enriching seed beds for dynamism and innovation. Professor Easterbrook has made the point that:[11] "When governments become sufficiently plentiful, and when the scope of laws matches the domain of their costs and benefits (that is, when costs and benefits are all felt within the jurisdiction enacting the laws), competitive forces should be as effective with governments as they are with private markets".

What I have said so far has touched on cultural objections to the creation of a European Civil Code. It can be argued that a Civil Code is intimately connected with a country's history and development[12] and the replacement of national Civil Codes by a supra-European one would involve jettisoning a lot of a country's historical legacy.[13] Of course, each and every part of a country's cultural and historical baggage is not necessarily worth keeping but national champions may find the wholescale submergence of national legal institutions in a pan-European order to be deeply troubling. The difference between national legal orders is perhaps at its most stark when it comes to the common law/civil law divide. Lawyers trained in the common law and civilian traditions may approach legal issues in different ways. Their legal mindsets are different. Civilians tend to start off with statements of general principles whereas the common lawyer

---

[10] See R. Van den Bergh, "Forced Harmonisation of Contract Law in Europe: Not to be Continued", in: S. Grundmann, J. Stuyck (eds.), *An Academic Green Paper on European Contract Law* (2002) 249 at 267:"[t]he advantages of competition between legal rules must not be underestimated: if rules differ, more preferences can be satisfied and learning processes remain possible. It is remarkable that the EC harmonisation measures concern rules of interventionist law, where preferences may be supposed to diverge most strongly".

[11] See F. Easterbrook "Federalism and European Business Law", (1994) 14 *International Review of Law and Economics* 125 at 127-128.

[12] See generally H. Collins, "European Private Law and Cultural Identity of States", [1995] *European Review of Private Law* 353.

[13] See S. Weatherill, "Why Object to the Harmonization of Private Law by the EC", [2004] *European Review of Private Law* 633 at 647: "This objection to harmonization is driven by the perception that legal culture, represented in part by the shape of private law, has undergone a long-term, frequently unplanned evolution in the Member States, reflecting a range of influences. To confine such richness within the straightjacket of harmonization is to rob Europe of its past. It is to sacrifice a multi-textured private law tradition to the narrow demands of economic integration built on regulatory homogeneity. A harmonized private law will not display the susceptibility to local preference that is the preserve of a more decentralized system. More broadly still, stretching far beyond the domain of private law, this dissenting vein is nurtured by the profound belief that Europe is strengthened by its diversity."

works more from the specific to the general. The facts of specific situation come first and through a process of analogy and induction can one come up with a statement of general principle. The civilian lawyer works the other way around and deduces the approach to be adopted in a particular case from an initial statement of general principle. These differences are often exaggerated for most areas of private law in the common law world have been deeply encrusted by statute, if not largely governed by statute. Often however, an appreciation of the effects of statute requires an understanding of the common law backdrop for, normally, common law norms will continue to apply in areas not regulated by the statute.

It has been suggested that the enactment of a European Civil Code means marginalising the common law canon of experience in favour of the civilian tradition. Lawyers trained in the common law tradition become second class citizens compared with their civilian counterparts. Generally the common law has no truck with general codes whereas Codes are a foundational element of the Civilian tradition. The very existence of a European Civil Code means bowing to the Civil Law in preference to the common law. These points have been put very forcibly by Pierre Legrand who speaks of "political correctness a l'europėene" or the desire to eliminate difference across laws or to pretend that it is not there. He goes on to say:[14] "Nowadays, there is only way in which one can be a 'good European' and it is to support the suppression of local particularism. Any expression of doubt in favour of cultural diversity, any critique of centralising legal integration processes is rapidly construed as inimical to the grand European project, its author being branded as a reactionary, someone who is on the wrong side of History. An extreme illustration of this discourse of 'closure' is, of course, the speech which then Chancellor Helmut Kohl delivered in Louvain in February 1996 where he said that European integration was a "question of war and peace in the twenty-first century.' Another German political leader opined that after Auschwitz it was no longer permissible to be 'against Europe'".

But not only this language but also the rhetoric seems overblown. For a start, the current consensus of opinion seems to be that the CFR/European Civil Code should serve merely as an optional instrument.[15] It should supple-

---

[14] See P. Legrand, "On the Unbearable Localness of the Law: Academic Fallacies and Unseasonable Observations", [2002] *European Review of Private Law* 61 at 66. Legrand (at p 67) suggests that the "diversity in private-law allocations of business risks across European laws reflects diversity in business expectations across national borders which, in turn, translates an "embeddedness" of thinking". He also sees the proposal for a European Civil Code as inherently reactionary. "How can codification ever transcend the reification that inevitably follows from the urge towards systematisation and the aspiration to deductive certainty (not to mention the accompanying phenomenon of fixation on the fact and on the letter of the code that comes with the adoption of any theological system)?" For a more measured but occasionally critical voice see M.W. Hesslink, *The New European Legal Culture* (2001).

[15] See generally Grundmann/Stuyck (n. 10) and in particular Part IV "An optional European Code supplementing, not substituting national laws".

ment national law rather than tying to supersede it. Contracting parties should be free to choose the optional instrument to govern their transaction if they wish. If presented in this way as a measure enlarging contractual choice it is hard to object to the CFR. Objections however, may still be raised. There may be additional costs and complexities.[16] Parties will have to expend time and energy in coming to grips with the CFR; understanding and appreciating its effects. The CFR will be a wholly new instrument not rooted in a national legal system and its proper interpretation may take some time thus generating uncertainties. Professor Collins has made the point that:[17] "With respect to the creation of an optional set of rules that could be chosen by the parties, the transaction cost approach cannot point to any advantages. The creation of [another] system of law, which the parties may select as their choice of law, neither reduces uncertainty nor ignorance. It has no benefits from a transaction cost point of view. Indeed, as is the case with any transnational and novel law, it is likely in fact to increase uncertainty, at least in the medium term, so that it would provoke increased transaction costs".

There are also possible "negative externalities" – spillover effects of the CFR on third parties. In other words, on non-contracting parties who have not bargained for the application of the CFR. Moreover, the laws of many countries contain mandatory provisions that contracting parties are not free to depart from. Making use of the CFR to contract around mandatory principles of national law would seem to set this notion at naught.

In considering the possible application of the CFR to proprietary securities the intimate connection with property law should be noted. Proprietary securities may be defined as rights against property to ensure the performance of some obligation. The typical obligation secured would be the payment of money e.g. the repayment of an advance. The standard justification for the inclusion of provisions on proprietary securities in the CFR seems to be no more than that they are part of private law, being generally the product of contract and have

[16] See H. Collins, "Transaction Costs and Subsidiarity in European Contract Law", in: Grundmann/Stuyck (n. 10) 269 at 281: "Transnational regulation can reduce transactions in commercial transactions only by becoming a compulsory uniform law, but the real benefits only emerge if the transnational regulation becomes reasonably certain or predictable".

[17] Note 16, 269 at 277. See also the views of a former English Law Lord, John Hobhouse, on international instruments (and presumably a Common Frame of Reference) "International Conventions and Commercial Law: In Pursuit of Uniformity", (1990) 106 *Law Quarterly Review* 530. He sees them as "inevitably and confessedly drafted as multi-cultural compromises between different schemes of law. Consequently, they will normally have less merit than most of the individual legal systems from which they have been derived. As such, they lack coherence and consistency and create problems regarding their scope. They introduce uncertainty where no uncertainty existed before. They probably deprive the law of those features which enable it to be an effective tool for the use of international commerce".

often been included in Civil Codes though usually not in an exhaustive way.[18] Also it might be easier to find agreement on the content of such provisions than on say provisions of Family law where moral and ideological differences run deeper. But it must be remembered that the security is a right over property and that property law is often considered to be a matter more or less within the exclusive domain of national governments. Many jurisdictions have a *numerus clausus* or closed list of property rights and it is not permissible for parties by contract to add to the list of property rights. The CFR may enlarge the scope of property rights under national law and if parties are free to adopt the CFR as the basis for their security arrangement, effectively they are pushing out the boundaries of the so-called closed list.

I would suggest that the case for a CFR and its application to proprietary securities is at best unproven. Intra-Community trade seems to function perfectly well without a common law of proprietary securities. There is no particular evidence of a hindrance to intra-community trade that needs removing by the promulgation of a code common to Europe.[19] Cross-border transactions may incur higher transaction costs than purely domestic transactions but legal concerns and issues can always be factored into the terms of the agreement. Non-legal considerations such as language barriers, lack of a common basis of trust and understanding, lack of local knowledge and lack of familiarity with local business practices are likely to be far more significant impediments to cross-border trade.[20]

Moreover, a degree of spontaneous or functional convergence may already be taking place with a view to facilitating trade insofar as one can judge by the number of international, as opposed to purely European, instruments being promulgated. It may be unwise to arrest this development by the imposition of an overarching legislative architecture at European level. With the economic case uncertain, ultimately one's views on the desirability or otherwise of a CFR and its particular application to proprietary securities probably depends on one's views on the respective weights to be attached to the values of national sovereignty and European integration. "The fundamental issue is whether some form of harmonisation of contract law can contribute to a form of better

18 See generally J. Basedow "The Case for a European Contract Act", [2001] *Journal of Business Law* 569. See also U. Drobnig, "A Subsidiary Plea: A European Contract Law for Intra-European Border-Crossing Contracts", in: Grundmann/Stuyck (n. 10) 343.

19 But see O. Lando, "Why Does Europe Need a Civil Code", in: Grundmann/Stuyck (n. 10) 207: "In Europe the existing variety of contract laws is a non-tariff barrier to the inter-Union trade. It is the aim of the Union to do away with restrictions of trade within the Communities, and therefore the differences of law that restrict this trade should be abolished".

20 See generally S. Macaulay "Non-contractual Relations in Business", (1963) 28 *American Sociological Review* 55; "The Real and the Paper Deal: Empirical Pictures of Relationships, Complexity and the Urge for Transparent Principles", (2003) 66 *Modern Law Review* 44. See also J. Michie, S. Deakin, *Contracts, Co-operation and Competition: Studies in Economics, Management and Law* (1997).

economic integration that nevertheless respects an appropriate degree of political sovereignty for nation states".[21]

The creation of a CFR/European Code smacks of a 19th century exercise in nation-building adding to the symbols of the European Union and strengthening and deepening the bonds of its citizens.[22] But to make an obvious point we are now in a new millennium with new fangled and multi centric modes of governance. 19th century solutions may not be apposite in the new era.[23]

Three additional points are perhaps worth mentioning while talking about codifying the law on proprietary securities on a Europe-wide basis as the CFR essentially involves. Firstly, in Continental Europe, the law in this area is, by and large, uncodified law. Legal recognition and expansion of security rights has occurred, in the main, through statutory supplements to the Civil Code and case law add-ons. As one commentator puts it: "the development of secured transactions law (...) largely took place (and continues to take place) outside the national Civil Codes. The legal regime is either entirely based on case law, as for example in Germany, or contained in special, fragmented legislation as, for example, in France, Italy and Spain".[24]

Secondly, England lacks a comprehensive Commercial Law code though, somewhat paradoxically, particular areas of commercial law are often spoken of as being codified from the 19th century.[25] For example, the common law rules pertaining to the sale of goods were largely codified in the Sale of Goods Act 1893 whereas the law of partnership – the principles of law that govern the relationship between persons who carry on business in common with a view to a profit – was codified in the Partnership Act 1890. There is no comprehensive statutory code in England however, when it comes to the law of proprietary security or, for that matter, the law of personal security.[26]

Thirdly, in discussing the possible content of the Common Frame of Reference, this paper asks whether the provisions of the UNCITRAL legislative guide of secured transactions serve as an adequate blueprint. While certainly not a

---

21 See Collins (n. 16) 269.

22 See generally T. Wilhelmsson, "The Legal, the Cultural and the Political – Conclusions from Different Perspectives on Harmonisation of European Contract law", [2002] *European Business Law Revew* 541.

23 On nation-building and the idea of civil codes see generally W. van Gerven, "Codifying European Private Law: Top Down and Bottom Up" in: Grundmann/Stuyck (n. 10) 405.

24 See E.-M. Kieninger (ed.), *Security Rights in Movable Property in European Private Law* (2004) at p 647.

25 See the article by the Law Lord, A. Rodger, "Codification of Commercial Law in Victorian Britain" (1992), 108 LQR 570. See also Roy Goode "Insularity or Leadership? The Role of the United Kingdom in the Harmonisation of Commercial Law", (2001) 50 *International & Comparative Law Quarterly* 751.

26 See generally on the presentational difficulties caused by this M. Bridge, "The Law Commission's Proposals for the Reform of Corporate Security Interests", in: J. Getzler, J. Payne (eds.), *Company Charges: Spectrum and Beyond* (2006) at p 267 who concludes at p 289: "Those who have participated in international gatherings will be acutely aware that the absence of a presentable package of English commercial law is a major hindrance to its international influence".

mirror image of existing English law in this area, the legislative guide more closely reflects the principles of the common law than it does civilian principles. If the Legislative Guide shapes in any significant way the content of the Common Frame of Reference on proprietary security then the position might be likened to that of a reverse takeover with the common law superseding civilian principles rather than vice versa. This is not because of any tremendous power enjoyed by the UK but rather by reason of the overweening influence of the major common law jurisdiction – the US.[27] American law and American lawyers heavily shaped the content of the Legislative Guide but it may prove a Pyrrhic victory. It is submitted that the Legislative Guide is too American in tone – too like Article 9 of the United States Uniform Commercial Code[28] – for direct and immediate translation into the Common Frame of Reference.[29] But even if the UNCITRAL guide is not followed closely, the CFR may still reflect more closely common law principles rather than civil law principles.

Assuming that secured credit is a good thing through fostering economic activity, it is submitted that the more general principles to be discerned from the English common law are more appropriate for inclusion in the CFR than the specific provisions of the Legislative Guide. Even here however a note of caution is appropriate for different States may wish to experiment with different degrees of freedom when it comes to sanctioning the creation and enforcement of security. The case for national autonomy is particularly strong in the area of consumer oriented transactions. But even in the commercial context, different States may have different views on the extent to which secured creditors should prevail over unsecured creditors and whether particular types of creditor e.g. trade creditors should prevail over other creditors e.g. finance creditors.[30] To

---

27 For comparisons betweens US and UK law in this area see G. McCormack, *Secured Credit under English and American Law* (2004).

28 Brief descriptions of Article 9 can be found in P. Winship, "Selected Security Interests in the United States", in: Norton/Andenas (n. 2) at p 267; R. Broude, "Secured Transactions in Personal Property in the United States", in: M. Bridge, R. Stevens (eds.), *Cross-Border Security and Insolvency* (2001) at p 45, and H.C. Sigman, "Security in movable in the United States – Uniform Commercial Code Article 9: a basis for comparison", in: Kieninger (n. 24) at p. 54.

29 It should be noted however that Professor Ulrich Drobnig who has been charged with the task of preparing the initial draft of the CFR on proprietary securities has, albeit many years ago, described Article 9 as being the "most modernised, rational and comprehensive system of security interests in the present world – see (1997) volume 8 *UNCITRAL Yearbook* at p 171.

30 See R. Goode, "Security in Cross Border Transactions", (1998) 33 *Texas International Law Journal* 47 at 48:"Common law jurisdictions, which are generally sympathetic to the concepts of party autonomy and self-help, have a liberal attitude towards security. This attitude allows security interests to be taken with a minimum of formality over both present and future assets to secure existing and future indebtedness (...) [T]hey allow universal security rather than require specific security. By contrast, civil law jurisdictions have been more cautious in their approach to non-possessory security and have been anxious about the false wealth which such practices are perceived as permitting (...) [Therefore, one can find in

develop this argument, it is necessary to look more closely at the provisions of the Legislative Guide and its overall philosophy. The discussion is divided into six parts. The first part considers the extent to which security rights should be recognised at all since they seem to strike at the principle of equality of treatment of creditors in a debtor's insolvency. The second part looks at comprehensive security rights; the third at possible carve-outs for unsecured creditors; the fourth at publicising the existence of security rights; the fifth at the treatment of quasi-securities and the final part considers the principles for working out priorities between competing securities. In each of these areas, the principles of the UNCITRAL Legislative Guide are looked at and how they might shape the content of the CFR.

III Justifications for Recognising the Existence of Security Rights

Lenders may wish to take security because it may give priority over other creditors in the event of the debtor becoming insolvent. It may also provide the lender with a measure of control over the assets. This is important for the lender may be able to dictate the time at which the assets are sold with a view to repaying the debt and also has a strong hand if the debtor proposes to restructure or reschedule the loan. If the lender has security it may mean that the debtor is more likely to carry out the loan commitments rather than other commitments because failure to honour the terms of the loan could lead to the loss of an asset that is crucial to the carrying on of the debtor's business. Moreover, having security opens up the possibility of the lender exercising self-help remedies i.e. being able to enforce the security without recourse to the courts. Self-help however, both as a concept and as tool for practical implementation remains controversial in many jurisdictions.

Notwithstanding a lender or creditor's desire to take security, security as an institution may strike one as being intuitively unfair in that it may involve one creditor being paid whereas other creditors remain unpaid.[31] Legal systems may however permit security, in certain circumstances at least, for a number of reasons. Security can be seen as a fair exchange for the credit. The secured creditor has bargained for security and, by implication, priority whereas other creditors have not and, therefore, it does not seem unfair to privilege the secured creditor over other creditors who could equally have contracted for security but

civil law jurisdictions] requirements of specificity or individualisation of collateral, the requirements of notice to the debtor as a condition of the validity (not merely priority) of an assignment of debts, and restrictions on self help remedies such as possession and sale of the collateral".

[31] For a strong critique of pari passu see generally R.J. Mokal, "Priority as Pathology: The Pari Passu Myth" [2001] *Cambridge Law Journal* 581 and see also V. Finch, *Corporate Insolvency Law: Perspectives and Principles* (2002) at p. 75-105.

chose not to do so. Having said that, there may be involuntary creditors i.e not in a contractual relationship with the debtor, who are not in a position to bargain for security. Also there are other non-adjusting creditors, or poorly adjusting creditors, where it is unrealistic to suppose that they could bargain for security or where the transaction costs of doing so are too great. These creditors in a weak bargaining position are perhaps most likely to be the ones that will be hit hardest by the debtor's insolvency. The insolvency may impact disproportionately on them in that they are not very capable of sharing or passing on the costs of the loss. Large financial institutions – businesses most likely to take security – by contrast are in a much better position to pass on the costs of the loss to their own customers.

International financial organisations have extolled the virtues of secured credit laws that permit easily availability of security but, at the same time, have generally focused on more instrumental justifications. For example, UNCITRAL has suggested that modern secured credit laws can have a significant impact on the availability and the cost of credit and thus on international trade.[32] In its view, the creation of a legal system that promoted secured credit not only aids in the cultivation and growth of individual businesses but also in general economic prosperity. Countries with inadequate secured transactions regimes may have suffered significant losses in gross domestic product (GDP) in consequence.[33] This proposition is developed by UNCITRAL as follows:[34] "The key to the effectiveness of secured credit is that it allows borrowers to use the value inherent in their assets as a means of reducing credit risk for the creditor. Risk is mitigated because loans secured by the property of a borrower give lenders recourse to the property in the event of non-payment. Studies have shown that as the risk of non-payment is reduced, the availability of credit increases and the cost of credit falls. Studies have also shown that in States where lenders perceive the risks associated with transactions to be high, the cost of credit increases as

---

32 *Draft legislative guide on secured transactions – Report of the Secretary General – Background remarks* A/CN.9/WG.VI/WP.2 at para 2.

33 Uncitral had previously done work on this general area in the 1970s commissioning Professor Ulrich Drobnig to produce a comprehensive report detailing the legal treatment of security interests in many jurisdictions: "Study on Security Interests", (1997) 8 *UNCITRAL Yearbook* 171; UN Doc.A/CN.9/SER. A/1977. Eventually however, UNCITRAL concluded that worldwide unification of the law of security interests in goods was in all likelihood unattainable. After working on the specific area of receivables financing in the 1990s leading to the UN Convention on the Assignment of Receivables in International Trade (New York, 2001) UNCITRAL has returned to more general work on secured credit in the new millennium.

34 *Draft legislative guide on secured transactions – Report of the Secretary General – Background remarks* A/CN.9/WG.VI/WP.2 at p 2 and see also the report by the Asian Development Bank *Secured Transactions Law Reform in Asia: Unleashing the Potential of Collateral* (2000). But for something of an alternative perspective see the article by the former English Solicitor General, R. Cranston, "Credit Security and Debt Recovery: Law's Role in Asia and the Pacific", in: Norton/Andenas (n. 2) at p. 219.

lenders require increased compensation to evaluate and assume the increased risk. In some countries, the absence of an effective secured transactions regime has resulted in the virtual elimination of credit for consumers or commercial enterprises".

In simple terms, the availability of security is said to encourage lenders to make loans that they would not otherwise make and, in this way, the pace of economic activity is increased. [35]

Moreover, security is said to lower the cost of credit because it reduces the risk faced by the lender and reduces the risk premium that a lender may build in to the matrix for calculating interest rates. In a particular case however, there may not be simple trade-off between interest rates and the cost of credit. Sub-prime borrowers may not only be charged high interest rates but also have to provide security as a condition of the loan. With blue-chip borrowers however, capacity to service the loan is not considered to be an issue and so security does not enter into the reckoning and moreover, the competition among lenders for a valuable source of business operates to keep interest rates low.

There has been an extensive debate, going back to the late 1970s, among academics, particularly in the United States, about whether secured credit is efficient. In the US, this debate gained added momentum in the context of the revision of Article 9. The prevailing legal norm, still reflected in Article 9, is based on full priority for secured credit over unsecured credit but there have been critics of this orthodoxy both from a "Right" "law and economics" camp and from a "Left" perspective. Those from the Right essentially argue that secured credit is not economically efficient or at least has not been proved to be economically efficient. Those from the Left have been dubbed "Symps" or Sympathetic Legal Scholars and they argue against secured credit, or at least full priority for secured credit, because of concerns that this might be unfair or damaging to the interests of unsecured, particularly nonadjusting or involuntary creditors. [36]

---

[35] See N. Cohen, "Internationalising the Law of Secured Credit: Perspectives from the U.S. Experience", (1999) 20 *University of Pennsylvania J Int'l Econ L* 423 at 429: "It might appear that the creditor can ameliorate the problem of losses from debtor default simply by raising the interest rate so that the profits from the transactions in which the debtors pay are high enough to outweigh the losses from those in which the debtors default. This solution can work only in a narrow range, though. After all, raising the interest rate makes it less likely that the credit transaction will be profitable for the borrower. If the borrower does not see the transaction as profitable, it will not take place. Thus, when the risk of loss from debtor insolvency is high, it will be difficult to construct a credit transaction in which both parties foresee profits".

[36] There is a full debate on this issue at a symposium reported at (1997) 82 *Cornell Law Review*.

IV Comprehensive Security Rights

Even if one accepts the bare bones of the proposition that security increases the availability, and lowers the cost, of credit, it does not necessarily mean that one should accept all tenets of the Legislative Guide. For instance, the guide has a comprehensive ambit both in terms of the range of persons to whom it may apply and also in terms of the assets that may serve as security. It exhorts States to be as comprehensive as possible in the design of secured credit laws and not to leave inadvertent gaps in coverage.[37] It is suggested that the law should apply equally to legal and natural persons though without affecting the scope of consumer protection legislation.[38] The main reason for such a recommendation is obvious – it complicates the law if differing sets of laws apply to the creation and recognition of security interests depending on whether the security giver acts for business purposes or as a consumer. The difficulty with the recommendation however, is that a particular jurisdiction may not have a very developed consumer protection regime to offset against the risks in the grant of security. Consumers may grant security without a full appreciation of the consequences in terms of the control that the creditor may exercise over their assets. Depending also on the bankruptcy laws in the jurisdiction, debtors may find themselves losing assets that are essential to their livelihood or sense of personality e.g. a family home. If there are no developed consumer protection principles in play, a more primitive form of protection is simply to deny the possibility of individuals creating security over certain types of property. A blanket ban of this nature is undoubtedly a blunt tool and may restrict the availability of credit. On the other hand, it provides consumers with a degree of respite from certain types of creditor enforcement action and in a world where "consumer overindebtedness" is seen as a pressing social problem, limiting consumer credit availability may be no bad thing.

Concerns about consumers, or about protecting the weaker party to credit relationships, may have motivated many of the limitations on the taking of security that are found in European jurisdictions. It is perhaps only a slight exaggeration to speak about a wilderness of single instances when talking about the taking of security in many jurisdictions. Often we have sector specific legisla-

[37] See recommendation 1 of the Legislative Guide ("Key Objectives"): "The law should be designed (a) To promote secured credit; (b) To allow utilization of the full value inherent in a broad range of assets to support credit in the widest possible array of credit transactions; (c) To enable parties to obtain security rights in a simple an efficient manner; (d) To provide for equal treatment of diverse sources of credit and of diverse forms of secured transactions; (e) To validate non-possessory security rights; (f) To encourage responsible behaviour on the part of all parties by enhancing predictability and transparency; (g) To establish clear and predictable priority rules; (h) To facilitate enforcement of creditor's rights in a predictable an efficient manner; (i) To balance the interests of affected persons; (j) To recognize party autonomy; and (k) To harmonize secured transactions laws, including conflict-of-laws rules."

[38] Recommendation 2.

tion that permits security in certain situations. This legislation may have been passed at the prompting of important political constituencies or pressure groups and it may be difficult to explain on more principled grounds. Interest groups who find their needs satisfied have no particular need to urge the enactment of more universal security instruments. If the case for a more comprehensive security regime was ever argued, then at least two considerations can be put forward for refusing to accept the case. The first is the proposition that a debtor should have a cushion or margin of free assets i.e. unsecured assets that are available to satisfy claims by unsecured creditors including involuntary creditors i.e. those who have not entered into contractual commitments with the debtor. The second is an ideological preference for the proposition that certain assets can never serve as the subject of security. For instance, many non-lawyers may find baffling the concept that a debtor can create security over assets that it does not yet own. On the other hand, Article 9 freely permits the creation of such security though initially there was some degree of ambivalence on this point in the US.[39] The English common law does likewise through the medium of the floating charge.[40]

These arguments against the recognition of comprehensive or universal security rights have also been made in the US and while Article 9 has no truck with the arguments, this outcome represents the result of a long process of historical development. Pre-Article 9 United States law did not have any place for a universal security right for the aforementioned reasons.[41] This comes through in a leading case *Zartman v First National Bank of Waterloo*[42] where the issue was whether a comprehensive security given by a company over its property extended to property that the company was permitted to dispose of in the ordinary course of business. The security, in express terms, covered after-acquired property but the court, nevertheless, denied effectiveness to the provision. It was said that entity could not create security over property that it did not yet own and secondly, the borrower's freedom of disposition sanctioned by the security meant that the security was fraudulent as against other creditors.

---

39 One of the architects of Article 9, Grant Gilmore, has said in "Security Law, formalism and Article 9", (1968) 47 *Nebraska Law Review* 659 at 672: "Article 9 draftsmen argued from the premise that, under existing security law, a lender could take an enforceable interest in all of a debtor's present and future personal property to the conclusion that the new statute should provide for the accomplishment of this result in the simplest possible fashion".

40 See generally on the floating charge R. Nolan, "Property in a Fund of Assets", (2004) Law Quarterly Review 120: J. Farrar, "World Economic Stagnation Puts the Floating Charge on Trial", (1980) 1 *Co Lawyer* 83; E. Ferran, "Floating Charges – the Nature of the Security", [1988] *Cambridge Law Journal* 213; S. Worthington, "Floating Charges – an Alternative Theory" [1994] *Cambridge Law Journal* 81.

41 Professor Grant Gilmore, has argued that if floating charges had been accepted in the US, then some of the pressure for change which brought about Article 9 would have been absent – see *Security Interests in Personal Property* (1965) at pp 359-361.

42 (1907) 189 NY 267.

This line of authority was confirmed at the highest judicial levels in the United States[43] but over time a sophisticated avoidance industry developed which had the effect of permitting large scale receivables and other financing.[44] This resulted in most types of personal property including both tangible and intangible property becoming available to serve as security. Like the current situation in Europe, this was often the result of legislative initiatives mounted by interest groups in the individual States[45]. A standard legislative feature in the US was to require the registration of each and every security that could be created so as to ensure third party effectiveness. The end result of the multiplicity of security devices was that in a single State, there might be a number of distinct filing systems with each of these covering a separate security device. In relation to some securities, there might be a single registry that covered all filings done in the State whereas in the case of other security devices, filing might have be done on a local or county basis. Filing or registration serves a public information function but the objective is defeated if the burden of inquiry becomes too great. With multiple registers, the inquiry becomes expensive and extensive in trying to find out the debtor's credit history and the possible existence of prior encumbrances. The father of Article 9, Professor Grant Gilmore has made the point that: "The typical pre-Code pattern included separate filing systems for chattel mortgages, for conditional sales, for trust receipts, for factor's liens and for assignments of accounts receivable. In such a situation the expense and difficulty of making a thorough credit check are obvious. Since the filing requirements were themselves frequently obscure and tricky, the chances were good that a lender who, through his counsel, was familiar with one device would inadvertently go wrong in attempting to comply with another and fail to perfect his security interest".[46]

Article 9 rationalised and systematised this state of affairs. Nomenclature was simplified with the effective abolition of the multiplicity of separate security devices and their replacement by the concept of a single security interest that could exist in all the debtor's property. Article 9 also embodied the proposition that there was no necessary incompatibility between the existence of a security interest in property and the debtor's freedom to dispose of the secured assets in

---

43 *Benedict v. Ratner* (1925) 268 US 353.

44 See generally Gilmore (n. 41) vol 1, chapters 1-8.

45 Article 9 has been described as "an anthological collection of the most celebrated security law controversies of the preceding forty years" in Gilmore (n. 39) at 671.

46 See the official comment attached to the 1972 version of Article 9-101. Gilmore (n. 41) notes at p 463: "The typical pre-Code pattern included separate filing systems for chattel mortgages, for conditional sales, for trust receipts, for factor's liens and for assignments of accounts receivable. In such a situation the expense and difficulty of making a thorough credit check are obvious. Since the filing requirements were themselves frequently obscure and tricky, the chances were good that a lender who, through his counsel, was familiar with one device would inadvertently go wrong in attempting to comply with another and fail to perfect his security interest".

the ordinary course of business. Article 9-205 states that a security interest is not invalid or fraudulent against creditors solely because the debtor has the right or ability to

a) "use, commingle, or dispose of all or part of the collateral, including returned or repossessed goods;
b) collect, compromise, enforce or otherwise deal with collateral;
c) accept the return of collateral or make repossessions; or
d) use, commingle, or dispose of proceeds;

or because the secured party fails to require the debtor to account for proceeds or to replace the collateral".

So, amongst other things, Article 9 brings together a multiplicity of separate security devices as well as permitting universal security. All this occurred in the 1950s and one might say that, given the time lag, Europe is overdue a similar development. On the other hand, the United States is a political as well as an economic union and there was probably a much higher degree of economic integration between the various States in the US than there is even today in the nation states of Europe. In Europe there is no common language. The path of historical development is clearly different and differences in national and regional culture run much deeper than they do in the US.

Be that as it may, it might be argued that it would be merely a modest first step for the CFR to simplify and rationalise the number of separate devices, without detracting from the potency of security, as well as legislating for the recognition of universal security. In one comparative study it is suggested that [47]"none of the jurisdictions of the EU Member States has developed a comprehensive, functional approach to security rights in movables. Instead, there exists in each jurisdiction a wide range of security devices, which differ from each other with respect to the character of the secured debt, the collateral that may be used, and the legal concept on which the security rights are based: title-based security rights such as retention of title, security transfer of ownership or leasing exist side by side with the possessory pledge and various devices that are based on the idea of the pledge such as non-possessory registered charges in individualised property or entities of assets."

Under the Legislative Guide security can be created over all types of movable property including property presently owned by the debtor as well as property that may be acquired by the debtor in the future.[48] Moreover, in the absence of agreement by the parties to the contrary, a security right in assets is stated

[47] See Kieninger (n. 24) at p. 648. See also U Drobnig "Present and Future of Real and Personal Security", [2003] *European Review of Private Law* 623; C. Bourbon-Seclet "Cross-border security Interests in moveable property", [2005] *Journal of International Banking Law and Regulation* 419.

[48] See Recommendation 2(a): "The law should apply: (a) To all types of movable property and attachment, tangible or intangible, present or future, including inventory, equipment and other goods, contractual and non-contractual receivables, negotiable instruments, negotiable documents, rights to payment of

to extend to the proceeds. The Legislative Guide aims to facilitate receivables financing and security may be created over future, fluctuating and conditional obligations owed to the debtor. Security rights can be created in bank accounts in favour of parties other than the depositary bank. The depositary is not permitted to block this though the security agreement cannot impose any duties on the depositary bank. The Legislative Guide however does not apply to security rights in "securities" (in other words, investment intangible such as shares or bonds) and it is also applicable in the case of immovable property with the exception of chattels that are attached to land and become so-called "fixtures".[49] The application of the Guide to intellectual property rights remains the subject of ongoing controversy.

V Carve-outs for Unsecured Creditors

One of the most significant features of the Legislative Guide is the validation of "all-assets security" i.e. security over the entire business operations of an enterprise.[50] This reflects an Article 9 approach but one might argue but it merely legislates for the equivalent of an English-style floating charge which has functional analogues in other European countries. European countries however, including England, generally carve out a proportion of all-assets security for the benefit of unsecured creditors.[51] In the associated commentary, the Legislative Guide does not recommend this approach of setting aside a proportion of security, or all-assets security, for the benefit of unsecured creditors.

This clearly indicates a preference for the approach adopted in the United States where the idea of carving out some security for the benefit of unsecured creditors failed to gain acceptance in the Article 9 revision process in 1998. Carve-out advocates pointed out that while the US Bankruptcy Code reflected a principle of recognising the priority of security rights to their fullest, nevertheless, there were a number of rules, doctrines and practices that effectively operated to erode the priority of secured claims in bankruptcy.[52] For example, Chapter 11 which governs proceedings for the restructuring of ailing businesses

funds credited to a bank account, proceeds under an independent undertaking and intellectual property rights".

49 Recommendation 5: "The law should provide that it does not apply to [indirectly held] securities and immovable property, although it may affect such assets, as provided in recommendations 24 and 45".

50 See Recommendation 17: "The law should provide that a security right may be granted in all assets of a grantor".

51 See what is now s 176A Insolvency Act 1986 and the Insolvency Act 1986 (Prescribed Part) Order 2003 which fixes the proportion of collateral set aside.

52 See L. Bebchuk, J. Fried, "The Uneasy Case for the Priority of Secured Claims in Bankruptcy" (1996) 105 *Yale Law Journal* 857; E. Warren, "Making Policy with Imperfect Information: The Article 9 Full Priority Debates", (1997) 82 *Cornell Law Review* 1373 at 1377.

imposed restrictions on the enforcement of security interests and during this time the value of the collateral may fall.[53] State legislatures also had power to sanction the creation of statutory liens with priority over the claims of secured creditors and this power had increasingly been exercised.[54] Advocates of a carve-out were sceptical at suggestions that their proposals would lead to a diminution in credit. They pointed out that a partial priority regime already obtained to a degree and that, in the final analysis, matters might turn on the extent of the carve-out.

Carve-out critics suggested that it would be factored into the borrowing base and secured creditors would extend less credit as a result. This would have a particularly adverse impact on marginal businesses resulting in more bankruptcies.[55] The lawyers responsible for the drafting of Article 9, Professors Harris and Mooney,[56] took on board the concerns expressed by commercial lender bodies and voiced the view that even a partial subordination of secured credit would cause many potential lenders to refuse to advance loans. They urged caution since the social and economic benefits of priority rights were indirect.[57] In their assessment, the denial of full priority might detract from the capacity of entrepreneurs to attract investors although it was impossible to identify particular companies that never came into existence as the result of a particular change in priority rights. Unpaid workers were easier to spot than workers who were never able to find a job because a particular project did not receive start-up financing.[58] It was suggested that while secured creditors might lose

53 See D. Baird, T. Jackson, "Corporate Reorganizations and the Treatment of Diverse Ownership Interests: A Comment on Adequate Protection of Secured Creditors in Bankruptcy", (1984) 51 *University of Chicago Law Review* 97, 112-114.

54 See K. Klee, "Barbarians at the Trough: Riposte in Defense of the Warren Carve-Out Proposal", (1997) 82 *Cornell Law Review* 1466 at 1474-1475.

55 See Klee (n. 54) at 1472: "For example, where the debtor is in a risky start-up venture or on the verge of insolvency, the risk to unsecured creditors might be so great that instead of seeking a high interest to compensate for increased risk, they simply will not extend new credit. The resulting liquidity crisis will force the debtor into bankruptcy, where unsecured creditors will recover less than if the debtor had not filed".

56 See S.L. Harris, C.W. Mooney, "A Property-Based Theory of Security Interests: Taking Debtors- Choices Seriously", (1994) 80 *Virginia Law Review* 2021; S.L. Harris, C. Mooney Jr, "Measuring the Social Costs and Benefits and Identifying the Victims of Subordinating Security Interests in Bankruptcy" (1997) 82 *Cornell Law Review* 1349 and see also S.L. Schwarcz, "The Easy Case for the Priority of Secured Claims in Bankruptcy", (1997) 47 *Duke Law Journal* 425.

57 For a strong riposte to this see E. Warren (n. 52) 1373 n 62: "Harris and Mooney state: 'For example, data may confirm that small businesses (and, accordingly, minority-owned businesses) would disproportion ately comprise that group [that would face constriction of credit]' (...) their support? Anecdotal evidence. This argument can be rephrased to say that banks want full priority to help their minority friends. Some critics may demand more than anecdotes to support this proposition."

58 See D. Baird, "The Importance of Priority", (1997) 82 *Cornell Law Review* 1420 at 1421.

profits under a carve-out regime, the biggest losers would be debtors, who would receive less funding, and potential contracting parties with such debtors.[59]

The US Attorney General's Office concurred with this general assessment stating that the carve-out proposal:[60]"could have detrimental effects on many highly leveraged sectors of the economy, such as small businesses and agriculture". Political realities meant that carve out proposals fell by the wayside in the United States. But the political realities in Europe are different and what plays well in Peoria, Illinois may not necessarily play well in Poitiers. Perhaps one can add that playing well in Peoria – the epitome of heartlands America – is often considered to be barometer of acceptability and commercial success for the Hollywood movie industry.

For many continental Europeans, England is considered to be something of a mirror image of the US but on this particular point there is a divergence. Under English law, all-assets security is possible through the medium of the floating charge[61] but under provisions in the Enterprise Act 2002 a certain percentage of floating charge realizations are set aside for the benefit of unsecured creditors. The percentage is calculated by secondary legislation on a sliding scale but subject to a global ceiling of £600,000.[62] Moreover, the carve-out is inapplicable if the company's net property is less than a prescribed minimum and where the insolvency representative considers that the cost of making a distribution to unsecured creditors would be disproportionate to the benefits. Defenders of the English provision suggest[63] it constitutes a fair concession to unsecured creditors without destroying the notion of security in its entirety. It is admittedly a blunt instrument since it benefits all unsecured creditors and not merely non-adjusting creditors i.e. those who are unable to adjust the explicit or implicit lending terms to take into account the fact that the borrower has granted security. [64] The fixed ceiling however, allows attendant risks to be calculated.

If the Legislative guide has an Anglo-Saxon bias then it is an American rather than an English bias. This United States orientation is also evident in the notice filing regime that the Guide imports for publicising the existence of security rights.

---

59 Harris/Mooney "Measuring the Social Costs and Benefits and Identifying the Victims of Subordinating Security Interests in Bankruptcy" (n. 56) 1349 at 1357.

60 (1997) 82 *Cornell Law Review* 1349 n 49.

61 See generally McCormack (n. 27) at pp 46-48 and 108-112.

62 See Insolvency Act 1986 (Prescribed Part) Order 2003.

63 D. Milman, D. Mond, *Security and Corporate Rescue* (1999) at p. 52. The 1982 Department of Trade and Industry Committee on Insolvency Law and Practice (the "Cork Committee") which recommended a carve-out for unsecured creditors specifically rejected the proposition that any such diminution of credit would occur (Cmnd 8558 at para 1535).

64 See V. Finch, "Security, Insolvency and Risk: Who Pays the Price?", (1999) 62 *Modern Law Review* 633 at 652.

VI Security Rights and Publicity

Under the Legislative Guide third party effectiveness of security rights requires registration of the security in a general security rights register.[65] Of itself, this notion is pretty controversial in that many jurisdictions, mostly notably Germany, are committed to the concept of registrationless regimes of personal property security. Even someone not ill-disposed towards the US Article 9 approach like Professor Ulrich Drobnig has downplayed the importance in this connection of the publicity principle stating "is the complicated technical system really necessary if all the information it offers is a notice that there may exist a security interest, so that intending creditors are put on notice but have to turn to the debtor in order to verify the true state of affairs. Is not nearly the same effect achieved in countries without a registration system where the courts proceed from a general presumption that business people must know that any major piece of equipment is bought on credit? Does not this presumption also put intending creditors on notice so that they also have to verify the true state of affairs: I remain to be convinced of the true necessity of a filing system".[66]

On the other hand, one might argue that a registrationless regime of personal property security only works well in a relatively closed credit market like Germany where there are a number of powerful players with a quasi-monopolistic control on credit.[67] In a closed credit market, leading banks have detailed information on the financial behaviour and credit needs of businesses. This is much less likely in a Europe wide credit market with financial institutions operating across national frontiers. Potential lenders simply do not have the business background and information on potential borrowers. If one does not have information that is publicly available through a filing system, then financial institutions who are trying to enter the credit market are also effectively excluded. They do not have the fund of built up knowledge and experience and have to rely more on credit reference agencies who may operate less trans-

---

65 Recommendation 184.

66 See Drobnig (n. 47) at 660.

67 For a somewhat sarcastic panegyric to the American system see J. White "Reforming Article 9 Priorities in Light of Old Ignorance and New Filing Rules", (1995) 79 *Minnesota Law Review* 529 at p. 530. "The filing system is an integral part of the most sophisticated secured lending system known to mankind. Only by an effective filing system can a secured lender know of other lenders and only by it can later secured lenders and unsecured lenders be encouraged to lend. Without such a system, lenders would grow wary, commerce would be hobbled, and the manifold commercial ends that are met by commercial lenders would be stunted, rendered more costly, or stymied altogether… I can see generations of law students writing this down and repeating this incantation in negotiations, in court, and elsewhere. This view even extends to Americans abroad who approach the English, Dutch and Germans with an air of superiority, asserting the superiority of our filing system and belittling the European efforts to put together a filing system worthy of the name".

parently than a public filing system. Advocates of the American approach might argue that it is more facilitative of entrepreneurial endeavour than the German i.e. it opens the availability of credit to persons who were previously not on first name terms with bankers.[68]

Article 9 uses the expression "perfection" as a general synonym for third party effectiveness of security rights. Filing is the standard method of perfecting an Article 9 security interest though other methods of perfection are permissible in certain circumstances including possession where physical possession of the property used as security is handed over to the security taker. Of course the transfer of physical possession is not practicable in most situations. The assets may be intangible or the debtor may need them for the carrying on of its business. In deference to the needs and wants of the capital markets, the revised Article 9 makes use of a notion of perfection by control.[69] In the case of certain types of financial collateral, including dematerialized or immobilised shares, the security taker can perfect the security though taking control of it. An example of control is where a securities intermediary agrees to respond to instructions from the secured party rather than from the debtor.

In its approach to the third party effectiveness of security rights, the Legislative Guide follows the basic tenor of Article 9. Filing or registration is given pride of place notwithstanding the general lack of appeal of this construct to civil law jurisdictions. Moreover, it is the US concept of notice filing that finds favour rather than the concept found in English law, and also more familiar to continental European jurisdictions, of transaction filing.[70] Under the notice filing regime, what has to be filed is not the security agreement itself but only a simple record – a financing statement – that provides a limited amount of information.[71] The filed notice merely indicates that a person may have a secu-

68 See A. Dunham "Inventory and Accounts Receivable Financing", (1949) 62 *Harvard Law Review* 588 at 611: "One banker though the questions [about sources of debtor information] 'silly' because his bank did not make a loan unless the borrower 'was properly introduced' and therefore a fraudulent borrower was an impossibility".

69 For the definition of control see Article 9-106. "Control" is recognised as a superior method of perfection over financial collateral than filing. Article 9-328 lays down that a secured party who is perfected by control will have priority over an earlier secured party who has perfected its security interest by filing.

70 For a succinct explanation of the distinction between notice filing and transaction filing see the Scottish Law Commission discussion paper *Registration of Rights in Security by Companies* (Edinburgh, TSO, October 2002) at p. 8.

71 According to the Scottish Law Commission, the only civil law jurisdictions to have introduced notice filing are Quebec and Louisiana; see Discussion paper *Registration of Rights in Security by Companies* (2002) at para 1.28 and see further: T.A. Harrell "A Guide to the Provisions of Chapter 9 of Louisiana's Commercial Code", (1990) *Loyola Law Review* 711; M. Bridge, R.A. Macdonald, R.L. Simmonds, C. Walsh "Formalism, Functionalism and Understanding the Law of Secured Transactions", (1999) 44 *McGill Law Journal* 567. Indeed, the Scottish Law Commission in a Discussion Paper state: "Existing models of notice filing presuppose Anglo-American property law and turn on distinctions between

rity interest in the collateral concerned but further inquiry by a searcher from the potential creditor and/or debtor will be necessary to ascertain the true state of affairs. The notice filing/transaction filing distinction may be explained on the basis that notice filing is party specific rather than transaction specific. The information filed is rather general in character being an invitation to further inquiry rather than being a synopsis of the transaction. The notice may be filed either before or after a particular transaction and a single filing is effective to cover multiple transactions. These are the perceived advantages of a notice filing system.

Advance registration allows a secured party to mark out its intentions in advance of the conclusion of the agreement and while negotiations between the parties are continuing. It is claimed that this is more convenient and flexible than "after the event" transaction filing.[72] The parties are given more time to attend to registration rather than having to do it post-transaction when there may be a lot of other formalities to deal with. Moreover, the facility whereby a single filing covers multiple transactions renders more concrete the possibility of making trade credit transactions registrable. In, for example, the supply of goods situation, there may be a number of separate transactions between the same buyer and seller, and if each one required individual registration, then cost and inconvenience would militate against registration being achieved in practice.

Many observers, and indeed legislatures, however, remain to be convinced about the merits of notice filing. Registration in advance of a transaction seems relatively small beer and, in any event, its benefits can largely be secured through a modification of a transaction based filing system that allows registration in advance but under which the registration lapses if a confirmatory filing is not made within a particular period of time.

Divorcing registration from particular individual transactions opens up the possibility that the register may become less reliable as a source of information. A searcher cannot be sure whether a particular entry on the register relates to an actual transaction between the parties or whether it relates to a transaction that was contemplated but never in fact materialised. The information that is publicly available is less than it would be under a transaction filing system and,

---

creation, attachment and perfection which are unknown in Scots law or in other systems drawn from the Germanic stream of the civil law tradition. A system of notice filing suited to English property law could not readily be modified or adapted to accommodate the very different structures and concepts of Scots property law"; see Scottish Law Commission Discussion Paper No 121 *Registration of Rights in Security by Companies* (2002) at para 1.28 and see also the Final Report by the Scottish Law Commission *Registration of Rights in Security by Companies* (Edinburgh, September 2004) at para 1.5.

72 The EBRD has been sceptical about the merits of allowing advance registration or pre-registration stating that "the advantages of allowing a potential creditor to take priority during the negotiations are debatable" – see *Publicity of Security Rights: EBRD Guiding Principles for the Development of a Charges Registry* (December 2004) at p 14 available on the EBRD web site www.ebrd.com/st.

in the modern information age, this state of affairs hardly seems justifiable. The Internet and modern methods of data capture should also allow easy registration of security instruments and any loss of financial privacy associated with such a procedure could be alleviated by the hiving off of commercially sensitive information to a separate document.

VII The Treatment of Quasi-securities

In nailing its colours to the mast of notice filing, the UNCITRAL Legislative Guide betrays, or to use a more neutral word, demonstrates the US influence in its drafting. The American antecedents are also obvious in the treatment of quasi-securities.

Permitting a single filing to cover a multitude of separate transactions only becomes something of an imperative if quasi-securities are made subject to a registration obligation. Requiring registration in this instance is not part of any common core of European Private Law. The dividing line between security strictly so-called and "quasi-securities" i.e. functionally equivalent legal devices such as finance leases and retention of title clauses in sale of goods contracts may be a thin one in particular cases but it is a line that is generally respected throughout Europe. In the main, albeit subject to exceptions, quasi-securities do not have to be publicised through registration as a condition of third party effectiveness.

The Article 9 approach is very different. Article 9 and legal regimes modelled upon it, such as those in New Zealand and in the common law provinces of Canada, pay greater attention to what is perceived to be the economic substance of a transaction rather than to its legal form. Article 9 abandons the old distinctions, still found for example in English law, between different ways of securing a claim and the use of absolute title as security.[73] Article 9 takes a generic approach towards a security interest. It sweeps away old legal terminology consigning traditional concepts used by lawyers to refer to security such as pledge, mortgage, charge and trust receipt to the realms of legal history. The unitary concept of an Article 9 security interest takes their place. Article 9 is also specifically stated to apply to certain transactions like factoring of debts and retention of title clauses in sale of goods contracts that, in traditional legal terms, do not involve the creation of security but nevertheless, in economic terms, serve the same financing purpose. In its deeming provision, Article 9 seems to be consciously extending the concept of security. Certain transactions are recharacterised as security rights and the security rights regime is then

[73] Article 9-109 states the scope of application of Article 9 and Article 1-201(37) defining "security interest" as meaning an interest in personal property or fixtures that secures either payment or else the performance of an obligation.

applied to them subject to certain modifications.[74] Finance leases, for example, by a legislative sleight of hand are deemed to constitute a security interest and if the lessor fails to "perfect" the deemed security interest against the lessee through filing then, effectively, the lessor will lose its ownership of the property if the lessee declines into insolvency.

The Legislative Guide takes the same functional track in its suggestion that the law should treat all devices that perform security functions as secured transactions including the transfer of title to tangibles or the outright assignment of receivables for security purposes.[75] This comprehensive approach would cover more or less all title transfer "security" devices and what is meant by this are rights of a proprietary kind that secure payment or the performance of obligations. There is a general principle enshrined in the Legislative Guide that public notice of quasi-security interests must be given by means of filing in a register that is open to public inspection.[76] There is a twist to the tale however in that the Legislative Guide admits the possibility of a "non-unitary approach". Under this approach, the substantive treatment of functionally similar security type transactions would be the same as for security strictly so-called but the legal characterization would remain different.[77]

One might criticise the recharacterisation approach for, in a sense, ignoring and overriding the parties' intentions. The parties never intended to create a security interest but are deemed by legislation to have done what they never intended to do. Critics would say that the Article 9 approach does not so much involve looking to the substance of the transaction. The intention of the parties as manifested in the form that they have drawn up represents the substance of the transaction and what Article 9 does is to disregard the substance.[78] Even

---

[74] See J. Ziegel, "The travails of English chattel security law reform – a transatlantic view", [2006] *Lloyds Maritime And Commercial Law Quarterly* 110 at 116 "a conditional sale agreement is only a short form of chattel mortgage and that in each case the seller or mortgagee merely retains or obtains title as security for performance of the buyer's obligation".

[75] Recommendation 2(e): which states that the law should apply to "all types of property right created contractually to secure the payment or other performance of an obligation, irrespective of the form of the relevant transaction, including the various forms of retention of title, financial leases and hire-purchase agreements, as well as transfers of title by way of security".

[76] For a detailed account of the Ontario PPSA see J. Ziegel, D. Denomme, *The Ontario Personal Property Security Act. Commentary and Analysis* (2nd ed 2000) and see also more generally G. McCormack, "Personal Property Security Law Reform in England and Canada", [2002] *Journal of Business Law* 113.

[77] See generally Part XII of the Legislative Guide.

[78] See the comment by I. Davies, "The reform of English personal property security law", [2004] *Legal Studies* 295 at 321: "The difficulty with the functionalism as applied in Article 9-type regimes is that it can be both over-inclusive and also under-inclusive at the same time. A more appropriate approach in any reform of English personal property security law is to operate within the existing legal landscape rather than to seek to transform it."

some supporters of Article 9 type regimes have acknowledged this argument:[79] "There are two features of the UCC, Article 9 approach that appear to be troublesome even to those who are attracted to it. The first is the total reconceptualisation that it requires in the context of types of transactions that traditionally are not viewed as secured financing devices .... The second feature (...) is the extent to which it requires a bifurcated approach to the characterisation of certain types of transactions. Since a title retention sales contract or a lease falls within a secured financing regime because it functions as a security device, it follows that the seller or lessor is not the owner of the goods sold or leased (...) What is troublesome is that outside this regime, the recharacterisation might not be acceptable with the result that same transaction is viewed differently depending on the legal issues being addressed".

In deference to primarily civilian sensibilities, and with a view to gaining greater international acceptance, the Legislative Guide is more subtle in its approach than the blunt tool of Article 9. Two options are available with one option (the unitary approach) being an Article 9 style regime with all its features trappings but another possibility is the non-unitary approach. The latter would entail States still applying a different formal characterisation to quasi-security devices. States however, would effectively be obliged to apply the same legal rules to both security and quasi-security with both types of transaction being subject to filing or registration obligations for third party effectiveness and both constituting an exception to the general first-to-file-has-priority principle underlying the Legislative Guide.

By and large, European jurisdictions, both civil and common law it should be said, do not apply registration requirements to quasi-securities such as finance leases, hire-purchase agreements and simple retention of title clauses. Adopting the Legislative Guide as a base for the CFR in this respect would constitute a major departure from current practice and one where the case for a change is not entirely clearcut. Registration is enshrined in the Legislative Guide as the general rule for quasi-securities. Certain exceptions are allowed but, again, these are much more in keeping with American Article 9 sentiments than with European legal traditions. Under Article 9, in the main, there is a certain grace period for registration of a quasi-security – 20 days from the date of creation, and this provision finds its way into the Legislative Guide. One might ask rhetorically why does the Legislative Guide more or less mirror Article 9 exactly in this respect? There are other international parallels closer at hand such as the European Bank for Reconstruction and Development Model Law on Secured Transactions under which a simple retention of title clause is categorized as an unpaid vendor's charge and is valid for 6 months without registration.[80]

---

79 R. Cuming, "The Internationalisation of Secured Financing Law", in: R. Cranston (ed.), *Making Commercial Law: Essays in Honour of Roy Goode* (1997) at p. 522-523.

80 See Article 9 of the EBRD Model Law which can be consulted on the "secured transactions" section of the EBRD website – www.ebrd.com/.

VIII Priority Rules

One of the perceived advantages of Article 9 is the presence of clear and rationally determined priority rules. There is the general principle that the first security interest to be filed has priority over competing security interests over the same property subject to an exception for purchase money security interests.[81] The latter outrank general security interests that extend to the same property. The purchase money security interest is basically the provision of funds to enable a debtor to acquire particular property with the debtor obtaining a security interest in the property. Under Article 9, there is a distinction drawn between general security interests and purchase money security interests with the latter enjoying a form of super-priority that has traditionally been enjoyed by those relying on quasi-securities such as title retention devices. Other financiers extending credit to facilitate the acquisition of property can now enjoy this super-priority status in certain circumstances[82]. If, for example, a debtor has created security over all its assets, including future property then, despite the general first-to-file priority principle, a financier whose credits facilitated the acquisition of "new property" by the debtor will take priority over the earlier creditor in respect of the new property.[83]

There are however, special requirements that have to be satisfied before a purchase money lender can obtain super-priority status and these requirements broadly differ depending on whether the property being acquired is inventory or capital equipment. The requirements are more difficult to establish in the case of inventory for there is what might be termed a prior notification requirement. The purchase money lender must notify earlier creditors whose security extends

81 Article 9-324 deals with the priority of purchase-money security interests and see generally on this area P. Shupack, "Defining Purchase Money Collateral", (1992) 29 *Idaho Law Review* 767; K. Meyer, "A Primer on Purchase Money Security Interests Under Revised Article 9", (2001) 50 *Kansas Law Review* 143. For an argument against the PMSI superpriority rules see A. Schwartz, "A Theory of Loan Priorities", (1989) 18 *Journal of Legal Studies* 209 at 250-254 who would limit super-priority in inventory and prevent PMSI super-priority in other collateral from trumping secured parties who do not have blanket liens.

82 Non-seller purchase money security was possible before the 1998 Article 9 revisions – see generally on this issue G. Nation, "Creation and Perfection of Non-Seller Purchase Money Security Interests: Current Law and Proposed Changes under Revised Article 9", (1998) 31 *Uniform Commercial Code Law Journal* 84.

83 Under Article 9-324(g) the holder of a purchase money security interest that secures the unpaid purchase price of collateral will prevail over the holder of a conflicting purchase money security interest that enables the collateral to be acquired. This means that a retention of title seller has priority over a lender that makes an enabling loan. For criticism of this rule see Meyer (n. 81) at 188 points to some possible inconsistency with Article 9-328 which deals with investment property. Priority in investment property is given to the secured party who has control. Article 9-328(2) provides that if two or more secured parties have control, priority is determined by who obtained control first.

to purchases of inventory that the new lender proposes to take a security interest in the inventory. With capital goods there is no such prior notification requirement. It suffices if the new lender registers its security interest either before the debtor acquires the capital equipment or within a short grace period thereafter. The financing of purchases of inventory is seen as more threatening to earlier lenders than the acquisition of new capital equipment".[84]

The latter is more likely to enable the debtor's business to grow and to generate profits that will enable earlier loans to be repaid. This factor is less obviously present in relation to the acquisition of inventory. Moreover, "line of credit" financing is, or was, standard practice whereby earlier creditors make periodic advances depending on the debtor's acquisition of inventory. Being notified that another creditor is financing the acquisition of inventory gives the earlier creditors the opportunity of curtailing their further advances.

In its provisions in this area, the Legislative Guide once again sticks to the contours of Article 9.[85] There is a first to file has priority principle as a general rule but subject to a special priority treatment of purchase money security interests. In the associated commentary, purchase money lending, or acquisition financing as it is referred to, is spoken of as potentially a more competitive source of financing than all-assets financing. The provisions on acquisition financing are said to embody a general policy objective of providing a source of affordable credit particularly for small/medium-sized enterprises; the facilitation of financing operations by creating transparency and ensuring the equal treatment of all acquisition financiers.[86] There is a broad definition of "acquisition security rights" to encompass all security rights in an asset that secure the obligation to pay any unpaid portion of the purchase price or other obligation incurred to enable the grantor of the security right to acquire the asset. The definition includes title retention mechanisms which are defined as arrangements that enable a person to acquire possession or use of assets subject to an obligation to pay their price to a person who retains title until the price is paid. This definition embraces finance leases and "hire-purchase" agreements (lease agreements with the option to purchase the goods) together with traditional retention of title clauses in sale of goods contracts. Pursuant to the "equivalence of treatment" principle, the same general rules on the creation of general security rights apply to the creation of acquisition security rights.[87] But the idea of

---

84 See H. Kanda, S. Levmore, "Explaining Creditor Priorities", (1994) 80 *Virginia Law Review* 2103 at 2139: "The rules intimate that the acquisition of new inventory and its associated debt is more threatening to earlier creditors than the debt-financing of new equipment but that debt tied to new inventory is still less threatening than new money unlinked to particular assets" and see generally Bridge/MacDonald/Simmonds/Walsh (n. 71) at fns. 99-108.

85 Recommendation 186.

86 See the statement of purposes in Part XII of the Legislative Guide.

87 Recommendation 183.

requiring registration for third party effectiveness of title retention mechanisms is likely to be controversial for many jurisdictions.

The economic justification for investing acquisition security interests or purchase money security interests (whatever expression is used) with super-priority status focuses on the fact that the debtor's total pool of assets has been increased. Existing debt is not simply being refinanced. With the infusion of funds the debtor is acquiring new assets and if existing security interest holders were allowed to claim priority in these new assets then it is argued they would receive a windfall benefit as they had done nothing to fund the acquisition of these assets.[88] Moreover, if an all-assets financier is allowed to obtain priority with respect to the debtor's after-acquired assets, then the financer may have an effective credit monopoly. If the financier is unwilling to advance any further funds then it may be very difficult for the debtor to procure financing from other creditors who may be loath to accept lower-ranking security or to lend on an unsecured basis. Moreover, financiers who are lending against specific assets may be in a position to offer more competitive interest rates than general all-assets financiers. The financiers who are lending against specific assets are lending against specific risk rather than general risk. They may be more easily able to establish the risk attached to specific assets, risk of default etc.[89]

There are counter-arguments. For instance, it might be argued that lenders against discrete assets are more likely to be smaller, secondary lenders and less likely to provide competitive interest rates than general lenders. Moreover, attributing a privileged status to purchase money loans seems premised on the assumption that the advance of funds which is specifically tied to the purchase of "new" assets is somehow more valuable for the debtor's business than the advance of funds for non acquisition reasons such as to pay the wages of employees[90]. One might question whether this is necessarily the case. In the context of Social Europe, should paying the wages of employees not be regarded at least as equally valuable? One might argue that the purchase money security interest exists in embryonic form in many European jurisdictions through the recognition of quasi-securities and, in the main, such quasi-securities have priority over security interests strictly so-called over the same property.[91] The move over to

---

88 For a law and economics perspective on this view see Kanda/Levmore (n. 84) at 2138-2141.

89 See A. Schwartz, "The Continuing Puzzle of Secured Debt", (1984) 37 *Vanderbilt Law Review* 1051.

90 See the comments in W.J. Gough, *Company Charges* (2nd ed. 1996) at p. 436: "It assumes that financial accommodation for the purpose of, for example, paying wages and salaries through cheques drawn on an overdrawn account is less important than for the purchase of stocks or plant and equipment. This is not a real world distinction. Credit, as a matter of business need, is indivisible in the sense that all business inputs, including wages, overheads, equipment and supplies are all vital to an ongoing business".

91 See also R. MacDonald, "Article 9 Norm Entrepreneurship", (2006) 43 *Canadian Business Law Journal* 240 at 283: "Collapsing the distinction between owing and owning, between true security and title deployed to secure the performance of an obligation, does not relieve a legislature of the need to determine whether, in a competition between secured creditors, a distinction should be drawn between a

an Article 9 regime however, would greatly expand the boundaries of purchase money super-priority with implications for other creditors, both secured and unsecured, that are not always fully appreciated. Purchase money super-priority is not an ever present feature of international model laws on secured transactions. The mechanism is not contained, for example, in the EBRD Model Law on Secured Transactions though under this Model Law, like many national laws, creditors are free to vary the order of priorities amongst themselves though without prejudicing the position of third parties. One might argue that if purchase money super priority is really beneficial to existing lenders then these existing lenders should be perfectly prepared, on a voluntary basis, to consent to a new lender having priority.

IX Possible Pointers in a Direction other than the Uncitral Legislative Guide

This paper has talked about various specific areas. These are justifications for the existence of security and the possible scope of security rights; the possibility or otherwise of carve-outs for unsecured creditors; publicity and the third party effectiveness of security rights; the treatment of quasi-securities and finally, priority between different security interests and special priority principles. These are very important areas where a comprehensive set of provisions or common frame of reference, call it what you will, on security interests is going to have to make provision. On these issues, the UNCITRAL Legislative Guide suggests a specific set of provisions that mirrors Article 9 of the United States Uniform Commercial Code quite closely. In none of the five areas however, except arguably the first, does the dispensation in the Legislative Guide approximate to what appears to be the legal consensus in Europe. Article 9 type reforms have been recommended in England by the Law Commission but the proposals have failed to pass muster among legal practitioners particularly those in the City of London. [92] The present system in their view works tolerably well though it could be with a bit of fine tuning from time to time. These lawyers have their precedent banks and store of received wisdom and have no desire to jettison these information banks in favour of reforms whose implications

creditor who was once an owner (a vendor) and a creditor who is merely a financier (a lender). Indeed, the priority afforded to the vendor's hypothec (or a 'purchase money security interest') merely replicates the logic of an instalment sale or a sale under a resolutory condition in regimes that continue to distinguish between security and title devices".

92 Strong opposition to the proposals was mounted by the Financial Law committee of the City of London Law Society. Its views can be found at www.citysolicitors.org and see also the article by its chair, Richard Calnan of the law firm, Norton Rose [2005] *Butterworths Journal of Iinternational Banking and Financial Law* 25 which summarises the views of the Financial Law Committee.

would be uncertain.[93] Moreover, it might also be the case that the transition to an Article 9 type regime would give US law firms a competitive advantage which in a global marketplace for legal services, domestic law firms would be anxious to avoid.

If one is looking for pointers towards the content of a CFR, it is submitted that there are more appropriate models than the UNCITRAL Legislative Guide. Guidance can from the EBRD Core Principles on Secured Transactions Laws.[94] While these principles cover the same ground as the Legislative Guide, and embody many of the same points, they are generally much less prescriptive. The Core Principles do not track the content of Article 9 to the same degree. There is much greater flexibility and tolerance of divergence in the Core Principles than in the Legislative Guide. For example, while the Core Principles talk about having an effective means of publicising the existence of security rights, unlike the Legislative Guide they do not come down in favour of notice filing as distinct from transaction filing. Article 9 enthusiasts extol the virtue of notice filing to the nth degree but this paper has pointed out that the arguments are not all one way. The same way with priority rules. Article 9 has a specific set of priority rules that may facilitate the extension of credit in an American context but these rules are not exactly replicated in Europe. The Core Principles, unlike the Legislative Guide, is fairly agnostic on the subject of priority though there is an overall emphasis on clarity. The Core Principles simply lay down that the law should establish rules governing competing rights of persons holding security and other persons claiming rights in the assets given as security. One might argue that this statement is a pretty meaningless platitude but, nevertheless, it leaves other priority possibilities open to Governments rather than the straight down the line prescriptions of Article 9 and the Legislative Guide.

X Conclusion

It is an open question what provisions, if any, should be included on security rights in the common frame of reference or indeed whether there should be a common frame of reference at all. Critics, of which there undoubtedly many in the UK, would argue that the CFR is merely the thin end

---

93 See generally H. Beale, "The Exportability of North American Chattel Security Regimes: the Fate of the English Law Commission's Proposals", [2006] *Canadian Business Law Journal* 178; Ziegel (n. 74) 110.

94 See generally F. Dahan, J. Simpson, "The European Bank for Reconstruction and Development's Secured Transactions Project: a model law and ten core principles for a modern secured transactions law in countries of Central and Eastern Europe (and elsewhere!)", in Kieninger (n. 24) at p. 98. See also G. McCormack, F. Dahan "The EBRD Model Law on Secured Transactions: Comparisons and Convergence", [1989] *Company, Financial and Insolvency Law Review* 65; L. Mistelis, "The EBRD Model Law on Secured Transactions and Its Impact on Collateral Law Reform in Central and Eastern Europe and the Former Soviet Union", (1998) 5 *Parker School Journal of East European Law* 455.

of the wedge or the tip of the iceberg, whatever analogy one wishes to use. It is the road to the ruination of a European Civil Code and another milestone in the creation of a European Superstate. The enactment of the CFR would involve a further erosion of national sovereignty.

As well as the constitutional, there are also economic objections. A common frame of reference, it is argued, might lead to sterile uniformity across Europe whereas, instead, Europe should serve as a laboratory for experimentation in terms of secured credit regimes.[95] Economic arguments are often pressed into the service of neo-liberal free market ideals but this need not necessarily be the case. If national governments are recognised as having continued autonomy in this area, it means that one State may favour an extensive regime of consumer protection in the secured credit sphere whereas another State may be content with more limited measures. States can try out different levels of security rights and gauge the impact of these on the cost and availability of credit. The CFR may straightjacket States into an unpromising and unprofitable uniformity. If the scope for innovation at a national level is denied, this may mean the loss of energy and creativity. [96]

There is at least a superficially convincing case that secured credit law in many European jurisdictions is in need of reform. Economic activity may be impeded by archaic rules that owe more to the hang ups of legal history than the needs of commerce. While functional convergence may already be in place in certain areas, market integration and economic imperatives may push States along the path of functional convergence even more.[97] One can certainly question the case for a CFR and its application to security rights. If one is prepared to accept the case however, at least for the sake of moving the debate forward, then questions of content loom large. In this task one should look, it is suggested, to the measure of convergence that already exists. Guidance can also be drawn from the EBRD Core Principles on Secured Transaction Laws. Regrettably, and notwithstanding the great effort that went into its preparation, it is submitted that similar inspiration cannot be found in the UNCITRAL Legislative Guide on secured transactions. It is argued that the UNCITRAL guide is too prescriptive in tone and too American in orientation to be much of a model.

Critics often complain that CFR would or could involve submerging the common law countries of Europe in a sea of Civil Law principles. The common law might lose its separate identity or at least suffer damaging and unquantifi-

95 For a reference to separate jurisdictions as legal laboratories see Brandeis J in *New State Ice Corp v Liebmann*, (1932) 285 US 262 at 311.

96 See H. Beale, "Finding the Remaining Traps", in: Grundmann/Stuyck (n. 10) 67 at 70: "diversity encourages experimentation and experimentation encourages legal development (...) [W]e should encourage pluralism. Diversity is one of the things that makes our society interesting to live in and I do not wish to limit pluralism unless it is strictly necessary to do so".

97 See Ogus (n. 9) at 418: "competition between jurisdictions will generate a tendency for national legal principles to converge in those areas of law designed primarily to facilitate trade".

able consequences from the importation of Civil Law principles. It is submitted that in the sphere of security rights this is not likely to be the case for the American, rather than the English, presence is omnipresent if not omnipotent.[98] Article 9 of the American Uniform Commercial Code has spawned a number of progeny when it comes to international efforts in terms of harmonization of secured credit law.[99]The Organisation of American States (OAS) Inter-American Model Law on Secured Transactions[100] is an obvious example but the example of the UNCITRAL Legislative Guide is perhaps even more striking, and certainly more universal. It is submitted that the EBRD Core Principles on Secured Transactions Law does a better job of accommodating both Civil Law and Common Law traditions and these principles should have a stronger influence on the shaping of the CFR. The Core Principles are also more nuanced and less dogmatic and prescriptive than the Legislative Guide.

---

98 For discussion of the "soft law" influence exerted by the United States see U. Mattei, "Hard Minimal code Now! – a Critique of 'Softness' and a Plea for Responsibility in the European Debate over Codification", in: Grundmann/Stuyck (n. 10) 215.

99 See generally MacDonald (n. 91) at 291 who suggests that "we need to locate our evaluations of commercial law reform within a better understanding of how local entrepreneurial networks and credit institutions function on the ground. The claim to universalism in accounts of modernization must be given up in favour of more differentiated analyses and prescriptions for particular times and for particular places. The boosterism of Article 9 norm entrepreneurs needs to be tempered by a realistic assessment of what can actually be accomplished in transnational commercial law reform".

100 This Model Law can be found on the OAS website and also at [2002] *Uniform Law Review* 262. See generally on the OAS Model Law B. Kozolchyk, J.M. Wilson "The New Model Inter-American Law on Secured Transactions", [2002] *Uniform Law Review* 69. See more generally A. Garro, "Difficulties in Obtaining Secured Lending in Latin America: Why Law Reform Really Matters" in: Norton/Andenas (n. 2) 251.

CHAPTER 10

European Tort Law

An Integrated or Compartmentalized Approach?

Willem H. van Boom*

1 Introduction

The 2007 Lleida Congress in honour of Reinhard Zimmermann centres around the Common Frame of Reference. Let me admit that I am not an experienced "CFR watcher", but that I was nevertheless struck by the fact that in the English language, the CFR memoranda and reports refer to a common frame of reference relating to *contract law*, whereas somehow in Dutch this is consistently translated into *verbintenissenrecht*. In Dutch legal terminology, however, "verbintenissenrecht" is the *law of obligations* rather than the law of contracts and therefore also includes tort law, restitutionary remedies, benevolent intervention and unjust enrichment. Some much for a common frame of reference! My first proposition here would be that a common frame of reference will inevitably get lost in translation.[1]

Having said that, as I understand the CFR undertaking is an attempt to restate and perhaps eventually "horizontally" harmonize the community's consumer contract law acquis even further by method of technocratic committee process in the best of EU tradition of comitology.[2] Moreover, it seems that along the way the CFR endeavour has somehow converged with the Principles project of the Study Group on a European Civil Code. Officially, the CFR does not include tort law issues. So we could stop here and not be bothered with tort law in relation to the CFR. There is, however, a good reason for looking into tort law as it may be operating "behind the scenes" of contract law. Indeed, the CFR undertaking does shed some light on the position of tort law. In the EU commission's second report on the CFR it is said that there is consensus among the CFR participants "that the CFR should contain the topics directly related to the existing EU contract law *acquis* in combination with general contract law issues which are relevant for the *acquis*"[3] and that during the CFR work "several voices advocated including certain general contract law issues that are relevant for the existing EU contract law *acquis*."[4]

---

* Professor of Private law at the Rotterdam Institute of Private Law, Erasmus University Rotterdam, The Netherlands. The author gratefully acknowledges helpful comments and suggestions by Simon Whittaker and Siewert Lindenbergh.

1 Cf. M.W. Hesselink, "The Ideal of Codification and the Dynamics of Europeanisation: The Dutch Experience", in: S. Vogenauer, S. Weatherill (ed.), *The Harmonization of European Contract Law – Implications for European Private Laws, Business and Legal Practice* (2006), p. 55 fn. 68. Note that C. von Bar et al., "Communication on European Contract Law: Joint Response of the Commission on European Contract Law and the Study Group on a European Civil Code", (2002) *European Review of Private Law* 193 fn. 14 seem to turn the argument around and imply that the Dutch translation is the better one.

2 For an overview of what the CFR is or may be, see, e.g., Hesselink (n. 1) at p.52 ff. with further references.

3 Report from the Commission – Second Progress Report on The Common Frame of Reference, COM/2007/0447 final, p. 8-9.

4 *Idem*, p. 11.

To include "general contract law issues" in the CFR work poses a problem of demarcation with tort law. It has been pointed out rightly before that the dividing line between tort and contract varies from country to country.[5] So, if the EU is designing a common frame of reference regarding contract law in general, it may have to decide under which heading to file problems of precontractual duties of care, of providing a quasi-contractual protection in tort to third parties, somehow linked to a contract, and the matter of dealing with legal relationships in chains of contracts. In short, it may have to engage in defining and dividing contracts and torts in some respects. Such a task seems rather difficult, to say the least.[6]

Having said that, it must be stressed that tort law *as such* is not on the regulatory agenda of the EU.[7] And rightly so. Who needs harmonized tort law? In the sense of a dogmatically coherent system of abstract rules, harmonized tort law seems rather superfluous. Why would we need a European standard on the issue of subjective or objective fault in tort law? Why would we need a uniform minimum age for tortious capacity of children? Why would we need to have uniformity on abstract notions of wrongfulness, duties of care and the like?

In the academic discussion on European harmonization of private law, the proponents of harmonization of tort law argue that a pan-European system of tort law would serve goals of equal treatment of wrongs and rights and equal protection of, e.g., business interests in Europe (level playing field, ironing out alleged "economic distortions"). Opponents tend to stress that business strategy in Europe is indifferent to the details of tort law systems and that differences between the legal systems stem from genuine differences in *preferences* of domestic legal policy.[8] Although I am not an expert, I would think that the latter

---

[5] See, e.g., R. Zimmermann, "Principles of European Contract Law and Principles of European Tort Law: Comparison and Points of Contact", in: H. Koziol, B.C. Steininger (ed.), *European Tort Law 2003 (Tort and Insurance Law Yearbook)* (2004), p. 10 f.; C. von Bar, U. Drobnig, *The Interaction of Contract Law and Tort and Property Law in Europe – A Comparative Study* (2004), p. 11 ff., p. 44 ff.

[6] Cf. G. Wagner, "The Project of Harmonizing European Tort Law", (2005) *Common Market Law Rev.* 1296.

[7] Cf. U. Magnus, "Europa und sein Deliktsrecht – Gründe für und wider die Vereinheitlichung des ausservertraglichen Haftungsrechts", in: H. Koziol, J. Spier (ed.), *Liber Amicorum Pierre Widmer* (2003), p. 221.

[8] For an overview of the main arguments pro and contra, see, e.g., M.G. Faure, "Product Liability and Product Safety in Europe: Harmonization or Differentiation?", (2000) *Kyklos* 467 ff.; M. Faure, "How Law and Economics May Contribute to the Harmonisation of Tort Law in Europa", in: R. Zimmerman (ed.), *Grundstrukturen des Europäischen Deliktsrechts* (2003), p. 31 ff.; G. Wagner, "The Virtues of Diversity in European Private Law", in: J. Smits (ed.), *The Need for a European Contract Law* (2005), p.3 ff.; Wagner (n. 6) 1269 ff. Cf. R. Van den Bergh, L. Visscher, "The Principles of European Tort Law: The Right Path to Harmonization?", (2006) *European Review of Private Law* 514; J. Smits, "European Private Law: A Plea for a Spontaneous Legal Order", in: D.M. Curtin et al., *European Integration and Law* (2006), p. 67 ff.

argument is not entirely sound from a European policy perspective: the basic idea of harmonization is in fact to discuss, negotiate and then agree on a pan-European preference (indeed, it is the basic idea of the EU itself).

Some authors justify non-intervention at the EU level with the "regulatory competition" rationale.[9] Suffice to say here that EU politics are not always driven by the concept of regulatory competition, especially when consumer interests are involved.[10] Moreover, the theory of regulatory competition in the field of tort law seems to overestimate the rationality of tort law systems and how they evolve. Rather than a flexible tax on corporate or individual behaviour, which can be raised or lowered annually in order to adjust to market circumstances, tort law is perceived by many to reflect socio-legal and cultural preferences which are not easily adjusted in view of some "legal competition" paradigm.

At the end of the day then, the only practically and politically relevant question therefore is whether there is both a *need* and a *political will* for harmonizing tort law in Europe.[11]

I very much doubt that there is an objective need for harmonizing tort law *in general*. Generally speaking, tort law is considered to be about protecting interests – life, property, economic interests to some extent – against wrongs, whereas contract law is about the exchange of goods and services. Initially, the harmonization of laws in the EU was considered to be an instrument of European economic policies. From the outset, harmonization efforts concerning contract law have made more sense than those concerning tort law. If domestic contract law systems are indeed an obstacle to smooth exchange within the European market, then there may be sound policy arguments for some level of unification of contract law. But this rationale for harmonization does not appear to be equally forcefully present in the case of tort law.[12] Tort law as it stands in Europe today seems to play such a relatively minor role in the decision making of both businesses and consumers, that it seems unlikely that differences in tort law would distort any economic level playing field. Admittedly, this might well be because on a more abstract level, tort law systems in Europe are rather similar. By and large, all these systems offer compensation in some cases of death and personal injury; they all protect property rights and they all tend to be reluc-

9 Cf. Wagner (n. 6) 1271.

10 For the law and economics analysis, see, e.g., M.G. Faure (n. 8) 467 ff.

11 Political will is even more relevant in light of the technical obstacle of competence of the EU to harmonize tort law. What would be the basis in the EU Treaty? On the issue of competence see, e.g., U. Magnus, "Towards European Civil Liability", in: M. Faure et al. (ed.), *Towards a European Ius Commune in Legal Education and Research* (2002), p.208 ff.

12 C. van Dam, *European Tort Law* (2006), p. 133 ff.; Van den Bergh and Visscher (n. 8) 514 ff. Contrast, e.g., G. Alpa, "'Principles of European Tort Law': A Critical View from the Outside", (2005) *European Business Law Review* 957 (stating that drafting Principles of European tort law is a "fundamental need for a society with European aspirations" (p. 960) and that in doing so "fundamental rights (...) will be better protected" (p. 974)); Magnus (n. 11) 205 ff.

tant in allowing unbridled claims for pure economic loss.[13] Moreover, by and large, tort law systems in Europe invariably tend to be less than fully predictable in outcome, expensive in operating, damned by business and cherished by the legal profession.[14] So, even in this respect tort law systems are rather alike.

Obviously, there are major differences between the legal systems at a concrete level.[15] Causation, heads of damage, the position of children in tort law, strict liabilities, they all tend to differ from country to country. But on a more abstract level and from a societal point of view, tort law systems in Europe seem to be rather similar in operation and relative unimportance. We tend not to commit torts every day, but we definitely do enter into contracts every day.

As a result, pressure groups advancing the harmonization of tort law as a body of law seem to be absent. This might have been different if there were stark contrasts between the various tort law systems in Europe and if this affected private interests considerably. Imagine for instance, that one member state in Europe adhered to a system of US-style class action with contingency fees and severe punitive damage in case of corporate wrongdoing. Then there might be a stronger political case for change, either for that particular member state to conform to others, or vice versa. Businesses would surely favour ironing out the extravagancies of this exotic system, and lawyers would undoubtedly take an opposing view since such an exotic system serves the bar's private interests best. In such an economic force field tort law harmonization would be a more of a political issue. In reality, it is not.

In the absence of pressure groups at a European level advocating change in tort law, it seems that the political relevance of harmonizing tort law in Europe is limited to isolated cases. I will return to this issue later. Suffice to conclude here that, if I am right in arguing that European tort law systems are indeed rather similar in the abstract, it seems logical for the EU not to engage in harmonizing tort law as a system but merely to repair the weak spots and iron out those parts of tort law that actually stand in the way of European internal market policies.

Having said that, there can be parts of tort law that might 'need' harmonization from a EU policy perspective. State liability for breach of community law is a good example of a specific category of torts that has in effect been harmonized

[13] In a similar vein, Magnus (n. 11), p. 206 ff. Admittedly, pure economic loss as such is treated very dissimilar in Europe, but even the legal systems most favourable for claims for pure economic loss (e.g., France) limit the extent of such claims with other instruments (e.g., proof of damage, calculation of damage, causation).

[14] On the typology of tort law in action, see, e.g., W.H. van Boom, "Compensating and preventing damage: is there any future left for tort law?", in: H. Tiberg, M. Clarke (ed.), *Festskrift till Bill W. Dufwa – Essays on Tort, Insurance Law and Society in Honour of Bill W. Dufwa – Volume I* (2006), p. 287 ff., with further references.

[15] Wagner (n. 6) 1281; J. Spier, O.A. Haazen, "The European Group on Tort Law ("Tilburg Group") and the European Principles of Tort Law", (1999) *ZEuP* 474 ("The legal systems of Europe have much in common, but the differences should not be underestimated.").

already – albeit with some aspects left to domestic tort law – in the interest of European legal unity. And there may be other examples, as we will see shortly. Then there is a case, not for harmonizing a *unitary* concept of European tort law, but for a *compartmentalized approach* in which some torts are subject to EU legislative or judicial attention and others are not.

In this paper, I will try to make a preliminary inventory of these torts that may "need" harmonization. Note that the verb "need" leaves a wide margin of appreciation and does not reflect objective necessity;[16] the EU will not stop functioning properly if these torts are not harmonized[17] (nor does it currently dysfunction without a uniform contract law, I might add). The idea is, however, that on the balance of costs and benefits of harmonization, for some torts the benefits of harmonization may outweigh the costs. So, in a way, the verb "need" should better be read as 'be ready for'...

In the process of identifying the torts 'ready for' harmonization efforts, I will address the points of departure that can currently be found in EU legislation for a body of European tort law (§ II). Then, I will turn to the areas which seem to be the most likely candidates for further harmonization in the near future (§ III). Finally, I will conclude on the feasibility of both an integrated and a compartmentalized approach in European tort law.

Finally, by way of "disclaimer" it should be noted that since the concept of tort law in itself is not a uniform concept, not all European tort law systems will consider some of the areas dealt with in this paper to be part of tort law. In the following I will try to identify these "border areas" where applicable.

II State of Affairs In EU Tort Law

Broadly speaking, the state of affairs of EU tort law is as follows. There are but a few EU Directives that directly pertain to tort law. Indirectly, however, a more considerable number of Directives have bearing on what is traditionally considered to be part of tort law. Carrier liability for death and personal injury, for instance, can be considered to be part of transport law but may also be considered to be part of EU tort law as it deals with protection acknowledged legal interests. Here, I will give a brief overview of the most relevant EU Directives pertaining to tort law.

1. *Products liability*

The 1985 Products Liability Directive[18] is the "cornerstone" of EU tort law, simply because it is the most comprehensive set of EU tort law rules available.

[16] As Spier and Haazen (n. 15) 477 rightly observe, little in this world is necessary in the strict sense.

[17] Note that tort law is not unified in the United States of America either, but rather left to the individual state legislatures and courts, notwithstanding informal ALI Restatement unification efforts.

[18] Directive 85/374/EEC of 25 July 1985 on the approximation of the laws, regulations and administrative provisions of the Member States concerning liability for defective products, as amended by Directive

The Products Liability Directive seems to be of major theoretical importance, but in practice, the impact appears to have been minimal. The Directive has become an integral part of European product safety policy nonetheless,[19] and the European Commission seems satisfied with the operation of the Directive.[20] Its value for identifying issues of importance in tort law should not be underestimated. The Directive gives a European floor to several important aspects of tort law, such as reasonable consumer safety expectations as a founding concept, defences under strict liability regimes, joint and several liability, fault of the injured person, limitation periods, and the compulsory nature of strict liability.

The Directive is by no means a complete harmonization effort, much is left to domestic legislation (How is damage calculated? What are the exact consequences of joint and several liability?). Moreover, the Directive is a compromise between consumer interests and business interests, which is demonstrated, e.g., by the fact that it uses a threshold for claiming and leaves the exclusion of the "development risk defence" to member states.[21]

2. Environmental damage

The 2004 Environmental Liability Directive[22] can hardly be considered to be part of general tort law, as it primarily addresses the relationship between polluting 'operators' and the State, more in particular recourse actions by the State and forced intervention and precautionary measures. All genuine private law aspects seem to have been removed in the legislative process.

3. Unfair trade practices

The recent Unfair Trade Practices Directive[23] is an extremely important Directive in the sense that it gives a pan-European floor to remedying so-called economic torts. It forbids unfair trade practices, i.e., commercial practices contrary to standards of "professional diligence" that distort consumer behaviour materially (e.g., misleading, aggressive practices, omission of vital information). Although the Directive does not present itself as a "tort Directive" and its ambit is confined to business-to-consumer practices, some member states did choose to implement the Directive –partially– as a species of a tort liability.[24]

1999/34/EC.

19 See the cross reference at Article 21 of the General Food Law Regulation 178/2002/EC.

20 See COM (2000) 893.

21 Article 9 (b) and 15(1) (b) Products Liability Directive.

22 Directive 2004/35/CE of 21 April 2004 on environmental liability with regard to the prevention and remedying of environmental damage.

23 Directive 2005/29/EC of 11 May 2005 on Unfair Commercial Practices.

24 E.g., Austria (Bundesgesetz gegen den unlauteren Wettbewerb 1984 (2007 Novelle)) and The Netherlands (Burgerlijk Wetboek, art. 6:193a ff.). On the influence of the Directive on domestic tort and contract law, see, e.g., G. Howells et al., *European Fair Trading Law; The Unfair Commercial Practices Directive* (2006), p. 71 ff.; cf. S. Whittaker, "The Relationship of the Unfair Commercial Practices

Moreover, the general standards used in the Directive can forebode a wider relevance for economic torts in general. Note that the Directive encapsules the earlier Directive 1984/450/EEC (amended by Directive 1997/55/EEC) on misleading and comparative advertising.

4. CSP liability

The Electric Signatures Directive[25] sets forth a third-party liability for Certification Service Providers. The interesting aspect here is that the EU uses tort law liability for pure economic loss vis-à-vis trusting parties as a deliberate tool for enhancement of the quality of CSPs.

5. Ultrahazardous activities

Here, the EU is involved in the well known Conventions on Third Party Liability in the field of nuclear energy.[26]

6. International traffic accidents

The Motor Insurance Directives[27] regulate, at least to a certain extent, the compulsory insurance contract terms, the insurance coverage amounts, the setting up of motor insurance funds for uninsured or unidentified tortfeasors, and the cross-border settlement (e.g., appointed claims representative) in traffic accidents. Regulating the terms of compensation under motor insurance contracts does not harmonize liability for motor vehicle accidents but it does seem to make Europe ready for the next logical step – harmonizing compensation systems for traffic accidents. For instance, Article 4 of Directive 2005/14/EC states:

> *"Member States shall take the necessary measures to ensure that any statutory provision or any contractual clause contained in an insurance policy which excludes a passenger from such cover on the basis that he knew or should have known that the driver of the vehicle was under the influence of alcohol or of any other intoxicating agent at the time of an accident, shall be deemed to be void in respect of the claims of such passenger."*

Directive to European and National Contract Laws", in: S. Weatherill, U. Bernitz (ed.), *The Regulation of Unfair Commercial Practices under EC Directive 2005/29; New Rules and New Techniques* (2006), p.139 ff.

25 Directive 1999/93/EC of 13 December 1999 (Electronic Signatures Directive); Article 6.

26 For an in depth overview, see T. Vanden Borre, "Shifts in Governance in Compensation for Nuclear Damage, 20 Years after Chernobyl", in: M.l Faure, A.t Verheij (ed.), *Shifts in Compensation for Environmental Damage* (2007), p. 261 ff.

27 Directive 2005/14/EC of 11 May 2005 amending Directives 72/166/EEC, 84/5/EEC, 88/357/EEC and 90/232/EEC and Directive 2000/26/EC relating to insurance against civil liability in respect of the use of motor vehicles (5th Motor Insurance Directive).

The basic idea here is that passengers should be compensated, but the effectiveness of this provision totally depends on how domestic tort law treats such contributorily negligent victims. In this sense, provisions such as Article 4 create the political leeway to take the next logical step of altogether harmonizing the effect of the contributory negligence defence.

7. General product safety

The General Product Safety Directive[28] (GPSD) imposes general duties of care on manufacturers (e.g., recall duties) that can be of relevance in ascertaining what duties of care a manufacturer is under, apart from the strict liability under the Products Liability Directive. In this sense the GPSD may help to develop a more abstract notion of professional negligence concerning manufacturers. For example, Article 5 of the GPSD provides that producers shall adopt measures enabling them to recall the defective product from consumers.

8. Carrier liability for personal injury and property loss

This field of transport law which was originally dominated by international treaties is now quickly becoming an integral part of EU private law.[29] It clearly aims at improving the position of travellers within the EU; improvement of the position in case of personal injury and loss of luggage is at the forefront of these developments. In short, the legislative framework is as follows:

- air carriage: Regulation 2027/97/EC of 9 October 1997 on air carrier liability (unlimited liability for death and personal injury; 100.000 SDR), amended by Regulation 889/2002/EC of 13 May 2002 (referring to the 1999 Montreal Treaty regime, extending the Regulation to cover luggage as well);
- sea and inland water: Regulation 2005/0592 of 23 November 2005 on liability of carriers of passengers by sea and inland waterways (referring to the Athens Convention 1974 and subsequent protocol 2002);
- railway carriage: Regulation proposal on international rail passengers' rights and obligations, COM(2004) 143 final (introducing harmonized liability regime);
- bus carriage: Proposal Regulation on the rights of international bus and coach passengers, scheduled for Fall 2007.

[28] Directive 2001/95/EC of 3 December 2001 on general product safety.

[29] See, with further references, J. Karsten, "Passengers, consumers, and travellers: The rise of passenger rights in EC transport law and its repercussions for Community consumer law and policy", (2007) *J. Consumer Policy* 117.

III Identifying Torts that are "Likely Candidates" for Further Harmonization

Harmonization and designing a CFR can go hand in hand. Indeed, the CFR work that is currently undertaken is sometimes considered to be a "Trojan Horse" for gradual and horizontal harmonization.[30] Harmonizing by means of a CFR based on an existing acquis is not possible in tort unless community tort law would be used as such a basis. I do not believe that to be the right starting point for our enquiry. Community tort law addresses the liability of EU bodies and national government agencies (e.g. in case of breach of EU law, insufficient and delayed implementation, et cetera). In some legal systems, liability of the administration differs considerably –both dogmatically and practically– from common tort law. The focus here is not liability of administrative authorities but rather tort law in general.[31] Therefore, I will not take this perspective.

If a "Common Frame of Reference for Tort Law" is to restate and rework EU substantive law, its goals should be utterly modest and humble at first. Indeed, *finding* the actual acquis may be challenging in itself. In fact, there is hardly any acquis at present. So, with some hesitance I suggest that there are four areas that may be ready for further harmonization (in decreasing degree of likelihood): economic torts, manufacturer duty of care, cross border tourist safety, and motor vehicle accidents.

In my view, then, a Common Frame of Reference for Tort Law should not work along similar lines as followed in the work on the "Principles of European Tort Law" and the "Principles of European Law – Liability for Damages". These two sets of principles were not based on the EU acquis but mostly on (what the participants perceived to be) the common core of national tort law systems.[32]

A first likely candidate is the category of economic torts. One can think of the protection of intellectual property through tort law, but also the liability for infringement of substantive rules of competition law and the liability for misleading advertising. Indeed, much has already been developed in terms of a European concept of economic torts as a consequence of the tendency to stimulate private enforcement of competition law. Having said that, the EU has not attempted harmonization of the underlying domestic tort law rules themselves. As a result, private enforcement of competition law through liability law (e.g. tortious lock out of competitors entering a specific market) is governed by

30 References to be found at Hesselink (n. 1), at p. 53 fn. 58.

31 For a combination of both perspectives, see, e.g., W. Wurmnest, *Grundzüge eines europäischen Haftungsrechts* (2003), p. 1 ff.

32 For an analysis of the working method followed in drafting the Principles, see R. Zimmermann, "Principles of European Contract Law and Principles of European Tort Law: Comparison and Points of Contact", in: H. Koziol, B.C. Steininger (ed.), *European Tort Law 2003 (Tort and Insurance Law Yearbook)* (2004), p. 2 ff.

domestic rules on calculation of damages, burden of proof, time limitation, et cetera. Needless to say that these rules may vary and the efficacy of the legal system at hand as well. The EU might find itself between a rock and hard place in this respect as the subsidiarity principle may not agree with perceived needs for a level playing field for European business and an efficacious level of enforcement. If the EU is serious about stimulating private enforcement in competition law across the board, it will have to address such divergence of national tort law rules. In essence, the same holds true for other economic torts – be it B-2-C or B-2-B torts.

The second category relates to manufacturer's duties of care. Naturally, the strict liability of the Products Liability Directive covers a lot of ground in this respect. Nevertheless, there may still be an additional converging force at work in this area, the General Product Safety Directive (GPSD). This Directive may eventually influence courts' perception of appropriate behaviour of manufacturers with regard to issues of after sales care, recall duties and similar duties of care vis-à-vis consumers in light of the safety of their products.[33]

Manufacturers are obliged under the GPSD to place only safe products on the market (Article 3 (1) GPSD), having regard to, *inter alia*, the state of the art and technology and reasonable consumer expectations. This latter requirement directly connects the GPSD to European tort law in the sense that the consumer expectation test is the pivotal concept in the Products Liability Directive.[34]

Under the GPSD, manufacturers are also required to inform themselves of the inherent risks of the product prior to marketing and to enable themselves to effectively redress potential defects that may come to light after marketing. The recall duty laid down in Article 5 GPSD is an instrument of last resort.

Obviously, the Directive does not require member states to implement the manufacturers' duties in national *tort* law. In fact, the Directive leaves it to the member states which system of enforcement to choose. If, however, national courts allow the substance of the Directive to trickle down into tort law or to converge with domestic concepts of recall duties, information duties, et cetera, the Directive may be the starting point of a concept of European manufacturers' duty of care.

Admittedly, there is the issue of full harmonization of European products liability under the Products Liability Directive. According to ECJ case law, the Directive does not allow the introduction of recall duties as a prerequisite for invoking one of the exonerating circumstances under Article 7 of the Directive, nor does it allow extension of the strict liability onto others than the manufacturer.[35] It does, however, seem to allow private enforcement of the GPSD to some

33 On the substance of the post-marketing obligations under the GPSD, see C. Hodges, *European Regulation of Consumer Product Safety* (2005), p. 129 ff.

34 See Art. 3 (3) (f) GPSD jo. Art. 6 Products Liability Directive.

35 See *Commission v France* (ECJ 25 April 2002, Case C-52/00 [2002] ECR I-3827); cf. *Commission v Greece* (ECJ 25 April 2002, Case C-154/00 [2002] ECR I-3879); *González Sanchez v Medicina Asturiana* (ECJ 25 April 2002, Case C-183/00 [2002] ECR I-3901).

extent as long as such enforcement is part of a pre-existing liability framework (such as fault-based liability) and does not constitute a competing system of liability for defective products.[36]

The third category concerns the safety of tourist services. Obviously, intra-community travel and tourism are an extremely important source of economic prosperity. There seems to be a political case for some level of harmonization of the compensation for death and personal injury suffered in cross-border tourism. Indeed, the EU has promulgated substantive rules on the liability of providers of package travel services –admittedly a contractual liability regime– and has recently intensified the harmonization efforts concerning liability of commercial carriers for transport accidents. As a result, personal injury caused by defective hotel services, holiday activity services and tourist transport services may well be on the way towards pan-European liability regimes.[37] The difficulty here is to define which services are included and which are not. Moreover, as it may be difficult to identify a "tourist" as such, the more practical approach would be to target those activities which "average tourists" engage in. This is the practical approach taken in the Package Travel Directive. A next step might be impos-

36 I do not believe that the strict and formal application by the ECJ of the full harmonization effect of Directive 85/374/EEC really stands in the way of such a development. Although the Court did rule that adding compliance to the recall duty to the conditions under which a manufacturer can exempt himself from liability was contrary to Articles 7 and 15 of the Products Liability Directive, it did not rule that construing a recall duty under national law as a local remedy for tortious breach of the material duties under the GPSD was contrary to Article 13 Directive. Moreover, it could be argued that "after sales duties" under general tort law principles (such as a recall duty) are altogether outside the scope of the Products Liability Directive. If, for instance, a public authority decides that a manufacturer should recall the defective product and the manufacturer refuses this may constitute both a criminal or administrative offence under the GPSD (depending on the domestic implementation of the GPSD) and a tortious breach of statutory duty vis-à-vis consumers that sustain injuries after such a breach. I would argue that since breach of statutory duties *as such* surely constitutes a source of tortious liability under domestic legal systems in the sense of Article 13 of Directive 85/374/EEC (i.e. Article 13 allows continuation of tortious liability for breach of statutory duties if such liability predates the Directive), the GPSD can be enforced through common tort law rules. Moreover, breach of the recall duty does not necessarily injure the same consumers as the defective products as such do, and therefore enforcing the GPSD through tort law does not constitute a competing system of liability for defective products. On the interpretation of Article 13 in light of the ECJ rulings, see, e.g., S. Whittaker, "Form and Substance in the Harmonisation of Product Liability in Europe", (2007) *ZEuP* 865; J.-S. Borghetti, *La Responsabilité du Fait des Produits* (2004), p. 563 ff.

37 On the political will to harmonize safety standards, industry standards, et cetera, see, e.g., "Report on a renewed EU Tourism Policy: Towards a stronger partnership for European Tourism" by the EP Committee on Transport and Tourism, culminating in an EP resolution calling on the EC to address the issue of a specific legal instrument covering the safety of tourist services (European Parliament resolution of 29 November 2007 on a renewed EU Tourism Policy: Towards a stronger partnership for European Tourism (2006/2129(INI))).

ing some sort of pan-European strict liability on hotel operators for death and personal injury suffered by guests during stays.

The final category is rather more political (and therefore more like a "minefield" rather than "green acres"): traffic accidents. With the increased movement of people in Europe, the chances of suffering injuries in traffic accidents abroad increase as well. Although traffic accidents are a major cause of death and injury in Europe, this field of the law is far from uniform. The EU has set up a comprehensive system of compulsory insurance and claim settlement, but has refrained from harmonizing liability rules. Indeed, a battle for the correct harmonization policy concerning traffic accidents has been predicted.[38] Notwithstanding the fact that currently no concrete steps towards harmonization of tortious liability for traffic accidents are being undertaken, the quality of cross border settlement has improved in the whole of the EU as a result of the Motor Insurance Directives. Moreover, the recent proposals for unification of carrier liability may also prompt further debate on unified tort liability for motor vehicle accidents. All this, however, does not conceal the fact that harmonizing traffic accident liability in general and the level of compensation in particular is extremely difficult. The level of compensation depends on the extent to which liability law is embedded – by means of, e.g., deduction for collateral benefits – in other compensation systems such as health care insurance, statutory sick pay and industrial accident compensation schemes. Therefore, harmonizing the level of compensation is so much more than just harmonizing tort law. I have strong doubts about the political feasibility of such a harmonization effort, although it is perfectly plausible that one day we will have a unitary set of conditions under which motor vehicle drivers are held liable for traffic accidents. Standards of conduct, fault, imputation of acts under influence of drugs, alcohol or physical impediment, contributory negligence, or even strict liability, all these categories may well be unified some day in a EU Directive. As mentioned, I feel that the assessment of damage and calculation of damages is a far less likely candidate.

IV And What About Remedies?

A certain level of indirect harmonization of domestic remedies for some torts can already be witnessed as a consequence of the operation of European law. Firstly, domestic tort law is in principle considered to be an integral part of the set of remedies available for breach of European substantive rules (*Courage v. Crehan*).[39] Secondly, the ECJ case law holds that if member

---

38 Wagner (n. 6) 1301.

39 ECJ 20 September 2001, C-453/99 ECR [2001] ECR I-6297 (*Courage v Crehan*) paragraphs 26 and 27. See also European Commission, *Green Paper "Damages actions for breach of the EC antitrust rules"* (EU Commission 2005), p. 4. On that case, see, e.g., A.P. Komninos, "New prospects for private enforcement of EC competition law: *Courage v Crehan* and the Community right to damages", (2002) *Common*

states choose to allow compensation through tort law as a remedy for such breaches, the tort remedy should be sufficiently dissuasive.[40] Seminal was the *Von Colson* case, a gender discrimination case concerning Directive 76/207/EEC (equal treatment) and the question involved was – from a European law perspective – what private law remedy the Directive necessitated. The Directive was in fact silent on this point, so in principle the member states were free to choose between different remedies. The ECJ ruled, however, that if a member state chooses the remedy of compensation for damage,

> *"then in order to ensure that it is effective and that it has a deterrent effect, that compensation must in any event be adequate in relation to the damage sustained and must therefore amount to more than purely nominal compensation such as, for example, the reimbursement only of the expenses incurred in connection with the application."*[41]

This case, and subsequent ECJ cases, seem to hold the principle that domestic remedies in tort must have a dissuasive effect and must amount to an adequate remedy.[42] So, if for instance consumers mostly suffer non-pecuniary loss in case of non-performance of travel package arrangements, then the national law of damages has to include this head of damage in assessing the amount of compensation.[43]

Market L Rev 460; A. Jones, D. Beard, "Co-contractors, Damages and Article 81: The ECJ finally speaks", (2002) *European Competition L.Rev.* 246; O. Odudu, J. Edelman, "Compensatory damages for breach of Article 81", (2002) *European L.Rev.* 327; G. Monti, "Anticompetitive agreements: the innocent party's right to damages", (2002) *European L.Rev.* 282; G. Wagner, "Prävention und Verhaltenssteuerung durch Privatrecht – Anmaßung oder legitime Aufgabe?", (2006) *Archiv für die civilistische Praxis* 402; Van Dam (n. 12) at p. 205 ff.

40 The phrase generally used in EU legislation is that sanctions must be "effective, proportionate and dissuasive."

41 ECJ 10 April 1984, Case 14/83 [1984] ECR 1891 (*Sabine von Colson and Elisabeth Kamann v Land Nordrhein-Westfalen*). On the dogmatic problems that the case presented under German law, see, e.g., G. Brüggemeier, "Haftungsfolgen, Entwicklungstendenzen im europäischen und deutschen Schadensersatzrecht", in: C. Ott, H.-B. Schaefer (ed.), *Die Präventivwirkung zivil- und strafrechtlicher Sanktionen* (1999), p. 171 ff. and Wagner (n. 39) at 389 ff.

42 Cf. ECJ 22 April 1997 Case C-180/95 [1997] ECR I-2195 (*Nils Draehmpaehl v Urania Immobilienservice OHG*) ruling that capping the total amount due by an employer in discrimination cases is inconsistent with the detterrence effect of the Directive. See also ECJ 23 May 1996, [1996] ECR I-2553 (*Hedley Lomas*) ruling that domestic tort law concerning state liability for breach of EU law may not be framed in such a way as in practice to make it impossible or excessively difficult to obtain reparation.

43 ECJ 12 March 2002, [2002] ECR I-2631 (*Simone Leitner v TUI Deutschland GmbH & Co. KG*) ruling that Article 5 of Directive 90/314/EEC on package travel is to be interpreted as conferring on consumers a right to compensation for non-material damage. In view of this EU perspective one may argue that Article 6:102 PEL Liab. Dam. ("Trivial damage is to be disregarded.") is in fact inconsistent with princi-

Another trend concerning remedies that is relevant to tort law in Europe, especially with regard to personal injury, is the tendency in EU substantive law to disallow (or to consider suspect) contractual limitation and exclusion of tortious liability for death and personal injury. See, e.g., Art. 5 Package Travel Directive, Art. 12 Products Liability Directive, Art. 3 (1) jo. Annex 1 (a) Unfair Contract Terms Directive.[44] This seems to signal the importance that the EU attaches to the compensatory function of liability: it is deemed to be a remedy of overriding importance that should not be lightly disregarded.

Another relevant issue that should not be disregarded, is the increasing attention given to remedies as tools of private enforcement. I refer to the discussion on the EC Green Paper on private enforcement in competition law,[45] but also to the collective redress mechanisms in the area of consumer rights.[46] This may be the dawn of a European collective action, serving as a counterweight to the global aspirations of the USA class action.

V Unlikely Candidates

Having identified those fields of tort law that are most likely to become subject of some harmonization effort at the EU level, we can now turn to a list of "least likely candidates". This list consists of four topics within tort law that I feel are the least likely to become the subject of harmonization efforts in the near future. These topics have been avoided by the European legislature and have been left to domestic private law for various reasons. The main legal reason is obviously that some of these topics fall outside the legislative powers of the EU.[47] The main political reasons are either the lack of political relevance of the topic or the absence of converging political minds. Let us now turn to the four "least likely candidates".

Firstly, there is the law of damages, notably in personal injury cases. As mentioned earlier, the levels of compensation in personal injury cases may depend on ancillary domestic compensation systems, such as workers' compensation, health insurance schemes and social security arrangements.[48] Harmonizing the law of damages and the rules for calculation of damage therefore

ples of EU law, because trivial damage should not be disregarded if that would lead to what economists would consider to be a state of "Underdeterrence".

44 Cf. von Bar and Drobnig (n. 5) at p. 155 ff.

45 European Commission, *Green Paper "Damages actions for breach of the EC antitrust rules"* (EU Commission 2005), p. 1 ff.

46 Directive 98/27/EC of 19 May 1998 on injunctions for the protection of consumers' interests; Regulation 2006/2004 of 27 October 2004 on cooperation between national authorities responsible for the enforcement of consumer protection laws (the Regulation on consumer protection cooperation).

47 On the boundaries of the EU legislative competence in tort matters, see, e.g., Magnus (n. 11), p. 208 ff.

48 G. Wagner, "Grundstrukturen des Europäischen Deliktsrechts", in: R. Zimmermann (ed.), *Grundstrukturen des Europäischen Deliktsrechts* (2003), p. 194-196 and p. 339. Cf. also the contributions to B.A.

seems virtually impossible. Moreover, the levels of compensation for non-pecuniary loss may depend on cultural diversity and implicit value judgements concerning life, freedom, privacy, and social solidarity.[49]

Secondly, there is employers' liability for occupational injury.[50] Although a popular area of tort law in some legal systems, employers' liability for accidents and occupational disease has been replaced in a considerable number of legal systems by tax-funded workers compensation outside private law.[51] Effectively, there is little to harmonize although there is a considerable amount of substantive EU legislation on occupational safety, which obviously leaves the nature of remedies to domestic law (criminal law, health inspectorate fining, etc.).[52] Moreover, the levels of compensation may depend on related compensation systems in personal injury. Worth noting is that this area of the law has in fact been excluded explicitly from PEL Liab Dam (Article 7:104 PEL Liab Dam).

The third unlikely category relates to industrial action (strike, lock out, et cetera). Liability for industrial action is unlikely to be harmonized as it is part of the domestic socio-economic balance of societal powers in employment issues, it is connected to collective bargaining processes and therefore the tort law aspects vary strongly from country to country.[53] Note that this item has also been excluded from PEL Liab Dam (Article 7:104 PEL Liab Dam).

The fourth and final category concerns general strict liabilities. A common core of general strict liabilities in Europe (for animals, children, employees, immovables, movable objects, hazardous activities) is not easily to be found. This is illustrated not only by the contrast between the recent French pre-proposal for the law on obligations in France and the Austrian and Swiss drafts,[54] but also by the stark contrast between England (virtually no strict liabili-

---

Koch, H. Koziol (ed.), *Compensation for Personal Injury in a Comparative Perspective* (2003), p. 1 ff. and to U. Magnus (ed.), *The Impact of Social Security Law on Tort Law* (2003), p. 1 ff.

49 Note that this may clash with the principle of *lex loci damni* in the Rome II Regulation (Art. 4 Regulation 864/2007 of 11 July 2007 on the law applicable to non-contractual obligations), which provides that in case of cross-border personal injury the law of the place where the damage originates is applicable (tort law of country A, where victim sustains injuries caused by tortfeasor decides the level of compensation for victim, even if the victim is resident of country B).

50 Cf. J. Spier, "European Group on Tort Law", in: M.C. Lopes Porto (ed.), *Um Código Civil para a Europa/A Civil Code for Europe/Un Code Civil pour l'Europe* (2002), p. 61.

51 See the contributions to T. Hartlief and S. Klosse (ed.), *Shifts in compensating work-related injuries and diseases* (2007), p.1 ff.

52 E.g., Directive 98/37/EC of 22 June 1998 (machinery).

53 Cf. Regulation 864/2007 on the law applicable to non-contractual obligations (Rome II Regulation), OJ L 199/40.

54 On those reform efforts, see, e.g., P. Apathy, "Schadenersatzreform – Gefährdungshaftung und Unternehmerhaftung", (2007) *Juristische Blätter* 205; P. Widmer, "Reform und Vereinheitlichung des Haftpflichtrechts auf Schweizerischer und europäischer Ebene", in: R. Zimmermann (ed.), *Grundstrukturen des Europäischen Deliktsrechts* (2003), p. 147 ff.; F. Werro, "The Swiss Tort Reform: a Possible Model

ties) and, e.g., Germany (a considerable number of strict liabilities in so-called "Sondergesetze"). Without such a core, harmonization seems unattainable at the moment.

VI Appraisal: Making Tort Law Tangible Through Compartmentalization

Cees van Dam recently argued that in the European tort law debate a general discourse on the policy issues involved is needed. He went on to state:

"In the end, this question is about what kind of Europe is to be preferred and pursued: should the emphasis be on the freedom to act, on corrective justice and regulating conduct, or should it be on protecting interests, on distributive justice and equality before the public and private burdens?"[55]

In answering these questions –which to my mind are indeed the correct questions – a compartmentalized approach seems the appropriate approach as far as tort law is concerned. Some torts are more likely candidates for harmonization efforts than others. The existing modest body of European tort law is, by necessity, an organically grown set of various rules, entered into force as a result of piecemeal legislative effort, sometimes of a contradictory nature in practice, and always lacking the dogmatic depths and overarching aspirations that national systems of private law tend to have. Working with this material necessitates a compartmentalized approach. By addressing the policy issues involved in each of these torts one by one, the EU can make tort law more tangible.

Rather than discussing e.g. the intricacies of what exactly is fault, the quest should be aimed at finding a *concrete balance* between the interests of those involved in *specific torts* – businesses, consumers, and the insurance industry. Such a compartmentalized approach would take us away from a conceptual policy discussion on "the" goals of tort law. It has been argued that at such an abstract level there will be no agreement between the "solidary systems" aimed at compensation and the 'individualistic systems' aimed at deterrence.[56] I think it therefore preferable not to concentrate on abstract discussions but rather to focus on a problem-solving-oriented, politically driven, piecemeal and compartmentalized strategy. These "solidary and individualistic systems" have been able to find compromise in other economic and legal areas as well, so social and

for Europe?", in: M. Bussani (ed.), *European Tort Law – Eastern and Western Perspectives* (2007), p. 81 ff.; I. Griss et al. (ed.), *Entwurf eines neuen österreichischen Schadenersatzrechts* (2006), p.1 ff.; P. Catala (ed.), *Avant-projet de réforme du droit des obligations et de la prescription* (2006), p.1 ff.

55 Van Dam (n. 12) at p. 137.

56 Wagner (n. 6) 1302-1303.

cultural divergence and differences in domestic preferences in the tort area as such should not preclude some level of harmonization in concrete cases.

Again, it is a matter of political will and perceived need. I have tried to demonstrate that some torts seem more ready for harmonization than others. That would also make them more fit than others for inclusion in some sort of CFR undertaking. This does not imply that harmonization is imminent with regard to these branches of the law of torts. If there is one thing even more unpredictable than tort law, it is politics.

By way of final remark it must be admitted that compartmentalization does not really address the needs of consistency[57] – as the historical development of the consumer law acquis has demonstrated – but aiming for consistency through an overarching construction of European tort law on dogmatic foundations may be several bridges too far at this point in time.

[57] Spier (n. 50) at p. 60 ("I strongly believe that one should not focus on isolated specific topics, ignoring the whole picture.").

CHAPTER II

A European Law on Unjustified Enrichment?

A Critical View of the Law of Restitution in the Draft Common Frame of Reference

Jan M. Smits*

I Introduction

The aim of this contribution is to discuss the European principles on unjustified enrichment as recently published in the Draft Common Frame of Reference.[1] These principles (or rather: model rules) were drafted with a view to the improvement and elaboration of the present European acquis in the field of private law. This contribution considers not so much the substantive details of the new model rules, but more the need for and the function of drafting principles in this area of the law. This is a legitimate approach as the law of restitution is traditionally not a core area of European legislative intervention. The private law acquis[2] rarely contains rules about restitutionary claims and their consequences.

This contribution sets off with a sketch of the background of the project on the Common Frame of Reference and the role of unjust enrichment therein (section 2). This is followed (section 3) by an overview of the main characteristics of the law on unjust enrichment in Europe: what do European legal systems have in common and in what do they differ? Section 4 subsequently describes the main model rules in the Draft CFR, while section 5 proceeds with raising questions about their role in a harmonised European private law.

II The Draft Common Frame of Reference and Unjust Enrichment

The rules on unjustified enrichment are part of the Draft Common Frame of Reference for European private law. This Draft CFR was presented to the European Commission on 28 December 2007. This was an important event and the result of four years of work by the *Study Group on a European Civil Code* and the *Research Group on the Existing EC Private Law* (the so-called 'acquis-group').[3] In its Communication on European Contract Law of 2004,[4] the European Commission had indicated that 'definitions, principles and model rules' for a European contract law would have to be prepared in order to improve

---

* Professor of European Private Law and Comparative Law, University of Tilburg and director of the Tilburg Institute of Comparative and Transnational Law (TICOM).

1 C. Von Bar, E. Clive, H. Schulte-Nölke (eds.), *Principles, Definitions and Model Rules of European Private Law: Draft Common Frame of Reference*, Interim Outline Edition (2008), also available at http://www.law-net.eu.

2 The most important directives can be found in J. Smits et al (eds.), *Wetseditie Europees Privaatrecht* (2006).

3 Both groups are the most important members of the *Joint Network on European Private Law* (CoPECL).

4 Communication (...) on European Contract Law and the Revision of the *Acquis*: the Way Forward, COM (2004) 651 final, OJ EC 2005.

the quality and overall consistency of the existing acquis. The first results are now published to invoke comments from all interested parties.

Of the ten books of the Draft CFR, Book VII is devoted to unjustified enrichment. It contains seven chapters with 23 different provisions ('model rules'). Unfortunately, comments and illustrations are not added to the provisions. This makes it difficult to assess them in an adequate way. The provisions almost literally follow the *Principles of European Unjustified Enrichment Law* as recently published on the internet by the Study Group on a European Civil Code.[5] The comments to these principles are not yet available either, but will be published in a volume in the series on *Principles of European Law*.[6]

According to its drafters, the Common Frame of Reference has several purposes.[7] First, it is a possible model for a political CFR: the presented text is an academic text and the European Commission has to decide whether it will use it as a building block when revising the present acquis or when drafting new rules. Second, the drafters regard the CFR as standing on its own as an academic text for legal science and teaching. They highlight that the Draft CFR will promote knowledge of private law in the jurisdictions of the European Union, and will in particular 'help to show how much national private laws resemble one another and have provided mutual stimulus for development and indeed how much those laws may be regarded as regional manifestations of an overall common European legacy.'[8] Third, in the same vein as the previously published Principles of European Contract Law, the CFR can be a source of inspiration for the national courts, the European Court of Justice and for national legislators.

It should be reiterated that the main aim of the final CFR (that is to be established in 2009) is to serve as a 'tool box' for the European legislator:[9] it can, 'where appropriate',[10] make use of the CFR to draft new directives or to review the existing *acquis*. The instrument is not in any way binding upon the European legislator or the Member States:[11] it is to derive its authority from the quality of its provisions.

5 Revised version of 27 February 2006, available at http://www.sgecc.net.

6 Published since 2006 by Sellier Publishers in München. The volume on unjustified enrichment is announced for 2008.

7 Draft CFR, p. 6 ff.

8 Draft CFR, p. 6.

9 Communication 2004, p. 14.

10 Communication 2004, p. 3.

11 Communication 2004, p. 6.

III Unjustified Enrichment in Europe: Similarities and Differences

The Member States of the European Union share several things when it comes to the law of unjustified enrichment.[12] Most importantly, there is the general maxim on which probably every European jurisdiction agrees to some extent. It is the maxim, also expressed in the Digest,[13] that no one should be enriched at another's expense. It is a maxim and not a legal rule because of its broad and abstract character (in which even the element of an 'unjust' enrichment is left out): the mere enrichment of a party does not give rise to a claim, but in specific cases the maxim *can* be used to allow a claim if some further requirements are met. These requirements differ from one jurisdiction to another.

With the general maxim (or principle) underlying the whole of the law of obligations, it is not too difficult to find, also in the law of contracts and torts, many cases that can be understood as preventing unjustified enrichment from taking place. This was well expressed by André Tunc when he related the general delict clause with the principle against unjust enrichment:[14]

> 'Le principe énoncé par l'article 1382 du Code Civil est l'une de ces grandes règles d'équité qui pourraient, à elles seules, résumer le Droit tout entier. On pourrait (...) concevoir (...) tout le droit des obligations régi par un seul principe: 'Chacun doit réparer le dommage qu'il cause, par sa faute, à autrui'; on pourrait d'ailleurs, substituant au principe de responsabilité celui tout aussi général d'enrichissement sans cause, se contenter d'écrire: "Nul ne peut s'enrichir injustement aux dépens d'autrui."'

This is the view in which the principle against unjust enrichment is used as a building block to understand the private law system better: it makes the system more intelligible. At the same time, in concrete cases, the principle can be used as an argument to allow compensation from a party that was unjustifiedly enriched – as long as the other requirements to allow the claim are met. In this

---

12 General overviews can be found in the writings of D. Visser (see below, n. 18), J. Gordley, A.T. Von Mehren, *An Introduction to the Comparative Study of Private Law: Readings, Cases, Materials* (2006), p. 552 ff.; R. Zimmermann (Hrsg.), *Grundstrukturen eines Europäischen Bereicherungsrecht*, (2005); J. Beatson, E. Schrage (eds.), *Casebooks on the Common Law of Europe: Unjustified Enrichment* (2003); D. Johnston, R. Zimmermann (eds.), *Unjustified Enrichment: Key Issues in Comparative Perspective* (2002); and E.J.H. Schrage (ed.), *Unjust Enrichment and the Law of Contract* (2001)

13 Pomponius, Dig. 50, 17, 206: 'Iure naturae aequum est neminem cum alterius detrimento et iniuria fieri locupletiorem.'

14 H. & L. Mazeaud, A. Tunc, *Traité théorique et pratique de la responsabilité civil délictuelle et contractuelle*, tome I, 6. éd., Paris 1965, p. 17.

sense, the general principle against unjustified enrichment is recognised in both the civil law and the common law tradition.[15]

A second aspect in which most European jurisdictions converge is the allowance of specific enrichment claims. At a general level, there are three requirements that have to be met before such a claim can be put forward. First, there has to be some enrichment, second this enrichment needs to be unjustified and third, the enrichment has to be at the expense of the claimant. But despite these three uniform requirements, there are also important differences in so far as to the so-called 'taxonomy' of unjust enrichment is involved.[16] There are at least three different taxonomies.

First, many civil law countries make a distinction between undue payment (*condictio indebiti*) on the one hand and unjustified enrichment on the other. This is true for, *inter alia*, France, Italy, the Netherlands and Spain. The (codified) action for undue payment intends to reverse a transfer (the payment was not due and it is irrelevant whether the value of the recipient's patrimony increased or not). Next to this action, many of the countries mentioned before allow for a general action for unjust enrichment or at least for claims in cases analogical to the ones accepted in their civil codes. These actions were usually developed in case law.

Second, there is the German distinction between several types of enrichment claims. This distinction finds its basis in the work of Wilburg and Von Caemmerer.[17] Apart from the *Leistungskondiktion* (the enrichment is based on performance or transfer without a legal basis) and the *Eingriffskondiktion* (the defendant encroaches on the property of the other party),[18] two other types of restitutionary claims are accepted. One is where the defendant's property is improved at the expense of the plaintiff, another where the plaintiff paid another person's debt.

Finally, there is a third way of looking at enrichment law. In the above distinctions, the focus is on the element of '*sine causa*': the enrichment is to take place without a legal basis before the plaintiff can claim any compensation. The other approach would be to focus on a *positive* reason that makes the enrichment unjustified: only if such a positive reason exists (the obvious unjust factors being mistake, duress, failure of consideration and illegality) can a claim be allowed. This is usually held to be the common law position: even with the acceptance

15 See for English law Lipkin Gorman v. Karpnale Ltd. [1991] 2 AC 548.

16 On taxonomy, see e.g. J. du Plessis, "Towards a Rational Structure of Liability for Unjustified Enrichment: Thoughts from Two Jurisdictions", 122 (2005) *South African Law Journal* 39.

17 See for an overview e.g. J. Gordley, *Foundations of Private Law: Property, Tort, Contract, Unjust Enrichment* (2006), p. 420.

18 See also D. Visser, "Unjustified Enrichment in Comparative Perspective", in: M. Reimann, R. Zimmermann (eds.), *The Oxford Handbook of Comparative Law* (2006), p. 969 ff., who emphasises (p. 997) the different national approaches are not too far apart. Cf. D. Visser, "Unjustified Enrichment", in: J.M. Smits (ed.), *Elgar Encyclopedia of Comparative Law* (2006), p. 767 ff.

of a general action, several types of restitution for wrongs remain to be identified. It was Peter Birks who played a big role in the emancipation of the English law of restitution and in distinguishing between various types of actions, even though – as is well known – he changed his opinion in 2003[19] and adopted the continental approach of only allowing a claim in case of enrichment "without a legal basis".

In my view, there is still a third aspect in which European jurisdictions converge. It is that the law of restitution differs in one important aspect of other parts of the law of obligations. While contract law and tort law are coherent sets of rules, the law of unjust enrichment is much less coherent. As James Gordley indicates: the law of restitution does not rest on a coherent principle, but on 'the need in disparate cases to fill the gaps left by other branches of the law.'[20] The traces of this *residual* character of restitution law can be found in all major jurisdictions. In Germany, the Wilburg/Von Caemmerer typology is for example not seen as exhaustive: there are other cases in which restitutionary claims should be allowed and it is difficult to structure these other cases in any consistent way. English law struggled for a long time with finding a proper place for the various enrichment claims. And in many jurisdictions there is an enduring struggle about the extent to which the enrichment action is a subsidiary one vis-à-vis contractual claims and claims in tort.[21] These are in my view signs of the unclear place of enrichment law in the whole of the law of obligations.

IV The Draft CFR: European Principles of Unjustified Enrichment Law

According to the drafters, the model rules contained in the Draft CFR are based on a comparative analysis of the law of the Member States and of the European Union.[22] This is in itself not a convincing methodology as it does not make clear which criterion was used to choose for one solution over another. It is suggested that in case of diverging solutions, the Draft CFR takes a middle road,[23] but this cannot have been the only criterion. I assume that more often a choice was made for the 'better' rule, but as long as the comments to the

19 P. Birks, *Unjust Enrichment* (2003), p. 87 ff. The position he previously held can be found in P. Birks, *An Introduction to the Law of Restitution* (1985).

20 Gordley (n. 17), p. 417.

21 Cf. H. J. van Kooten, "The Structure of Liability for Unjustified Enrichment in Dutch Law, with References to German, French and Italian Law", in: Zimmermann (Hrsg.) (n. 12), p. 221 ff.

22 Draft CFR, p. 12.

23 Draft CFR, p. 12: "as far as there are differences between the underlying values in individual jurisdictions, or between the Member States' laws and EC law, the DCFR mediates between them and takes a balanced position."

provisions are not available we do not really know why one rule was found to be better than another.

This means we have to base our analysis of the model rules on the text of the draft itself.[24] My focus is on the two main provisions in Book VII of the draft. Article VII-1:101 offers the basic rule:

"(1) A person who obtains an unjustified enrichment which is attributable to another's disadvantage is obliged to that other to reverse the enrichment.

(2) This rule applies only in accordance with the following provisions of this Book."

This is followed by Article VII-2:101 on the circumstances in which an enrichment is unjustified:

> "(1) An enrichment is unjustified unless:
> (a) the enriched person is entitled as against the disadvantaged person to the enrichment by virtue of a contract or other juridical act, a court order or a rule of law; or
> (b) the disadvantaged person consented freely and without error to the disadvantage.
> (2) If the contract or other juridical act, court order or rule of law referred to in paragraph (1) (a) is void or avoided or other wise rendered ineffective retrospectively, the enriched person is not entitled to the enrichment on that basis.
> (3) However, the enriched person is to be regarded as entitled to an enrichment by virtue of a rule of law only if the policy of that rule is that the enriched person is to retain the value of the enrichment.
> (4) An enrichment is also unjustified if:
> (a) the disadvantaged person conferred it:
> (i) for a purpose which is not achieved; or
> (ii) with an expectation which is not realised;
> (b) the enriched person knew of, or could reasonably be expected to know of, the purpose or expectation; and
> (c) the enriched person accepted or could reasonably be assumed to have accepted that the enrichment must be reversed in such circumstances."

Three aspects of these principles deserve further attention. First, if compared with the national systems of enrichment law, it is clear that the Draft CFR does not follow any of the existing national taxonomies. It turns away from the two tier structure in civil law jurisdictions of the *condictio indebiti* on the one hand and other enrichment claims on the other. The German distinction between *Leistungskondiktion* and *Nichtleistungskondiktion* is not followed either. Instead,

[24] Some information on the choices made can be found in S. Swann, "The Structure of Liability for Unjustified Enrichment: First Proposals of the Study Group on a European Civil Code", in: Zimmermann (Hrsg.) (n. 12), p. 265 ff.

there is an integrated system in which all enrichment claims are governed by a set of uniform requirements.[25] However, not all restitutionary claims found a place in Book VII: the restitutionary effects of avoidance and termination of contracts are laid down in the arts. III-3:511 ff. The main rule that a party is entitled to claim restitution of benefits conferred under the contract before termination was already part of the Principles of European Contract Law.[26]

Second, it is worth noticing that the provisions look at the enrichment claim from the perspective of the defendant (the enriched person). The question always is whether this defendant received the enrichment unjustifiedly, prompting the court to look at the various factors of Article VII-2:101. This approach comes close to the position of English law, in which an unjust factor also needs to be identified before a claim can be brought. However, the difference with English law seems to be that the factors identified in Article VII-2:101 are formulated in a much more abstract way than the factors in English law.

Third, it is important to realise the draft does not adopt the principle of subsidiarity.[27] Instead, there is free concurrence of actions between the enrichment claim and other claims. In national jurisdictions, such concurrence is often seen as a possible threat to other fields of private law because it may undermine the coherent structure of this domain: if the enrichment claim is freely available, it may mean that the law of contract and tort are circumvented by parties turning to an enrichment claim instead. This is why in Italy and France the enrichment claim is a subsidiary one.[28] The drafters do not seem to have this fear: they insist that enrichment law only has a supplementing function.[29]

V Questioning the Harmonisation of the Law on Unjustified Enrichment

What to think of the approach of the Draft CFR? Does the drafting of provisions on unjustified enrichment really contribute to the harmonisation of European private law? The obvious answer seems to be affirmative, but on closer look this conclusion may be false. My argument consists of two building blocks. The first has to do with the function of enrichment law as such, the second with the possibility of harmonisation of this area of the law.

The first point relates to the function of enrichment law. What does this area of the law *do* if compared to the law of contracts, torts or property? In my view, enrichment law is principally different from other areas of private law in that it has a *residual* function: as indicated already in section 3, it fills the gaps left by

25 Swann (n. 24), p. 275.

26 Cf. arts. 9:307-309, 4:115 and 15:104 PECL.

27 Also see Article VII-7:102 Draft CFR.

28 This is less clear in Dutch and German law. See Beatson, Schrage (eds.) (n. 12), p. 425 ff.

29 Swann (n. 24), p. 277.

other branches of the law. It is true that the principle against unjust enrichment underlies most of the law of obligations, but whether the principle comes to the surface or not is very much dependent on the intricacies of the national system in question.

English law offers a well-known illustration of how the general principle was long hidden behind the heading of quasi-contract: consequently, there was no need for a separate law of restitution. In modern jurisdictions, it also depends on the existing boundaries of contract and tort to what extent the law of unjust enrichment manifests itself. An example of this is the typical case in which goods are supplied or services are performed without a formal contract. Thus, in the English case of *British Steel v. Cleveland Bridge and Engineering*,[30] British Steel negotiated with Cleveland Bridge about the supply of nodes. During the negotiations, Cleveland Bridge issued a letter of intent asking British Steel to start the work. Almost all the nodes were delivered, but not paid for, while the parties were still negotiating. British Steel then claimed payment, in the absence of a contract, on basis of the reasonable value of the nodes. Judge Robert Goff found reason to allow payment but had trouble in finding the proper legal basis for this. After all, starting the work did not mean there was a contract: the parties were still negotiating and it was impossible to say with any certainty what the terms of the contract would have been. In the end, Goff found the following to be the proper reason for allowing a claim:[31]

"In my judgment, the true analysis of the situation is simply this. Both parties confidently expected a formal contract to eventuate. In these circumstances, to expedite performance under that anticipated contract, one requested the other to commence the contract work, and the other complied with that request. If thereafter, as anticipated, a contract was entered into, the work done as requested will be treated as having been performed under that contract; if, contrary to their expectation, no contract was entered into, then the performance of the work is not referable to any contract the terms of which can be ascertained, and the law simply imposes an obligation on the party who made the request to pay a reasonable sum for such work as has been done pursuant to that request, such an obligation sounding in quasi contract or, as we say now, in restitution."

This case illustrates how the principle against unjust enrichment can be accommodated as a restitutionary claim in one jurisdiction and as a contractual claim in another. It is for example likely that in Dutch law the above facts would justify a claim in contract. The underlying principle against unjust enrichment thus fulfils the function of a gap filler and a corrector to what is already there. Stephen Swann, one of the main drafters of the European principles of unjustified enrichment, therefore characterises enrichment law as "parasitic":[32] "it

30 [1984] 1 All ER 504 (QB).

31 [1984] 1 All ER 504, at 511.

32 Swann (n. 24), p. 265; cf. p. 266: "an essentially gap-filling and corrective role."

assumes certain outcomes in other fields of private law and provides a corrective mechanism whereby as between the parties at least beneficial entitlements are brought into line with the overall justice of the situation.'[33] Unlike contract law or tort law, it is – still according to Swann – "a second order rather than a first order set of legal principles."[34]

The second building block in the argumentation relates to harmonisation. If an important function of enrichment law is to correct and to supplement the other sources of obligations, will it then be possible to harmonise this area of the law? My answer would be that this is dependent on what we mean by harmonisation. If harmonisation means that existing national legal systems are replaced by a binding European code, it is certainly possible to carve out a proper place for enrichment law. In a well worked out system of obligations, the supplementing role of the enrichment claim can be properly defined – as it is now reasonable well defined in national jurisdictions. But such full harmonisation is not the aim of the Draft CFR. The Draft CFR will primarily be used as a toolbox for new European legislation or as source of inspiration for national courts and legislators. Closest to our idea of a civil code is that it may form the basis for an optional code.[35] But in all these varieties, the so-called multi-layered structure of European private law will be reinforced: present efforts towards the harmonisation of private law do not lead to an elimination of national jurisdictions, but to a continuous *living together* of European and national rules. This prompts the need to think about which rules serve a certain purpose better at the European or at the national level.

If one continues this way of reasoning, it is likely that contract law will best be regulated at the European level because of its close relationship with the European internal market. But this is different for enrichment law: if large parts of enrichment law serve the function of correcting and supplementing the existing law of obligations, this function is in my view best fulfilled at the national level.[36] The way in which the principle against unjustified enrichment is applied is so dependent on the internal structure of a national legal system (the way in which the sources of obligations communicate with each other) that it is almost impossible to have one ideal set of European principles. Stephen Swann employs the wording of 'constructing a castle in the air' as long as there are no common foundations underlying the European law of obligations.[37]

There is one obvious counterargument. This is that one cannot harmonise contract law without at the same time harmonising adjacent areas of private law

[33] Swann (n. 24), p. 267.

[34] Swann (n. 24), p. 268.

[35] Draft CFR, p. 37.

[36] The obvious exception concerns rules that relate directly to the restitutionary effects of avoidance and termination of contracts. Another possible exception concerns restitutionary claims in European competition law

[37] Swann (n. 24), p. 268 ff.

such as tort, property and restitution. The reason for this would be that contract is only one source of obligations and as the law of obligations forms a coherent whole in the Roman tradition, also the other parts of the law of obligations should be covered. I do not find this argument very convincing. First, because English law is much less familiar with the idea of one law of obligations. Second, and more importantly, because European private law will continue to have a multi-layered character: European and national rules will continue to exist next to each other. Some form of incoherence is the inevitable consequence of this.

Does this mean one should not incorporate rules on unjustified enrichment in the CFR? This would go too far. There certainly is a need to deal with the restitutionary effects of avoidance and termination of contracts (now laid down in the arts. III-3:511 ff.). But outside of this area, the CFR should not offer a fully-fledged self-contained and self-referential legal system[38] of restitution law as we know in national legal systems. In view of the function of the CFR as a *toolbox* for European and national legislators and courts, it should be enough to state the principle against unjustified enrichment. Interested parties can then use this principle as an *argument* whenever necessary. In my view, it is too early to draft detailed rules: we first need to establish a truly European legal science and a European argumentative community.[39]

VI Conclusions

The above questions the need for harmonisation of the law on unjustified enrichment. The main function of enrichment law is to correct and supplement the existing law of obligations. With differing internal structures of the various sources of obligations in national jurisdictions, a European law on unjustified enrichment cannot have firm foundations. The risk is then indeed[40] to construct 'a castle in the air.' Seen from this perspective, the rules of the Draft CFR suffer from so-called 'methodological nationalism':[41] they suggest that rules relevant for the European harmonisation process are of the

[38] The expression is taken from P. Legrand, "Against a European Civil Code", 60 (1997) *Modern Law Review* 45.

[39] It gives me great pleasure to refer to the work of Reinhard Zimmermann, the most important proponent of this idea and the person in whose honour the conference at which this paper was given, was held. See, e.g., R. Zimmermann, "Comparative Law and the Europeanization of Private Law", in: M. Reimann, R. Zimmermann (eds.) (n. 18), p. 539 ff. and id., "The Civil Law in European Codes", in: D.L. Carey Miller, R. Zimmermann (eds.), *The Civilian Tradition and Scots Law* (1997), p. 293: "the essential prerequisite for a truly European private law would appear to be the emergence of an 'organically progressive' legal science, which would have to transcend the national boundaries and to revitalize a common tradition."

[40] Swann (n. 24), p. 268: see above, section 5.

[41] See on this concept C. Joerges, "The Challenges of Europeanization in the Realm of Private Law: a Plea for a New Legal Discipline", 14 (2004) *Duke Journal of Comparative and International Law* 149, and R.

same standing as national rules. By drafting the rules of the CFR in the way we are familiar with at the national level – as rules to be applied in a national legal community – one forgets that we need different ways to represent the law at the European level. If the conceptual foundations of European private law can no longer be tied to the nation-State, a focus on *arguments* instead of on *rules* is the better approach.

Michaels, "Welche Globalisierung für das Recht? Welches Recht für die Globalisierung?", 69 (2005) *RabelsZ* 525.

CHAPTER 12

A European Law of Trusts?

M.J. de Waal*

I Introduction

The topic of this contribution is: "A European law of Trusts?" The question mark already denotes an element of uncertainty. That this is indeed the case with regard to the issue of a European trust law will become readily evident in the analysis that follows. Before the analysis, however, a preliminary question: what qualifies this particular contributor to write on a topic such as this? In the final instance perhaps only two things: first, the fact that the experience can be shared of a legal system where the common law trust has been received but then totally transformed into a "proper" trust, fully compatible with civilian notions; and, secondly, the fact that the perspective of an outsider brings with it the advantages of distance and, hopefully, also a degree of objectivity.

What, then, is the aim of this contribution? To put it briefly, it is an attempt to answer the following two questions: first, where are we now regarding a European trust law or, put differently, what is the current state of European trust law?; and, secondly, are we perhaps beginning to see the contours of a next phase of development? In answering these questions the focus will necessarily fall on the broad picture – with only one brief excursion into the minutiae of trust law.

Why is the debate as to a European trust one of such perennial fascination? The following, somewhat provocative, statement by the Italian trust law expert Maurizio Lupoi can be taken as a point of departure:[1]

> "The mere fact that trusts exist in civil law countries should prove the point that there is no basic incompatibility with civil law structures. Why, then, is the opposite view held so unanimously? The simple answer is that common law scholars have not attempted a comparative study of the civil law institutions, while civil law scholars have not attempted a comparative study of trusts. Each of the two groups has taken at face value what the other propounds...Common law scholars put on robes that were not their own and handled tools with which they were not familiar. They tried to steer a conceptual course instead of a remedial course. A shipwreck ensued and the debris is still there to be seen. Civil law scholars, however, quickly adhered to notions they thought they could simultaneously understand and dismiss, chief among them the notion of equitable ownership."

The key to the problem really lies in the concept mentioned in the last sentence of the statement, namely that of "the notion of equitable ownership" (or, put differently, that of the dichotomy between legal and equitable ownership). What is often found then is, from the common law perspective, the insistence that

[A] BCom LLB LLM LLD (Stellenbosch), Professor: Department of Private Law. University of Stellenbosch.

[1] M. Lupoi, "The Civil Law Trust", (1999) 32 *Vanderbilt Journal of Transnational Law* 967 at 968.

the trust can only be explained on the basis of such a divided ownership; and, from the civil law perspective, the acceptance that, due to the absence of such a concept in the civil law, there can be no such thing as a civil law trust. This is the conventional wisdom that has for a considerable time stifled a rational discourse as to the possibilities of a trust outside of the common law.

However, it is probably fair to say that we have now broken free from the constraints of this position. How did it happen? This question relates to the first issue identified above, namely that of the current state of European trust law.

II The Current State of European Trust Law

1 Discarding preconceived notions

The important breakthrough, without doubt, came through historical and comparative research. A crucial catalyst was the realisation that the "trust idea" is a universal one on which no legal system can claim a monopoly. As Graham Moffat observes[2]:

> "At its broadest, the proposition can be advanced that social organisations, indeed society itself, rests on a creative combination of qualities of ideas, of which trust is as important a component as the assumed rational choice imperatives of contractualism. Thus the idea of trust is present in all complex economic systems."

And the basic trust idea is, of course, a simple one: assets are put under the control of a person, not for the benefit of the latter, but for that of someone else or for a particular specified purpose. Thus David Johnston[3] has shown convincingly that, already in Roman law, there were "trust-like devices" (for example, *fideicommissum* and *fiducia*) as well as "trustee-like persons" (for example, executors, tutors and the *familiae emptor*).

This purely historical research has been followed by a number of important comparative historical analyses. Arguably the most prominent example of this type of work is the volume edited by Richard Helmholz and Reinhard Zimmermann: *Itinera Fiduciae: Trust and Treuhand in Historical Perspective.*[4] The other essays in this volume go a step further than the purely historical research of Johnston (that is also included). They tend to show that there are indeed connections between the English trust and Continental institutions such as *fideicom-*

---

2 G. Moffatt, "Trusts Law: a Song Without End?", (1992) 55 *The Modern Law Review* 123 137.

3 D. Johnston, "Trusts and Trust-like Devices in Roman Law", in: R. Helmholz, R. Zimmermann (eds) *Itinera Fiduciae: Trust and Treuhand in Historical Perspective* (1998), p. 45ff.

4 N. 3.

missum, *fiducia* and *Treuhand* – that there is a "common core" that unites them.[5] Another example is the work of Lupoi, who sees an even stronger connection. He argues that the English Chancellors (without mentioning their sources) drew on thirteenth and fourteenth century civil law authority in their development of the English trust.[6] And, finally, one can mention Patrick Glenn who contends that the introduction of the trust into a civilian context is not a question of the importation of a foreign legal institution, but rather of "revivifying ideas of the common law of Europe".[7]

But the renewed academic interest in the idea of a European trust (be it from an historical or a comparative perspective) did not occur in isolation. It apparently coincided with (or was perhaps in some instances inspired by) a practical issue, namely the fact that European lawyers were, in a globalising world, increasingly confronted with the common law trust – especially in the commercial sphere. This development has been described in the following terms:[8]

> "In business and the financing of commerce globalization has given rise to a renewed interest in civil law quarters in common law trust doctrine and the purposes to which that trust form can be put. Security provision and investment, both personal and commercial, are the pre-eminent subject-matters of interest, but the interest extends to the use of the common law trust for property 'holding' purposes. It is surprising how often a simple express trust to hold property for the transferor, subject perhaps to a conditional interest in another or others, can be of value in banking and commercial dealings."

To this were added the obvious attractions of the common law trust as an instrument in estate planning, tax planning and the management of family wealth.[9]

It is therefore not surprising that prominent studies now started focusing on modern "functionally equivalent, but doctrinally different"[10] European civil law institutions that could perhaps be utilised for at least some of the purposes just mentioned.[11] In these works one would therefore find discussions along these lines of, for example, the German *Testamentsvollstreckung* and *fiduziarische*

---

5 R. Helmholz, R. Zimmermann, "Views of Trust and Treuhand: An Introduction", in: Helmholz and Zimmermann (n. 3) at p. 30.

6 Lupoi (n. 1) at 975.

7 H.P. Glenn, "The Historical Origins of the Trust", in: A. Mordechai Rabello (ed), *Aequitas and Equity: Equity in Civil Law and Mixed Jurisdictions* (1997), p. 749 at 776.

8 See "Introduction to the Principles of European Trust Law", in: D.J. Hayton, S.C.J.J. Kortmann, H.L.E. Verhagen (eds), *Principles of European Trust Law* (1999), p. 3 at 5-6.

9 *Ibid.*

10 *Ibid* at p. 4.

11 See, for example, the work mentioned in note 8 *supra* and D.J. Hayton, S.C.J.J. Kortmann, A.J.M. Nuytinck, A.V.M. Struycken, N.E.D. Faber (eds), *Vertrouwd met de Trust. Trust and Trust-like Arrangements* (1996).

Treuhand; the Dutch *fiducia cum amico* and *bewind*; the French *fiducie*; and the Spanish *fiducia cum amico* and foundation. The analysis and comparison of these institutions have even led, in one instance, to the distillation of a set of "principles of European trust law".[12]

Despite this somewhat ambitious formulation, one refrain coming from the analysis of these institutions is that not any single one of them can by itself perform all those functions for which the common lawyer employs the trust.[13] The function which these institutions undoubtedly do fulfill, however, is the important one of placing assets under the control of another for the benefit of a beneficiary or for a specified purpose. However, the dilemma, in the words of Tony Honoré, is that "there is a difference between a law of entrusting and a law of trusts".[14] In other words, these institutions are not yet "proper" trusts. And the typical explanation for this – here in the words of Hein Kötz with reference to the German position[15] – sounds familiar:

> "The idea of having two persons occupying owner-like positions with regard to the same thing in such a way that one of them, as 'legal owner', has powers of disposition 'at law', and the other, as 'equitable owner', has certain rights recognised 'in equity' is a concept that seemed to Maitland 'almost essential to civilization'. Yet there is nothing quite like it in German law."

But it is, of course, exactly at this point where one is confronted with the intriguing reality of the "proper" trust institutions in a number of civilian and mixed jurisdictions. How can these trusts be explained and what lessons do they hold for the European civilian systems that do not yet have "proper" trusts? Exactly this question was the focus of yet another wave of more recent comparative trust law research[16] – research which, in my view, can provide the key to the development of a "proper" European trust.

What does this research tell? The first and fundamental thing is that the basic structure of these trusts is fully compatible with civilian principles. The typical pattern is one where the trustee is owner of the trust assets and the trust beneficiary is the holder of a personal right against the trustee. There is, of course, no question of an ownership divided between the trustee and the trust beneficiary. But already this simple statement is anathema to the common lawyer's understanding of the trust. The point is that in the common law the

[12] See the work mentioned in n. 8.

[13] See, for example, H Kötz, "National Report for Germany", in: Hayton, Kortmann, Verhagen (n. 8) at p. 85.

[14] T. Honoré, "Obstacles to the Reception of Trust Law? The Examples of South Africa and Scotland", in: Rabello (n. 7), p. 793 at 794.

[15] N. 13.

[16] See, for example, M. Lupoi, *Trusts: A Comparative Study* (2000); J.M. Milo, J.M. Smits, *Trusts in Mixed Legal Systems* (2001). See also n. 17.

divided title is seen as fundamental for the protection of the trust beneficiary in a variety of situations, chief among them the insolvency of the trustee and the appropriation or sale of trust assets in breach of trust. In other words, one can have no "proper" trust without it. However, the work done on especially the trust in mixed jurisdictions such as Scotland and South Africa (but also Louisiana and Quebec) has shown the opposite: one can have a "proper" trust if at least the following "core elements" are present[17]:

a) a trustee who fills a fiduciary position;
b) separation between the trustee's personal estate and the trust estate;
c) the operation of real subrogation; and
d) the construction of trusteeship as an office.

The effective protection of the trust beneficiary – the fundamental idea behind the divided ownership – is also exactly what these core elements are aimed at.[18] The fiduciary position of the trustee obliges him to act in a very specific way with regard to the trust property and the trust beneficiary. Recognition of the concept of separate trust and private estates means that the trust beneficiary will enjoy effective protection in the instance of, for example, the trustee's insolvency. The operation of real subrogation guarantees continuity of the trust estate and it also provides further protection should the trustee commit a breach of trust (by, for example, lawfully or even unlawfully alienating or replacing trust assets). And, finally, the acceptance of trusteeship as an office means that a measure of state control is brought to bear upon the trustee. If these elements are present and they are combined with the normal civilian remedies of the law of delict, enrichment law and the doctrine of notice, the aim of sufficient protection for the trust beneficiary can indeed be achieved – in other words, one can have a "proper" trust.

Is there a reason why these core elements cannot be present in a European institution that can then be properly called a trust? I cannot see any. But then one must be careful of the pitfalls of conventional wisdom, as pointed out by Lupoi in the quotation in the first paragraph above. This will be illustrated by a brief analysis of one of these core elements, namely real subrogation, that is often held up as yet another barrier between the common law trust and the development of a "proper" civilian trust.

---

17 See, for example, M.J. de Waal, "The Core Elements of the Trust: Aspects of the English, Scottish and South African Trusts Compared", (2000) 117 *South African Law Journal* 548; M.J. de Waal, "In Search of a Model for the Introduction of the Trust into a Civilian Context", (2001) 12 *Stellenbosch Law Review* 63; G. Gretton, "Scotland: The Evolution of the Trust in a Semi-Civilian System", in: Helmholz, Zimmermann (n. 3) at p. 507; G.L. Gretton, "Trusts without Equity", (2000) 49 *International and Comparative Law Quarterly* 599; Honoré (n. 14); K.G.C. Reid, "National Report for Scotland", in: Hayton, Kortmann, Verhagen (n. 8) at p. 67; A.N. Yiannopoulos, "Trust and the Civil Law: the Louisiana Experience", in: V.V. Palmer (ed), *Louisiana: Microcosm of a Mixed Jurisdiction* (1999), p. 213.

18 De Waal (n. 17, 2001) at 67.

2 Illustration: An Excursion into the Concept of Real Subrogation

2.1 The General Concept of Subrogation

The general concept of subrogation is not really difficult to explain. The Latin verb *subrogare* (to subrogate) is in the dictionary given to mean: "to suggest that a person be chosen as substitute for another".[19]

This, of course, is what is known as *personal* subrogation. Perhaps the most common situation in which personal subrogation operates is in the context of insurance. An insurer who pays the loss to the insured is entitled to stand in the shoes (that is, to substitute or subrogate) the insured and claim in his stead from the wrongdoer. There is nothing mysterious about this and one finds the doctrine of subrogation in this form in many common law and civil law jurisdictions.

It is therefore somewhat surprising, even disconcerting, to read the following claim in a leading work on equity in English law:[20]

> "[Subrogation]...is a doctrine with *common law* and *equitable* origins whereby one person is entitled to stand in the shoes of another and assert that other's rights."

Note the claim in this passage as to the origin of the doctrine: it is a common law and, especially, an equitable doctrine. I will return to the significance of this shortly.

2.2 The Concept of Real Subrogation

2.2.1 General

It has been argued convincingly that the concept of two separate estates (mentioned above as the second of the "core elements") provides the key to understanding why one can have a proper trust regime in a civil law system, without having to resort to the vexed concept of a divided ownership.[21]

But what happens if an original trust asset is replaced with another asset? Here one can use three simple examples with relating questions. First, a trust asset in the form of a painting is sold in accordance with the provisions of the trust. (In other words, no breach of trust has occurred.) Does the money received for the asset now become a trust asset? The same question arises if

---

19 *Cassell's New Latin-English/English-Latin Dictionary* at "subrogo".

20 J. E Martin, *Hanbury & Martin: Modern Equity* 16th ed (2001), p. 696 (my italics).

21 See, for example, De Waal (n. 17 2000) at 559-563; Gretton (n. 17, 2000) at 608-615; Reid (n. 17) at 68-69; K.G.C. Reid, "Patrimony not Equity: The Trust in Scotland", (2000) 8 *European Review of Private Law* 427.

the money is used to buy another asset, say a gold coin. Does the gold coin now become a trust asset? Secondly, a trustee in breach of trust sells the painting and appropriates either the money or the asset bought with it (the coin) to his own private estate. Does the beneficiary retain any rights with regard to either the money or the coin? Third, the trustee in breach of trust sells the painting to a *mala fide* third party, spends the money and becomes insolvent. Would the trust beneficiary retain any right with regard to the erstwhile trust asset (the painting), now in the hands of the third party?

A proper trust regime would hardly be possible unless satisfactory answers to these questions can be provided.

2.2.2 English Law

In English trust law questions such as these are often linked with the concept of personal subrogation as set out above, but then under the guise of a different doctrine, namely that of "tracing". In yet another leading work on equity one finds this approach formulated as follows:[22]

> "Subrogation is a restitutionary remedy concerned with the replacement of one claimant with another. [Tracing]...is a process which offers both some striking similarities with and differences from the remedy of subrogation. Equitable tracing claims are based on a breach of trust which results in the original property rights of the claimant being pursued into substitutes for that property or into mixtures of that property with other property. Equitable tracing constitutes the substitution of one piece of property for another; whereas subrogation constitutes the substitution of one *claimant* for another."

The essence of what is explained here as *tracing* lies in the phrase "the substitution of one piece of property for another". And again the subtext is that the mechanism by which such a substitution would be possible is somehow based on principles of equity.

Now if that were true, it would have been a nearly insurmountable obstacle to the recognition of a proper trust in civil law systems. Why is that so? The answer is obvious. Once one accepts that the concept of two separate estates is the foundation on which a proper trust regime in a civil law system can be erected, one must go a step further. Then one must also have a mechanism to deal with the obvious eventuality of a replacement of (or turn-over in) assets in the trust estate (as illustrated in the first set of examples above). This mechanism is found in the concept of real subrogation. Real subrogation, in its basic form, means that the proceeds of a trust asset (if the asset has been sold) or the substitute asset (if the proceeds have been used to buy something else) will also be subject to the trust. One could also say that the proceeds or the substitute, as

[22] A. Hudson, *Equity & Trusts* 3rd ed (2003), p. 909.

the case may be, will form part of the trust estate. George Gretton has encapsulated this whole point very well:[23]

> "Real subrogation is the key to the doctrine of patrimony [separate estates], and patrimony is the key to the trust."

But, again, listen to Maitland's claim in this regard:[24]

> "The idea of the trust-fund which is dressed up (invested) now as land and now as current coin, now as shares and now as debentures seems to me *one of the most remarkable ideas developed by modern English jurisprudence*."

2.2.3 Certain Assumptions Regarding Real Subrogation

However, it does appear that certain assumptions regarding real subrogation in civil law systems often do form another (unnecessary) obstacle to the recognition of the trust in such systems. Time will allow for only two brief examples.

The German institution that corresponds perhaps most closely with the trust is the *Treuhand*. For example, the *Treuhänder* (trustee) becomes owner of the assets, he fills a fiduciary position and he must keep the assets separate from his own estate (in other words, in principle there are two separate estates).[25] Yet we are told that, though it does apply to deceased estates, the doctrine of real subrogation probably does not extend to the *Treuhand*.[26] Why not? The answer is not clear. Kötz admits that "there is nothing in the structure of German law that would preclude" the extension of the doctrine also to the *Treuhand*.[27] Be that as it may – without real subrogation the *Treuhand*, in Gretton's words, "falls short of the trust".[28]

---

23 Gretton (n. 17, 2000) at 610. From a different perspective it has been said that the importance of real subrogation lies therein that it "ensures the continuity of the trust estate": see Honoré (n. 14) at p. 805. B. Rudden, "Things as Things and Things as Wealth", (1994) 14 *Oxford Journal of Legal Studies* 81 at 87 gives the following explanation of the concept of real subrogation: "But from the point of view of the portfolio, the sales and subsequent purchases effect merely a real subrogation whereby the things sold are transmuted into the sale price which then becomes the things bought".

24 H.D. Hazeltine *et al* (eds), *Maitland: Selected Essays* (1936), p. 134 as quoted by Rudden (n. 23) at 87 (my italics).

25 Kötz (n. 13) at p. 89-90.

26 It is important to note that the doctrine is explained as follows by Kötz (n. 13) at 94 (italics added): "If a trustee disposes of assets and acquires other assets with the proceeds, the new assets are trust assets *regardless of whether or not the trustee's disposition was in breach of trust*".

27 Kötz (n. 13) at p. 94-95.

28 Gretton (n. 17, 2000) at 613.

According to Matthias Storme the most important obstacle ("belemmering") to the introduction of the non-discretionary trust in Belgian law is the limited possibility of creating, through a private juristic act, a separate estate ("afgescheiden vermogen" or "doelvermogen") of which the characteristics are, first, beneficiaries that enjoy priority regarding the assets of this estate as against other creditors and, secondly (and more important for present purposes), real subrogation that will determine the object of the priority (that is, the separate estate).[29] Storme's view is that it is through this real subrogation that the right to the assets of the separate estate can be seen as a real right to the value thereof.[30] In other words, subrogation is the mechanism by which the value of the separate estate can be preserved, regardless of the exact composition of the estate.[31]

In the preceding exposition one can, I think, identify at least three basic assumptions that call for a reaction.

The first assumption is that real subrogation is an equitable doctrine that should be understood and applied on the basis of equitable principles. This is an assumption that should be rejected out of hand.[32] True, real subrogation in the form of *equitable tracing* is a doctrine with exactly such a basis and such an application. But that is not the only form in which real subrogation exists and should be understood.

The second assumption, which is most probably inspired by the first, is that real subrogation can only operate properly if the beneficiary has a real right to the assets in the separate estate, and thus in the assets that are subrogated (or substituted) for the original assets. But this is also wrong.[33] It is indeed the basis on which equitable tracing operates, but it certainly is not the basis on which real subrogation in the context of both the Scottish and South African trusts does. In both these mixed systems the beneficiary has, at most, a *personal right* against the trustee and not a real right to the trusts assets.[34] And there can be no doubt that in the trust regimes of both these jurisdictions the principle of real subrogation is recognised as well as applied – albeit not in exactly the same fashion, as will be illustrated shortly.

---

29 M. E Storme, "Van Trust gespeend? Trusts en Fiduciaire Figuren in het Belgisch Privaatrecht", (1998) 35 *Tijdschrift voor Privaatrecht* 703 at 712.

30 Storme (n. 29) at 712: "Het is deze zakelijke subrogatie die maakt dat het recht op de goederen van een afgescheiden vermogen kan worden beschouwd als een (zakelijk) recht op de waarde ervan."

31 Storme (n. 29) at 712: "De subrogatie is een middel tot behoud van dezelfde waarde van een vermogen, ongeacht de precieze samenstelling...ervan."

32 Yiannopoulos (n. 17) at 221: "Tracing of assets is not a typical common-law institution. The civilian institution of real subrogation performs a similar function." See also Honoré (n. 14) at p. 816-817.

33 A. M Honoré, "Trusts: The Inessentials", (2003) 4 *Trusts: Trimestrale di Approfondimento Scientifico e Professionale* 497 at 504: "It is a mistake to explain this...as resting on a right *in rem* of the trust beneficiary arising by virtue of his or her equitable interest in or ownership of the trust assets."

34 South African law does recognise the so-called "bewind" trust in terms of which the trust beneficiary is owner of the trust assets. But trusts in practice do not usually appear in this guise.

Before the third assumption can be stated, a brief explanation is called for. Although it is not always appreciated, real subrogation can present itself in one of two forms. First, it can be restricted to only *lawful* replacements of trust assets. In other words, it only operates where a trustee sells trust assets in accordance with the provisions of the trust provisions. In such a case the money or substitute asset bought with the money will become trust assets (that is, will form part of the separate trust estate). This is what Bernard Rudden calls the "peaceful" function of real subrogation.[35] However, real subrogation can also be extended to cover *unlawful* replacement of trusts assets. In other words, it also operates where a trustee in breach of trust sells a trust asset and appropriates the money or the substitute asset bought with the money to his personal estate. This is what Rudden calls the "hostile" function of real subrogation.[36] Now the third assumption apparently is that you cannot have a proper trust if you have real subrogation only in the first form (that is, restricted to lawful replacement of trust assets). This, once again, is a wrong assumption. Of that the South African trust is an example.[37] The Scottish trust, on the other hand, provides an example of a trust where you have real subrogation in the second form. And it is again the Scottish trust that is proof that one can have real subrogation even in this form without having to resort to the notion that the beneficiary must have a real right (read: "equitable ownership") in the trust assets.

2.2.4 General Lessons from the Mixed Jurisdictions?

What can one learn from this brief excursion? In my view, by way of summary, the following:

a) one must always be somewhat suspicious of the conventional wisdom regarding legal institutions. As I have tried to illustrate above, the South African and Scottish trusts teach us that much of the wisdom in connection with real subrogation in the context of trusts is either plain wrong or must, at the least, be substantially qualified;
b) a certain degree of pragmatism is always healthy. This may be somewhat difficult in purely civilian systems where the lawyer is used to operate in a systematic constellation of principles and rules. But also here the exercise above shows us that one can devise innovative and pragmatic answers without in any way compromising the basic principles and rules. Perhaps the mixed system's acquaintance with the common law's more pragmatic, case-by-case approach makes this easier;
c) one must take comparative research seriously. Many answers to problems that may seem intriguing have already been worked out elsewhere.

---

35 Rudden (n. 23) at 91. See also De Waal (n. 17, 2000) at 564-565.

36 *Ibid.*

37 See in general E. Cameron, M. de Waal, B. Wunsh, P. Solomon, E. Kahn, *Honoré's South African Law of Trusts* 5th ed (2002), p. 30.

A last remark is necessary here. In the examples used above a third scenario has been mentioned. That is where the trustee in breach of trusts sells the trust asset to a *mala fide* third party, spends the money and becomes insolvent. The question was whether the trust beneficiary would retain any right with regard to the erstwhile trust asset, now in the hands of the third party.

Here one has moved beyond the scope of real subrogation in the civilian sense, both in its "peaceful" and its "hostile" functions. For the English trust lawyer it would be unthinkable to deal with this problem without resort to that other special child of English trust law, the constructive trust. But here again South African and Scots law show that there are indeed other possibilities. However, that is a topic that cannot be pursued within the context of this contribution.[38]

III Seeing the Contours of a Next Phase of Development?

So where does one move from here? In order to answer this question I think one must look beyond the traditional "trust-like" institutions mentioned above and towards a number of possible new areas of development in the European context. Let me mention a few that in my view deserve special attention:

a) recent developments in the commercial sphere regarding investment vehicles (usually established under company law) such as pension funds, collective investment schemes, debenture holders and securitization;[39]
b) developments in Dutch law relating to the use of the *fiducia* in the financial sphere – especially as a possible finance vehicle – as well as special challenges posed by the practice of "securitization" without the use of a formal trust mechanism;[40]
c) the continued development of the Italian "domestic trust";[41]
d) developments in German law relating to the so-called *Treuhandkonto*; and[42]
e) the introduction of a *fiducie* by legislation into French law.

---

[38] For an introduction to this issue see in general De Waal (n. 17, 2000) at 564-565.

[39] See in general M. Graziadei, U. Mattei, L. Smith (eds), *Commercial Trusts in European Private Law* (2005) and, especially, the remarks in the introductory chapter at p. 5.

[40] See, for example, S. Scott, "An Introduction to the Securitisation of Claims Incorporating a Collective Security Arrangement", (2006) 18 *South African Mercantile Law Journal* 397.

[41] See, for example, S. Wagner, "Enthebung und Neuernennung von Trustees in Italien", (2006) 14 *Zeitschrift für Europäisches Privatrecht* 158.

[42] See, for example, K. Schmidt, "Das Rätsel Treuhandkonto – Gedanken über 'Unmittelbarkeit', 'Mittelherkunft' und 'Offenkundigkeit' als Kriterien der Verwaltungstreuhand", in: E. Bucher, C.-W. Canaris, H. Honsell, T. Koller (eds), *Norm und Wirkung: Beiträge zum Privat- und Wirtschatsrecht aus heutiger und historischer Perspektive (Festschrift für Wolfgang Wiegand zum 65. Geburtstag)*, (2005) p. 933; H.G. Ganter, "Die Rechtsprechung des Bundesgerichtshofs zu Treuhandkonten in der Insolvenz des Treuhänders",

In my view the challenge now is to examine these developments in order to establish whether the contours of a "proper" European trust are not already discernable. A possible methodology could be to audit specific institutions at the heart of these developments against the core elements identified above and to establish whether these core elements are emerging or perhaps already present.

My own (admittedly preliminary) impressions are that the results could be surprising. For example, here is only one conclusion based on a recent and wide-ranging study of "commercial trusts" in European private law (in this quotation regarding the distinction in these new commercial contexts between a purely creditor-debtor relationship and one that could be described as a "trust relationship"):[43]

> "Evidence that the transferor [in trust jurisdictions that formed part of the study, such as England, Scotland and Ireland] did not intend to let the transferee have free hands with the assets will point to the conclusion that the relationship was one of trust, not of debtor and creditor. Is the same factual element relevant in other European systems, where the parties are always thought to be bound by contract? Here is an aspect of contract law that is seldom mentioned: in many jurisdictions of continental Europe, property transferred to the manager for a specific purpose will not be available to its creditors...This outcome is clearly at odds with the idea that ownership is an all-or-nothing affair. Continental legal systems show a variety of approaches when faced with the problem of describing the precise legal status of property transferred to the manager for a specific purpose. Some openly admit that the legal status of that property does not conform to the model set out in the definitional provisions of the civil codes on ownership. A different notion of ownership is emerging here. It may be named by commentators or judges with the help of expressions like 'economic ownership', 'fiduciary ownership', etc. Nonetheless, the tension between the classical civil law notion of ownership, that is the right to use, enjoy and dispose of things to the fullest, and the special features of ownership under the circumstances described above, is still there."

One should not be led astray by the somewhat unfortunate reference here to "different notions of ownership". The mixed legal systems tell one that it is normal ownership, but held in a fiduciary capacity and apart from the personal estate of the owner. What one sees here, in my view, is nothing else than the emergence or indeed presence of the first two core elements identified above, namely the fiduciary position of the trustee and the concept of separate estates. The special protection afforded to the beneficiary (or creditor) under these circumstances need not and, I think, cannot be explained in any other way.

---

in: H. Haarmeyer, H. Hirte, H.-P. Kirchhof, F. Graf von Westphalen (eds), *Verschuldung; Haftung; Vollstreckung; Insolvenz (Festschrift für Gerhart Kreft zum 65. Geburtstag)* (2004), p. 251.

[43] N. 39 at 541-542.

The fourth core element of trusteeship as an office holds absolutely no doctrinal difficulties and is essentially a simple matter of legislative regulation – as is very well illustrated by, especially, the South African example (but also by a variety of others in civil law and mixed jurisdictions).[44]

And I hope that I have been able to illustrate that the perceived obstacle represented by the third core element, the concept of real subrogation, is yet another red herring that can be discarded on the basis of proper comparative research. One can therefore say that European civil law already has all the concepts necessary for a "proper" trust.

However, a valid question at his stage could be: but does it all really matter? What are the special benefits of a "proper" European trust? I can think of many (some of which I have already stressed), but let me mention just one particular benefit relating to the theme of this conference and to the work of the laureate Reinhard Zimmermann: the quest for the identification of a European *ius commune* and also the possible unification of laws. The potential role of trust law in this regard is well motivated in the study on commercial trusts in European private law just mentioned:[45]

> "This is why, thinking to the 'ought to be', trusts represent an advisable alternative road to an efficient marketplace. The data collected in this study show that trust law successfully competes with contract law to tackle problems of economic agency. There is little doubt, therefore, that issues of unification of contract law in Europe are affected by the availability or not of the trust structure and of a well-developed law of trusts."

And would this not be the crowning glory of Reinhard Zimmermann's work if the two great common law and civil law traditions can come together in this way?

Let me then conclude with the bold assertion of an outsider. We are at the very boundary of such a "proper" European trust law – perhaps we have already crossed that boundary without realising it.

---

44 See in general De Waal (n. 17, 2001) at 63ff.

45 N. 39 at 556.

CHAPTER 13

Contract and Transfer of Property*

Isabel González Pacanowska and Carlos Díez Soto

I Contract and Transfer of Property: Different Approaches

This contribution will focus on the relationship between invalidity and termination of a contract aimed at transferring property of movables, more in particular, an onerous contract, such as sale or barter, and its effects on property.

It is a field in which issues concerning contract law and property law appear to be inextricably mingled. As Kaser pointed out, the juridical relationship between sale contract and transfer is one of the central problems of private law, placed at the crossroads of the Law of obligations and the Law of things. The basic principles applied in this field decide, to a great extent, the organization of Patrimonial Law.[1]

On the outset, the relationship between contract and property transfer usually allows a rough division of European systems into two different groups: consensual systems *versus* those requiring an additional element – *traditio* – in conformance with Roman law tradition. Depending on the interference of contractual invalidity – or termination – on such additional requirements, systems are further subdivided into abstract *versus* causal. Indeed, in what has been described as a "unitary approach" – the model being Article 1583 of the French *Code* – when a contract is void or an avoidable contract has been avoided, or in case of termination, the seller is deemed to have never lost property – or automatically regains it – and may rely on the typical protection of property by means of *reivindicatio*. This effect would take place in three constellations of cases: as to the parties, as to subsequent transferees – notwithstanding the rules on good faith acquisition of movables *a non domino* – and, finally, as to the buyer's creditors, who would have to submit to a third party action of the seller.[2]

The second approach places a *prima facie* clear division between the contractual-obligatory level, and the property ("real") effect. Contract produces obligations, but the transfer of property requires something more, *traditio*. Which we are of course rather familiar with, being the traditional Spanish approach that is also to be found in modern Civil Codes: Catalonian Law[3] or the Dutch Civil

---

* Isabel González Pacanowska is Professor of civil law, University of Murcia, Carlos Díez Soto is Professor of civil law, Technical University of Cartagena (UPCT). The present paper has been made with the aid of the Research Project SEJ 2005 07603 ("Los privilegios crediticios como mecanismo de protección del crédito"), financed by the Spanish Ministry of Education and Science.

1 M. Kaser, "Compraventa y transmisión de la propiedad en el Derecho romano y en la historia de la dogmática moderna", (1962) t. XIII *Anales de la Academia Matritense del Notariado* 572.

2 See C. v. Bar, U. Drobnig, "Study on Property Law and Non-contractual Liability Law as they relate to Contract Law", submitted to the European Commission – Health and Consumer Protection Directorate General – SANCO B5-1000/02/000574 at: http://ec.europa.eu/comm/consumers/cons_ int/safe_shop/fair_bus_pract/cont_law/study.pdf. In particular, nº 193, *et seq.* (this part provided by Rainer, in collaboration with J.F. Stagle And U. Drobnig).

3 Article 609 CC in Spain; Article 531-3, 5th Book of the CC Catalunya (Llei 5/2006, of 10 May). See F. Badosa Coll, "Els sistemes adquisitius a Catalunya", XIV Jornades de Dret Català a Tossa, to be found at http://civil.udg.edu/tossa/2006/textos/pon/2/fbc.htm.

Code[4]. *Traditio* usually requires transfer of possession, but the forms of *traditio* may be construed rather broadly. *Traditio brevi manu* and *constitutum possessorium* are widely accepted, but even consent of the parties may suffice. Indeed, Article 1464 of the Spanish Civil Code (hereinafter CC) accepts "mere consent" of the parties as a way of transferring ownership when a movable asset has been sold, but cannot possibly be physically delivered. Legal writers have granted this provision a wide scope, in that consensual *traditio* is to be loosely admitted if it suits the parties' convenience, notwithstanding the limited effect such transfer may have in conflict with the seller's creditors or in double sale conflicts.[5] It could be said that this rather flexible attitude towards the fulfilment of the *traditio* requirement allows party autonomy to play a decisive role when deciding on the exact moment in which property of movables is transferred, at least in onerous transactions.[6] Furthermore, transfer of property may be excluded – despite delivery – by the addition of retention of title clauses.[7]

---

4 Article 3:84 par. 1 B.W.

5 See L. Díez-Picazo, "La tradición y los acuerdos traslativos en el Derecho español", (1966) *Anuario de Derecho Civil* 562. This, however, may be accepted as to the relationship between the parties. If it also has effects against third parties is another question. Case Law seems prone to refer to this rule the justification of property of movables, albeit the actual owner has never entered into possession, as will happen in financial lease contracts, where the delivery of the asset by the seller directly to the lessee, together with the related lease-contract, is deemed enough to transfer ownership to the financial lessor (decisions of the *Tribunal Supremo* – hereinafter STS- 12 March 2001 [RJ 2001/5970], 7 October 2002 [RJ 2002/9265]); the same applies – via *constitutum possessorium*- to justify ownership of the lessor in a lease-back contract (STS 20 November 1999 [RJ 1999/8615] . On the contrary, the Spanish Supreme Court seems inclined to reject third party actions from a buyer of goods that have remained under possession of the seller and are under execution issued by the latter's creditors; the mere agreement is not enough to hold the transfer against creditors of the seller if the assets have remained on the premises of the transferor, unless the asset had been actually delivered or the contract had been consigned on a notarial deed: STS 28 October 2003 (RJ 2003/7771), 25 February 2004 (RJ 2004/854). A similar solution is applied when transfer is based on *datio in solutum*: STS 1 December 2004 (RJ 2004/7904), 10 March 2005 (RJ 2005/3186), 28 March 2006 (RJ 2006/1864). In the field of double sale of the same asset, Article 1473 CC states that ownership is transferred to the buyer who first acquired possession in good faith; the proper coordination between this rule and Article 464 CC (good faith acquisition *a non domino* for the purchaser of movables) will protect the second buyer to whom physical possession is transferred in conflict with a first buyer who only received *traditio ficta*. See T. Rubio Garrido, *La doble venta y la doble disposición* (1994), p. 86 *et seq.*

6 In this way, the differences between consensual and *traditio* systems practically cease to exist. In English Law, the Sale of Goods Act 1979, section 17, states that property in specific goods will pass when the parties intend it to, and in ascertaining that intention the court is directed to have regard to the terms of the contract, the conduct of the parties and the circumstances of the case.

7 National legislations may settle extra requirements (such as a notarial deed, or entry into a Register) in order to hold retention of title clauses against third parties. According to the decision of the ECJ 26 October (ECJ 2006/311), such demands do not signify infringement of Article 4.1 Directive 2000/35.

In any case, the additional requirement appears to be linked to the contract, in that invalidity will clearly hamper the proprietary effects of delivery. The effects of termination, on the contrary, appear to be more disputed, and we will deal with them later on.

A step further – in what has been called a "split approach" – introduces the well known Savigny's discovery of the "real agreement", not dependent on the invalidity or termination of the underlying contract. Property, therefore, is not only acquired by the buyer, but the latter retains it until the seller brings forth an action in order to claim retransfer of the goods, on the basis of unjust enrichment. The model is the German BGB and the so-called "*Abstraktion Prinzip*". This picture is rather oversimplified, as the independence of contract and real agreement shows many nuances: not only in the relationship between the parties (as defects of the contract may also affect the real agreement, *Fehleridentität),*[8] but also as to subsequent transferees, if they are not in good faith. In principle, however, the buyer's creditors will not be bothered by a third party action from the seller before he has regained ownership, despite avoidance or termination of the underlying contract.[9]

II The European Law Context

Now the question may be: How could European law deal with these issues? To what extent does the dependence/independence of property law affect the rules on contract Law?

There is a debate, as S. van Erp has written, on whether property law should be harmonised at all. Indeed, Article 295 of the EC Treaty states that "this Treaty shall in no way prejudice the rules in member States governing the system of property ownership", but "this does not mean that property law cannot be touched at all by European law". To S. van Erp harmonisation seems useful in areas directly affecting cross-border business dealings, such as security interests with regard to movables and claims, as well as mortgages on immovables. The difficulty is that harmonisation "cannot be undertaken without looking also at the whole fabric of property law and the interaction between property law and the law of obligations, especially contract law". S. van Erp also has suggested an approach – a "bottom-up" approach – in order to find common thought patterns. When looking for such common patterns, he lays out a distinction between leading principles, ground rules and technical rules. Leading rules such as *numerus clausus*, and the principle of transparency, in which information for

8 Or other cases, such as an agreement to subordinate the efficacy of the real agreement to the validity of the underlying contract, which, in turn, seems to be accepted restrictively, in order not to undermine the "Abstraktionsprinzip". For a clear overview, see K.H. Schwab, H. Prütting, *Sachenrecht*, 29th ed., (2000), p. 12 ff.

9 See C.v. Bar/U. Drobnig (n. 2) n. 494.

third parties is of vital importance – are a filter necessary for the characterisation of a right as indeed a property right. Ground rules concern further consequences following the conclusion that the right is a property right, and decide how these rights relate among themselves. Such ground rules are, basically, *nemo plus iuris ad alium transferre potest quam ipse sibi habet*, and *prior tempore potior iure*, together with protection rules, such as embodied by reivindication. Technical rules, finally, provide in more detail how property rights function and are of a more elaborate nature. As S. van ERP points out, the diverging technical rules are the greatest difficulty in discerning what the various property law systems in Europe have in common. Indeed, "it is sometimes very hard to understand what is happening in a particular legal system "under the surface", but "this approach is vital to tracking the common features".[10]

We intend to deal with some technical rules regarding contract and transfer of property by placing at the crossroads rules on contract and rules on property, considering the mutual influence thereof in void contracts, or in case of termination for non-performance and breach of contract, taking into account two basic constellations: effects between the parties to the contract, on the one hand, and effects on third parties, on the other. Considering third persons, however, a further subdivision seems necessary, in that conflicts with subsequent transferees, on the one hand, and creditors of either of the parties, on the other, may offer diverging solutions.

In doing so, it might be interesting to contrast, on the one hand, the Principles of European Contract Law on these issues (quoted as *PECL*), and, on the other, the draft of Book VIII of the Common Frame of Reference[11] (the *Draft*). As authors of the Spanish Report for the Working Group on acquisition and loss of ownership in movables, some views will be inevitably influenced by our own "legal construction traps". However, perhaps the *Draft* itself may allow it, as Article VIII.- 2:101 ("*Requirements for the Transfer of Ownership in General*"), states that:

"(1) The transfer of ownership in a movable requires
a) the transferor's right or authority to transfer ownership in the movable and
b) delivery, an equivalent to delivery, an agreement as to the time ownership is to pass or, where provided so by national law, an entry into the register based on
c) an obligation to transfer ownership".

10 S. van Erp, "European and national Property Law: Osmosis or Growing Antagonism", *W. v. Gerven Lectures (6)* (2006) 6, 13, 14 ff.

11 The Working Group on "Transfer of movables" belongs to the SGECC. It was created in 2001, and is currently directed by Prof. Dr. B. Lurger (University of Graz) and Prof. Dr. W. Faber (University of Salzburg). The publication of their work on "Acquisition and Loss of ownership in movables" is due for the end of 2009. National reporters have been asked to cover a great deal of issues. The authors thank Dr. W. Faber, who has provided us with the latest version of the Draft (July 2007).

Indeed, not a consensual, but a *traditio* approach. Furthermore, focusing on the case in which the said *obligation* may arise from a contract (as stated in VIII.-2:103) the *Draft* has also provided rules for *Transfer based on invalid, ineffective, avoided or terminated* contracts (VIII, Article 2:203), stating that when the contract (*obligation*) is (1) "invalid, ineffective or avoided"... "ownership never passes or is deemed to have never passed to the transferee (retroactive proprietary effect) (This rule applies to the relationship between the parties as well as to the relationship to third parties)". On the contrary, pursuant (2), "where a movable has been transferred based on an obligation that is terminated afterwards, termination has no proprietary effects". Finally, according to (3), "this article does not affect any [obligatory] right to recover the movable [or its value] based on other provisions of this Code [or other rules comparable to these provisions]".

So it seems, not an abstract, but a *causal* approach. We may now perhaps confront the interference of these rules with contractual law, and encounter some of the problems.

III Void and Avoidable Contracts

Invalidity of contract entails a certain degree of complexity (not to mention the "black cat and blind men theory"[12]). Concepts and grounds differ. We could, however, use as a standpoint the notion of "absolute nullity", as opposed to avoidable contracts. Not only because it is a basic division in many European systems, as well as in the Spanish one, as based on the Roman tradition, but also because it has found its way into the PECL.

Contracts are deemed to be *avoidable* for defects related to consent of one of the parties (mistake, fraud, threat or duress). In addition, there is usually a time limit within which the contract can be avoided. According to Article 4:113 PECL, "a reasonable time, with due regard to the circumstances, after the avoiding party knew or ought to have known of the relevant facts or became capable of acting freely". Most European countries fix a precise time limit[13], which in Spain is four years (Article 1301 CC). The time limit may only apply if the contract has been executed, not when the grounds for avoidance are raised as a defence. According to some authors, the time limit is to be referred to recovery of what was given.[14] Furthermore, only a party to the avoidable contract – more precisely,

[12] See R. Zimmermann, *The Law of obligations* (1996), p. 678.

[13] Despite important variations (e.g., twenty years for Scotland, versus one year for Portugal). See *Principles of European Contrac Law, Parts I and II*, prepared by the Commission on European Contract Law, edited by O. Lando, H. Beale (2000), p. 275 *et seq.*

[14] Indeed, Spanish legal writers have long disputed on the exact configuration of avoidable contracts, as the CC provides for a four year limit for the "action of nullity" (Article 1301 CC) and declares the said action to be "extinguished" if the avoidable contract is "confirmed". Some hold the contract to be provision-

the one who suffered the defect of consent- is entitled to effectively avoid it, or, instead, confirm it.[15]

Absolute nullity, on the contrary, is not usually confined to a fixed set of grounds. Yet it is, for one thing, clearly related to contradiction with the general limits of private autonomy, namely mandatory rules – which, however, may provide for a different type of consequence – or, more generally, concepts of immorality, public order and similar. Such seems to be the approach of the PECL (Part III, Chapter 15) on "illegality", by declaring of no effect the contract "to the extent it is contrary to principles recognised as fundamental in the laws of the member States of the EU" (Article 15:101). Exclusion of effects may also be the case of contracts infringing mandatory rules, as provided for by Article 15:102 PECL.[16]

It is usually understood – by Spanish scholars at least – that absolute nullity is "definitive", as the contract, as it was originally concluded, cannot become valid. Therefore, a court order declaring the contract to be void may be obtained without limitation period; in addition, not only by the parties to the contract, but also by third persons who may be interested in destroying the appearance of legal effects (*"quod ab initio vitiosum est non potest tractu temporis convalescere"*). In Spanish case law it is rather frequent to encounter creditors of one of the parties to a sham contract invoking the "absolute nullity" of the contract in order to defeat the apparent buyer and owner of the asset who, in turn, is exercising a third party action (*tercería de dominio*) to release the asset from the claws of the creditors.[17]

The parties to an avoidable contract, once avoided, or to an initially void ("absolute nullity") contract, are mutually obliged to return whatever they received. The Spanish Civil Code has a specific set of rules (Article 1303-1317)

ally *valid* (at least it is binding for the party who was not "impaired" in any way) unless the party who suffered the defect – and most deserving protection- files a claim within the time limitation period in order to have the contract invalidated and thereby recover what was given to the other party. For others, an avoidable contract is initially invalid, unless subsequently confirmed; if not, the protected party may at any time plead for a declaration of nullity in order to be declared unbounded; the four year limitation period is then applied to the restitution-recovery claim. See J. Delgado Echeverría, Mª.A. Parra Lucán, *Las nulidades de los contratos. En la teoría y en la práctica* (2005), p. 54 ff.

15 See PECL Article 4: 112. Pursuant Article 4: 114 (Confirmation), if the party which is entitled to avoid a contract confirms it, expressly or impliedly, after it knows of the ground for avoidance, or becomes capable of acting freely, avoidance of the contract is excluded. The Spanish CC deals with confirmation in arts. 1309-1313.

16 Article 15:102: "Contracts infringing mandatory rules. (1) Where a contract infringes a mandatory rule of law applicable under Article 1:103 of these principles, the effects of that infringement upon the contract are the effects, if any, expressly prescribed by that mandatory rule. (2). Where the mandatory rule does not expressly prescribe the effects of an infringement upon a contract, the contract may be declared to have full effect, to have some effect, to have no effect, or to be subject to modification".

17 STS 14 February 2006 (RJ 2006/2776).

dealing with these issues. The Spanish Supreme Court has often referred to such recovery rules as a legal consequence of nullity, which may even be provided for by court of its own motion.[18]

The *PECL* also provide – as an "effect of avoidance"- for mutual restitution that may be claimed by either party in case of avoidance (Article 4:115 PECL)[19]; a similar rule is laid down for contracts rendered ineffective for "illegality" (Article 15:104 PECL).[20]

Such claims refer to the relationship between the parties to the void/avoidable contract. And, at least in the Spanish Civil Code, are submitted to several nuances and exceptions, which we will not be dealth with here. The problem is how the rule excluding transfer of property in these cases interferes with personal or obligatory restitution claims. Indeed, the "notes" and "comments" added to the PECL highlight that the rules on mutual obligation of restitution in case of avoidance "do not deal with questions of property and take no position on whether avoidance produces an automatic re-transfer of property, with a concomitant right to restitution of any property transferred as such, or merely to a personal right to restitution. Nor do they deal with the position of third parties who may claim an interest in the property".[21] Furthermore, the rules on concurrent restitution in case of "illegality" "contain no provisions about the transfer of property and ownership under illegal transactions".[22]

Rules regarding recovery based on property and those regarding recovery as a result of obligatory remedies differ. The success of *reivindicatio* requires the asset to still exist, proof of ownership and possession of the defendant. The defendant, in turn, may be the party to the contract or a subsequent transferee, who will have to return possession, unless protected by rules of *a non domino* acquisition. In relation to creditors of the buyer, the owner would be entitled to oppose to the seizure in individual executive proceedings, by means of the so-called "third party ownership action", or would be indeed treated as an owner – *separatio ex iure dominii* – in insolvency proceedings.[23] Moreover, a *reivindicatio*

---

18 See, among many others, STS 22 November 2005 (RJ 2005/10198).

19 Article 4:115 PECL: "Effect of Avoidance. On avoidance either party may claim restitution of whatever it has supplied under the contract, provided it makes concurrent restitution of whatever it has received. If restitution cannot be made in kind for any reason, a reasonable sum must be paid for what has been received".

20 Article 15:104 PECL: "Restitution. (1) When a contract is rendered ineffective under Articles 15:101 or 15:102, either party may claim restitution of whatever that party has supplied under the contract, provided that, where appropriate, concurrent restitution is made of whatever has been received... (4) If restitution cannot be made in kind for any reason, a reasonable sum must be paid for what has been received".

21 See PECL, Parts I and II, *op. cit.*, p. 278.

22 See PECL Part III, *op. cit.*, p. 224.

23 For Spanish Law, see Article 80 LC. A. Recalde Castells, in I. Quintana Carlo, A. Bonet Navarro, J.A. García Cruces González (dirs.), *Las claves de la Ley concursal* (2005), p. 404.

or claim *in rem* may perhaps not encounter a specific time limitation period and will only be set back by original (or *a non domino*) acquisition of property by the defendant.

On the contrary, the personal duty of restitution derived from contract avoidance only falls on the other party to the contract and, as a rule, can only be claimed by his counter-party[24]. It is not barred when it cannot be made in kind for any reason, nor does it require the *accipiens* to still be in possession;[25] the *solvens* may have not even been the owner in the first place. Since the obligation of restitution is mutual, the defendant may be granted the right to withhold performance as long as he does not get back his own prestation. Finally, personal claims of recovery are submitted to fixed time limitation periods (in the Spanish Civil Code, fifteen years, Article 1964 CC).

However, with respect to the relationship between the parties to a void/avoidable contract, *both* remedies may seem *prima facie* available.[26] The mutual interference of rules on protection of property (namely *reivindicatio*) and rules providing legal (personal) obligations of mutual restitutions is a debated issue among Spanish legal scholars.[27] Perhaps part of the discussion may be useful here. We will not deal in depth with the different opinions, as it involves taking

---

24 In Spanish Law, however, a third party may obtain restitution when the contract is declared to be void within criminal proceedings. See Delgado Echeverría/Parra Lucán (n. 14), p. 243, 324 ff.

25 Pursuant Article 1307 CC, the defendant must pay the *"value the thing had when it was lost, plus interest from this date"*. The field of application of Article 1307 CC, however, is widely debated. According to Delgado Echeverría/Parra Lucán, restoration of the "value" of the thing when it cannot be restored in kind, for any reason, should only apply to the *accipiens* of bad faith, in order to harmonise this article with those ruling *condictio indebiti*. Whereas a good faith *accipiens* who is unable to return in kind, will benefit from the rule laid down for *condictio indebiti*, in that he will only have to return to the extent of his own enrichment. Case law usually provides for restitution of the price the *accipiens* received from a subsequent transferee. It must also be taken into account that the *solvens* may have a personal claim of recovery against the *accipiens*¸ and a *rei vindicatio* against a subsequent transferee; if the former is chosen, legal opinion agrees that the *reivindicatio* is not available. See Delgado Echeverría/Parra Lucán (n. 14), p. 255 ff.

26 As L.P.W. van Vliet emphasises, "it is not superfluous for a causal transfer system to give the transferor two remedies: a *rei* vindication and in addition a *condictio indebiti*. True, normally the owner will rely on his revindication as it is an action which works as against everyone. Yet, the object transferred may be lost, consumed or sold to a *bona fide* third party. Moreover, the transferee may have acquired ownership of the thing, as a result of original acquisition. The transferor will then have to resort to the *condictio*". See *Transfer of movables in German, French, English and Dutch law* (2000), p. 189.

27 We will only attempt here to summarise some of the opinions on this matter, taking into account the fact that the Spanish Civil Code has devoted specific rules on restitution in case of void contracts (arts. 1303-1314 CC), apart from the rules on *condictio indebiti* (arts. 1896-1897). The relationship between *reivindicatio* and *condictio indebiti* is quite controversial. However, in other *causal* systems, such as Italy, it seems that the *solvens*, provided the necessary requirements concur, could choose between either remedy. See E. Moscati, "Caducazione degli effetti del contratto e pretese di restituzione", (2007) *Rivista*

into account, *inter alia,* the different requirements of ordinary and extraordinary acquisitive prescription, as well as the different rules regarding restitution of fruits, improvements, expenses and the like in cases of *reivindicatio*, contractual inefficacy and *condictio indebiti*.[28] A general overview, however, provides some insight.

The different approaches, for the sake of clarity, we shall describe as priority, complementariness and exclusivity, although this terminology is not usually used.

Priority would mean that it has to be decided whether obligatory remedies cannot be defeated by property rules, or the contrary. If the first, as long as personal claims have not expired, the defendant cannot rely on property rules to avoid restitution. If the second, the defendant could seek protection in the rules on acquisitive prescription (*usucapio*), before the period of (extinctive) prescription of the personal claim has run out. Both opinions have been defended by Spanish scholars, when discussing the effects of absolute nullity. For some authors, while the time limit for the obligatory right of restitution (which according to our CC is fifteen years, Article 1964 CC) has not yet elapsed, the other party may not benefit from the (maximum) six year period of acquisitive prescription of movables (Article 1962.1 CC).[29] For others, on the contrary, the possessor of the movable must indeed be granted protection by acquisitive prescription – should he/she have possessed for the six year period as an owner (*posesión en concepto de dueño*) – as any other solution would mean treating him worse than any other third person, who would be perfectly protected by *usucapio*, despite not related at all with the owner.[30] However, it could be said that not

di Diritto Civile 481 *et seq.*; P. Gallo, *Arrichimento senza causa e quasi contratti (I remedi restitutori)* (1994), p. 127 ff.

[28] Further references of Spanish Law can be found in our Report on Transfer of Movables in Spanish Law, to be published.

[29] Delgado Echeverría/Parra Lucán (n. 14), p. 247 ff.: "Entre las partes deben prevalecer las consecuencias de la nulidad de la relación contractual". C. López Beltrán De Heredia, *La nulidad contractual. Consecuencias* (1995), p. 283: "Si el vendedor perdió la acción reivindicatoria al ganar el comprador la propiedad por usucapión, mientras subsista la posibilidad de recuperar el precio mediante el ejercicio de la acción personal restitutoria, ha de subsistir la posibilidad de recuperar la cosa, mediante el ejercicio de esa misma acción personal". If the contract is *avoidable*, Article 1301 CC fixes a four year time limit for the "acción de nulidad". Time, however, may start running many years after the contract was concluded and executed. For instance, when the contract was celebrated by an incapacitated person, the period begins after the *solvens* has acquired full legal capacity; if under threat or violence, only when the *solvens* is free of such illegal constrictions. The other party to the contract may not avoid restitution resorting to acquisitive prescription (six years for movables). See P. De Pablo Contreras *et alii*, *Curso de Derecho Civil*, T. III, *Derechos Reales* (2004), p. 421.

[30] M. Pasquau Liaño, *Nulidad y anulabilidad del contrato* (1997), p. 297, 363: "El transcurso del plazo necesario para la usucapión a favor del adquirente en virtud del contrato nulo, si es más breve que el propio de la acción de nulidad (o la de restitución), habrá consolidado la adquisición, que quedará inmune no

even this bars the personal claim for the value, as any other kind of original acquisition (*specificatio* or *commixtio*) certainly does not.

Pursuant Article VIII 2:103 (1) of the *Draft*, when the contract is "invalid, ineffective or avoided", "ownership never passes or is deemed to have never passed to the transferee (retroactive proprietary effect). This rule "applies to the relationship between the parties as well as to the relationship to third parties". Nevertheless, Article VIII 2:103 (3) of the Draft declares that this article "does not affect any [obligatory] right to recover the movable [or its value] based on other provisions of this Code [or other rules comparable to these provisions]". Perhaps this may allow us to decide that an obligatory right of recovery may still be available, despite the defendant tries to rely on acquisition of property by means of *usucapio*.

Priority of personal claims, furthermore, entails another consequence. When the Law, despite not admitting enforceability of the contract, refuses to grant restitution claims to one or to both of the parties[31], protection under the *reivindicatio* is likewise to be denied.[32]

Deciding for "priority" of personal claims, however, does not settle the matter. Property rules may still be put forward as "complementary" as opposed to the exclusivity of personal claims. If the latter, once the period of time for prescription of personal (obligatory) recovery claims has elapsed, the owner, notwithstanding the nullity of the contract, will not be entitled to exercise the *reivindicatio* against the other party to the contract. Indeed, among Spanish scholars it is usually admitted that, since the Civil Code provides for a four year

sólo respecto de la acción real reivindicatoria, sino también respecto de la restitución derivada de la nulidad". By the same author, see "La acción de nulidad sí prescribe", in J. Delgado Echeverría (Coord.), *Las nulidades de los contratos: un sistema en evolución* (2007) 245. See also M. Yzquierdo Tolsada, *Las tensiones entre usucapión y prescripción extintiva* (1998), p. 198; and, by the same author, "Tipología del justo título en la usucapión. Crónica de una cuestión pendiente", (2001) *Anuario de Derecho Civil* 605, 624, 633.

31 As in arts. 1305 and 1306 CC, when the causa is "*torpe*". If this amounts to a criminal offence attributable to both parties, neither of them is entitled to recover, and the assets – object of the contract- will be treated as instruments of the crime (Article 1305.1); whereas if one of the parties was innocent, he will be able to recover and not compelled to perform (Article 1305.2). If the "*causa torpe*" was not a criminal offence, neither of the parties can demand recovery (Article 1306.1); yet if only one was to blame, the innocent party is again entitled to demand back what was rendered (Article 1306.2). Courts apply the *in pari turpitudinis...* rule rather restrictively. On this restrictive approach see Delgado Echeverría/Parra Lucán (n. 14), p. 291 ff.

32 See A. Carrasco Perera, "Restitución de provechos", (1987) *Anuario de Derecho Civil* 1067: Despite Article 348,2 CC being a general rule about restitution, regardless of the fact that possession was acquired directly from the owner or through a third person, "la nulidad del título por el que el dueño le transmite la cosa directamente al poseedor le permite reivindicar; y a la inversa, cuando la Ley, a pesar del título ineficaz, excluye la restitución, no sólo excluye la restitución por el título contractual viciado, sino que impide reivindicar (por ej., arts. 1305 y 1306 CC)".

limitation period in order to challenge avoidable contracts, once this period has passed, property remains definitely by the transferee.[33] Others hold this opinion even for the so-called "absolute nullity", considering that the recovery claim is then submitted to the maximum prescription period of fifteen years, to which no any other claims based on property may outlive.[34] Most authors, however, allow property rules to be called in aid as "complementary", despite the (extinctive) prescription of the personal claim in cases of absolute nullity, admitting that *reivindicatio* will be only defeated by rules on acquisitive prescription. Hence, when the personal action has expired after fifteen years (Article 1964 CC), the owner may still be enabled to *reivindicatio* until the possessor gains good title by continuous possession. This, in case of immovables, would take thirty years.[35] The defeated possessor – whose own claim for mutual restitution will have by then also expired- is granted, in turn, a subsidiary remedy based on unjust enrichment.[36]

The Spanish Supreme Court seems to give support to the "complementary" approach, in that it allows the party to an "absolutely null" contract to claim restitution as the lawful owner. Yet, in most occasions, it seems that the Supreme Court is simply abiding by the traditional opinion that declares the action of nullity – and consequential restitution- to be *imprescriptible*.[37] The owner may vindicate or plead for restitution as a consequence of the declaration of nullity and will recover possession – provided the "title" of the possessor has been proved to be void, if necessary- unless the defendant has fulfilled the requirements of (extraordinary) acquisitive prescription. This in some cases is

33 It is however disputed. The majority consider the four year period the maximum time limit afforded to the "impaired" party in order to challenge and avoid the avoidable contract, that, in the absence of avoidance, is to be considered, to all intents and purposes, as "valid".

34 Pasquau Liaño (n. 30), p. 244, 246: "Me cuesta entender por qué, por ejemplo, quien enajena un inmueble de su propiedad mediante un contrato nulo dispone de treinta años para recuperarlo, y, sin embargo, el adquirente a título oneroso a virtud de ese mismo contrato dispone únicamente de quince años para recuperar el precio que pagó... tratándose del mismo negocio y de la misma causa de nulidad".

35 Pursuant the rules on extraordinay *usucapio*, Article 1959 CC. See López Beltrán De Heredia (n. 29), p. 282; Delgado Echeverría/Parra Lucán (n. 14), p. 249 *et seq*. The party defeated by *reivindicatio* would be entitled to recover the price (eventually paid) on the basis of unjust enrichment.

36 López Beltrán De Heredia (n. 29), p. 283.

37 STS 10 December 1987 (RJ 1987/9285). Expressly excluding restitution in case of nullity to be submitted to a specific time limitation period: STS 25 March 2002 (RJ 2002/2665) ["*En cuanto a la prescripción extintiva no es aplicable el Article 1964 CC porque la acción básica ejercitada en la demanda de nulidad radical de un negocio jurídico es imprescriptible (...). Es de reiterar que la acción ejercitada se fundamenta en el Article 1459, números segundo y quinto, párrafo tercero, del CC (...). En segundo lugar resulta incuestionable que la aplicación de la norma prohibitiva referida produce la nulidad radical del negocio (Article 6.3 CC) (...). Y finalmente, resulta incuestionable que la nulidad radical o absoluta, a diferencia de la anulabilidad, no es sanable por transcurso del tiempo...*"]; STS 30 November 2005 (RJ 2005/7739).

rejected, not for lack of time, but for lack of the possessory concept (*"posesión en concepto de dueño"*).[38]

IV Termination

Most European systems do not require the purchase price to have been rendered in order to transfer property. Therefore, if the title or underlying contract is valid and the *traditio* is duly performed by the seller in any of the forms admitted by the law, the buyer will thereby acquire property, despite not having yet complied with his own obligations. Hence, retention of title is not usually implied[39], but must have been expressively provided for by the parties in order to allow the seller to retain ownership until the counter-performance has been completely fulfilled. Lack of performance, however, entitles the aggrieved party to cancel the relationship and thereby what has been done under the contract must be unravelled. Thus, if property had been transferred, provided the asset is identifiable (*corps certain*), it must be restored.

The *PECL*, in fact, deal with the effect of termination and mutual restitution as to the relationship between the parties. According to Article 9:308 PECL, "on termination of the contract a party which has supplied property which can be returned and for which it has not received payment or other counter-performance, may recover property". Furthermore, Article 9:309 PECL states that on termination of the contract "a party which has rendered a performance which cannot be returned, and for which it has not received payment or other counter-performance, may recover a reasonable amount for the value of the performance to the other party". Thus merely a "personal" obligation *inter partes*, as these rules "deal exclusively with the relationship between the parties and not with the effect which the contract may have on the property in goods sold or bartered. Whether a creditor of the buyer, the buyer's receivers in bankruptcy or a *bona fide* purchaser may oppose the restitution of goods sold is to be determined by the applicable national law".[40]

The *Draft* of the Working Group, on the other hand, provides for the "property" rule. As quoted above, (VIII, Article 2:203 (2)), it declares: "Where a movable has been transferred based on an obligation that is terminated afterwards, termination has no proprietary effects".

Termination, actually, works on the effects of a valid contract. The general opinion sustains that the contract has provided – where necessary.- a *valid title* as a requirement for transfer of property. Moreover, termination does not restrain

---

38 See further references in Yzquierdo Tolsada, *Las tensiones* (n. 30), p. 133 ff, 194 ff.

39 Notwithstanding some systems that do consider retention of title to be implied in case of deferment of price, when the asset has been already delivered. Such as in the Law of Navarre (*Compilación del Derecho Civil Foral de Navarra*, 1973, Ley 565).

40 PECL, Part II, p. 423.

the effects of the contract to continue – at least – as the source of rules on the consequences of termination governing the parties' relationship. Indeed, it has been said that general statements to the effect that termination operates either retrospectively or prospectively are of limited value: "It is true that termination operates (at least) prospectively in that one of its effects is to release the parties from future primary obligations. Equally it is true, that, in imposing on the parties reciprocal duties of restoration, termination has certain retrospective effects".[41]

One of the major divergences between different legal systems in this field deals with one of the legal effects of termination, namely the retransfer of property. Causal systems would appear to be here again opposed to abstract ones, in that for the former, termination is "retroactive" – property is deemed to be automatically retransferred as if the seller had never lost it – whereas in an abstract system termination only creates a personal duty of restoration. The *Draft*, therefore, would seem to have departed from its *causal* approach, in declaring that *termination has no proprietary effects*. Yet, the scope of the rule seems aimed at solving a particular problem, that is, the protection of a subsequent transferee who acquired *before termination*. In other words, the third party transferee – provided the necessary requirements for transfer had been fulfilled *before* termination – acquired *a domino*, which marks an important difference with cases of void/annulled contracts.

Indeed, despite the *causal* approach of many systems – in requiring a valid contract – as to the transfer of property, it seems to be widely admitted that *bona fide* purchasers for value will not be bothered by subsequent termination of their transferor's title. It is true that this might be achieved by applying rules on acquisition *a non domino* of the good faith purchaser of movables and the rule *possession vaut titre*.[42] However, the protection of the subsequent transferee can also be the consequence of a specific provision of the Law, either excluding retroactive effect in case of termination, or by declaring that it cannot impair (proprietary) rights acquired by third parties for value and in good faith. The latter is the solution of the Spanish CC (Article 1124 *in fine*).

Resolución (termination) for breach of contract in Spanish Law, following the implied condition theory of natural lawyers that in turn was adopted by the French *Code* (Article 1184)[43] is systematically placed among the rules on

---

41 G.H. Treitel, *Remedies for breach of contract. A comparative account* (1988). Article 9:305 PECL (*Effects of Termination in General*), is indeed designed to underline that termination "*should not have retroactive effect*", as "it would be very inconvenient to treat a contract which has been terminated as cancelled in the sense of never having been made". However, it is also clear that in some situations "it is appropriate to undo what has taken place before termination"; in particular, either party "may need to be able to recover...property which has been transferred". See *Principles of European Contract Law, Parts I and II* 420.

42 Article 2279 *Code Civil*; Article 464 Spanish CC.

43 See R. Zimmermann (n. 12), p. 803.

resolutive (subsequent) condition, which is always implied in reciprocal obligations where one of the parties does not fulfil his undertaking. It is not, however, an automatic effect, as the aggrieved party – provided his own performance has been fulfilled or was prepared to tender – may choose a different remedy, namely, specific performance, plus, in both cases, compensation of damages. The right to terminate a contract, furthermore, does not necessarily require a court's decision, but – provided the breach is fundamental – may be exercised by notice to the other party.[44] A request before the court, however, will frequently come, whenever the defaulting party does not agree to comply with the notice.

In addition, the traditional view on the effects of termination, at least in "instantaneous" contracts,[45] is that it works retroactively, but without prejudice to the rights lawfully acquired by third parties for value and in good faith. Indeed, the Spanish Supreme Court has declared that protection of third party transferees against termination of the title of their own transferor, as laid down in Article 1124 *in fine* CC, is not a particular case of acquisition *a non domino*. Furthermore, according to the provisions of the Act on Land Register (Article 11 LH) and case law on movables, if the third party transferee was simply aware that the price had not yet been paid, this would not entail bad faith in itself.[46]

Therefore, it seems to be clear that protection of subsequent acquirers for value and in good faith in case of termination of contract may be fairly supported with, or without, a specific rule on (no) proprietary effects of termination.

That said, it seems that it still remains to be decided if property goes back automatically or not. A rule of "no proprietary effects" of termination appears to have other consequences, in that it may imply that the effects of termination are purely personal in the relationship between the parties. Despite the aggrieved party having given due notice to the other party (or the court declaring extrajudicial termination to have been correct), property would not be immediately regained, but the defaulting party would be under the (personal) obligation to retransfer. Among Spanish legal writers it is a debated matter. The traditional view purports automatic retransfer, whereas other authors contend that prop-

---

44 As in *PECL*, Article 9:303. Notwithstanding diverging opinions, *resolución* does not require necessarily a court's decision. The faculty of the aggrieved party to terminate the contract is usually described as *"derecho potestativo"* or *"facultad de configuración jurídica"*. For extensive information and references see L.P. San Miguel Pradera, *Resolución del contrato por incumplimiento y modalidades de su ejercicio* (2004).

45 As opposed to those entailing "continuous" performance over a period of time. An account of the traditional view, with nuances, in L. Díez Picazo, *Fundamentos del Derecho Civil Patrimonial*, v. II, *Las relaciones obligatorias*, Civitas, 4ª ed. (1993), p. 724. J.L. Lacruz Berdejo *et alii*, *Elementos de Derecho Civil*, T. II, v. 1º, *Derecho de obligaciones*, 3ª ed., revised by F. Rivero Hernández (2003), p. 200.

46 STS 5 May 1983 (*RJ* 1983/2668), STS 15 February 1990 (*RJ* 1990/687). In case of sale of immovables, the Supreme Court has decided for the protection of a third party transferee in good faith, despite his own acquisition had not been entered into the Land Register, and even if he had had notice of the resolutive contractual clause of his own transferor: STS 10 February 2006 (*RJ* 2006/1700).

erty cannot revert automatically, as – in turn – it could not be transmitted *solo consensu* in the first place. Therefore, reacquisition of property calls again for delivery or a court order imposing restitution.[47]

This issue, however, may be tackled differently with regard to creditors of the buyer or to the buyer's receivers in bankruptcy – or bankruptcy administrators –. Even admitting that the seller may not be granted – on termination – with a *droit de suite* against third party transferees in good faith, if he will also be abated by the other party's creditors appears to be a different question, the answer depending primarily not on the automatic (or not) recovery of property on termination, but rather on the rules on preferences in individual executions and the law of bankruptcy.

Furthermore, where termination had already taken place before the seizure of the asset by the transferee's creditors or before the commencement of bankruptcy proceedings, without the buyer having restored property to the aggrieved party, a rule of "no proprietary effects" of termination (or excluding automatic retransfer) would seem to leave the seller with only an unsecured claim in order to recover what he gave – despite the termination of the contract before the seizure or insolvency proceedings – unless protected by a retention of title clause. Yet this type of conflict – again – cannot be decided but by detailed comprehension of the national law on insolvency proceedings.

Indeed, national regulations on insolvency of the transferee and remedies of the seller are varied, and cannot be dealt with here. It is enough to say that the seller (not protected by retention of title clause) may on some occasions recover the goods, regardless of proprietary rules. A rather brief overview appears to offer, *inter alia*, the following remedies:

- if the goods have not yet even been physically delivered, the seller may be granted the right to withhold performance (*exceptio non adimpleti contractus*);
- despite *traditio* having been fulfilled by way of the so-called "documents of title" or "titles of tradition" – such as bill of lading or way bill – , the national law of bankruptcy may entitle the seller to order *stoppage in transitu*, and thereby recover the possession of the unpaid goods;[48]
- furthermore, the unpaid seller could resort to a *quasi-reivindicatio*, in order to claim goods delivered to the bankrupt buyer, provided such a claim is made within reasonable time limits, after bankruptcy has been declared;
- finally, although recovery of property or some kind of *separatio ex iure*

---

47 See V.L. Montés Penadés, *Comentarios al Código Civil y Compilaciones Forales*, Dir. M. Albaladejo, T. XV, Vol. 1º (1989), p. 1248 ff (quoting Pintó Ruiz). M. Clemente Meoro, *La facultad de resolver los contratos por incumplimiento* (1998) 553 *et seq.* Mª.J. Montfort Ferrero, *La restitución en la resolución por incumplimiento de los contratos traslativos del dominio* (2000), p. 330 ff.

48 As admitted by the Spanish former Law on insolvency. See F.J. Arias Varona, *El derecho de separación en la quiebra* (2001), p. 328 ff.

dominii is denied, the seller may still be placed in a better position than other creditors, by means of a specific preference granted by law, even in the absence of contractual clauses providing retention of title.

The solution of the Spanish law on insolvency proceedings (*Ley Concursal*, 9 July 2003, hereinafter *LC*) is not so clear. We will focus here on termination of contract *before* the commencement of insolvency proceedings. According to Article 69 *LC*, in case of movables (or immovables) sold against a deferred price and termination for lack of performance before the declaration of bankruptcy, the bankruptcy administration is entitled to "rehabilitate" the contract, but only when termination took place within the three months prior to the commencement of the proceedings. Such "rehabilitation" requires giving notice to the other party and payment of what was already due, while the rest of the price – originally deferred – is to be treated as a debt of the active mass. The transferor – who previously had terminated the contract – , is entitled to oppose to rehabilitation not only when he had already recovered possession before the declaration of bankruptcy, but also when – prior to this moment – he had filed a judicial claim for termination of the contract and/or recovery of the asset (Article 69.2 LC).

It is undisputed that the Bankruptcy Law is clearly granting effects to the extrajudicial termination of contract,[49] as only in this case may the administrators force rehabilitation on the aggrieved party. Should they choose not to do so, or if indeed the other party decides to oppose to it in the aforementioned circumstances, it is still not clear if the seller may claim for delivery of possession of what – due to the prior termination – could be his own property (*separatio ex iure dominii*), or, on the contrary, has only an unsecured credit in order to claim restitution.

Some authors, when describing the *separatio ex iure dominii*, as granted by Article 80 LC, whilst admitting that nullity, avoidance, or even rescission by means of the *actio pauliana* by creditors of the seller allow the said *separatio*, reject this effect for termination[50]. However, it could be supposed that the effects of termination and property re-transfer in conflict with other creditors of the buyer might be decided not according to a strict property rule, but focusing on the requirements that make termination opposable to third parties. We may consider that, even if we do think it all depends on property having returned or not to the seller, the rather flexible way in which property – of movables, at least – could indeed be re-transferred (even by mere consent), does not mean that such re-transfer is going to be held *erga omnes*. As mentioned above, it does not work like that *on the way there*, as normally further requirements (such as

---

[49] See M.J. Marín López, in R. Bercovitz Rodríguez-Cano (Coord.), *Comentarios a la Ley Concursal*, Vol. 1, (2004), p. 810.

[50] See A. Recalde Castells, in I. Quintana Carlo, A. Bonet Navarro, J.A. García-Cruces González (Dirs.), *Las claves de la Ley Concursal* (2005), p. 404.

notarial deed or unquestionable date) are demanded by the courts in order to prejudice creditors. Therefore, the main question may be focused on termination itself and the requirements that need to concur, in order to hold the priority of the aggrieved party against other creditors.

V Conclusive Remarks

The determination of the consequences of invalidity and termination should not be primarily based on the formulation of general rules granting – or not – proprietary effects to the different causes of inefficacy (which might lead to excessive consequences in order to guarantee the third parties a protection level that might well be achieved by different and more subtle ways), but should take into account the different constellations of cases that may be given, and the convenience of considering the different interests that may be put at stake in each case. It is particularly important to analyse separately, on the one hand, the relationship between the parties to the contract; on the other hand, the relationship between the original transferor and the third parties who may have acquired from the transferee; and, finally, the relationship between the transferor and the transferee's creditors, be it in the context of insolvency proceedings or in that of singular execution proceedings.

The regulation of the consequences of inefficacy in contracts aimed at transferring property should not fail to consider the relationship between real, on the one hand, and obligatory rules and actions, on the other. By way of principle, it could be held that, as between the parties to the contract, the application of the specific rules that regulate the (reciprocal) restitution of prestations should hold priority, excluding the resort to real defenses (such as those based on acquisitive prescription). The main argument in favour of this approach might be found in the principle of speciality: the rules demanding (reciprocal) restitution are based on the consideration of the specific relationship established between the parties to a contract, regardless of the fact that this contract has turned out to be invalid or has been terminated by one of the parties for the other's lack of performance. On the contrary, the rules regarding acquisition and protection of property, as well as those regarding extinctive prescription of real actions, have a more general scope, and should therefore govern the relationship between the parties to the contract and third parties.

The protection of third acquirers against the consequences of inefficacy of the contract should be primarily focused on the assessment of the circumstances of the third party's own acquisition. In cases of invalidity, it may be decided by looking at the rules regarding original acquisition or *a non domino* acquisition. If the contract is terminated, the primary rule may forbid any prejudice with respect to third acquirers in good faith. The legal requirements to be granted protection might vary depending on the particular circumstances: onerous and valid title should be required in any case (leaving aside the cases of acquisitive prescription), but the kind or content of good faith demanded might not always be the same.

When it comes to the creditors of the transferee, the question of their eventual protection as against the inefficacy of the transferring contract requires a more complex analysis. In cases of invalidity, it does not seem adequate to grant the creditors the right to pursue assets that -according to the generally admitted concept of invalidity, where the protection of general interest or of a private interest *deserving* a special protection are involved- have never belonged to their debtor (the transferee). Therefore, it should be admitted that the transferor – provided he obtains a judicial declaration of nullity or challenges (avoids) the contract in due time – will always be allowed to obtain restitution of the assets, be it through the exercise of a third party action based on ownership against execution or through the *separatio ex iure dominii* in cases of insolvency. Obviously, the limit of the transferor's protection in these cases will be the turning up of a third acquirer in good faith as a consequence of the execution and judicial selling of the assets.

In case of termination of the contract based on non-performance of the transferee's obligation, a distinction can be made depending on the time when the transferor's – judicial or extrajudicial – declaration of termination was made. If the termination took place *after* seizure of the assets by the transferee's creditors or after the transferee's declaration of bankruptcy, the transferor shall be considered as a concurrent creditor himself, subject to the preference system provided for by the rules on bankruptcy or on singular executions. Depending on the circumstances and the applicable rules, he might be considered as an ordinary creditor – left to be paid in bankruptcy money – or as a preferential creditor, eventually endowed with the right to separately execute his right to recover the assets (e.g., when he has a retention of title clause or some equivalent).

On the other hand, if termination took place *before* the assets were seized or the transferee was declared bankrupt, it might seem reasonable to grant the transferor a better position – provided the termination itself and the date thereof turn out to be opposable to third parties, e.g., through its formalization in notarial deed or in a judicial document. As a matter of fact, it is well known that the seller (including the unsecured one) that has delivered the assets but has not received payment has been traditionally protected, even against the buyer's bankruptcy, through different means; which seems to prove that an indiscriminate protection of the transferee's creditors should not be assumed as an undisputed principle.

Now, a rule based on the exclusion of any proprietary effects in case of termination of the contract for lack of performance can not be founded generally on the convenience of protecting third parties' interest: it has already been explained that the third party acquirers may be protected against the consequences of the transferee's title's inefficacy, as long as their acquisition meets the requirements established by law in each case. On the other hand, the transferee's creditors are – relatively – protected against the termination of their debtor's title, provided such termination takes place after the asset was seized or the bankruptcy was declared, by the specific rules governing bankruptcy and singular execution. In short: the final consequence of the exclusion of proprietary effects in termination seems to be the indiscriminate protection of the creditors of the transferee against the termination performed by the transferor *before* seizure or bankruptcy declaration took place, which may seem arguable, at least where the date of termination can be ascertained and is, as a consequence, opposable against third parties.

CHAPTER 14

European Private Law without European Law on Civil Procedure?

Rosa Miquel Sala*

I Introduction

The great development in the field of European Private Law in the last twenty years has transformed national laws in an irreversible way, since the legal systems of the Member States are no longer the result of the exercise of the own sovereignty but they are very much influenced by European rules. Harmonization through Directives has been successful in creating (not without problems[1]) a common consumer's protection, and this seems to lead to a final integration of the different national rules on Private Law, but it is still too early for a European Civil Code to be enacted. Nonetheless, the efforts made by lawyers from all over Europe have made possible a future Common Frame of Reference in the area of Contract Law. Leaving the doubts about the possible applications of these rules aside, a unified Contract Law is quite possible in the medium term if the constitutional rules are conveniently reformed.

However, I will not focus on the integration of Private Law, but on a closely related topic, for the harmonization of civil procedure is a necessary corollary to the rapprochement of substantive laws. Nowadays, each Member State has the power to fix its own standards and procedural norms, and therefore to decide, for example, about the recognition of foreign judgments. The existence of different procedural regimes implies an obstacle for free competition because a cumbersome regime of civil proceedings which favours the evasion of goods by the debtor can be a handicap for national traders.[2] Moreover, Procedure Law plays a big role when granting the respect of constitutional rights in a trial. These and other arguments can be given to conclude that the adoption of common contractual rules for all of Europe can be only a minor success if a simultaneous integration of procedural rules is not achieved, but in this respect it is maybe much more important to point out that also the fundamental liberties signalized by the Primary Law need uniform procedural standards to apply with the same force in all the Member States.

This paper aims to straighten out which is the best way for the already existing European Law on Civil Procedure to develop according to the foreseeable progresses of European Private Law. It is structured as follows: The following section tries to give an overview of the evolution of the so-called European Procedure Law, paying special attention to rules on jurisdiction. Section III is devoted to the four ways which have led to the Europeanization of national civil procedures. Then a comparison will be made between the policies in material and procedural law and the possible future strategies. Finally, the protection of fundamental rights during the trial in the hypothetical context of a unified Procedure Law will be briefly discussed.

---

* Universität Bayreuth.

1 See later IV. 1.

2 See Recital 8 of the Regulation 861/2007.

II Foundations of European Procedure Law

1 Overview

The rapprochement of the different civil procedures in Europe begins in 1957, as the EEC Treaty states in Article 220: the goal of simplifying the formalities governing the reciprocal recognition and enforcement of court judgments. The main result was the successful Brussels Convention on Jurisdiction and the Enforcement of Judgments in Civil and Commercial Matters in 1968. It was not until 1994, when a group of experts, the "Commission European Judiciary Code", published a study (Storme Report)[3] on the approximation of the laws and rules of the Member States concerning certain aspects of the procedure for civil litigation. So the idea of a European Code of Civil Procedure was already in the wind, but it was too early for a specific text to be adopted.[4]

The Treaty of Amsterdam provided the basis for the great development of European Law in the last decade. It set the goal of achieving an area of freedom, security and justice.[5] This also required that individuals and businesses should not be prevented or discouraged from exercising their rights by the incompatibility or complexity of legal and administrative systems in the Member States.[6] A brief look into the past is sufficient to realize how much the European Institutions have done in the field of International Procedure Law: ten years ago the Brussels Convention was the only important rule; nowadays a lot of Regulations, Directives and Decisions cover many aspects of this area of law.[7] The legislative task has developed by now towards two big directions, namely International Civil Procedure and Transnational Civil Procedure,[8] leaving internal procedures almost untouched.[9] As a result, European Procedure Law has become a kind of

---

3 M. Storme (ed.), *Rapprochement du Droit Judiciaire de l'Union europèene/ Approximation of Judiciary Law in the European Union* (1994).

4 K. Kerameus, *Die Angleichung des Zivilverfahrensrechts in der Europäischen Union vor dem Hintergrund der Schaffung eines Europäischen Zivilgesetzbuches*, in: *Untersuchung der Privatsrechtsordnungen der EU im Hinblick auf Diskriminierungen und die Schaffung eines Europäischen Zivilgesetzbuch*, (Workpaper, JURI 103 DE, October 1999; PE 168.511), p. 85-95 (94); S. Leible, "Die Angleichung der nationalen Zivilprozessrechte – 'Vom Binnenmarktprozess' zu einer europäischer ZPO?", in: P.- C. Müller-Graff (red.), *Der Raum der Freiheit, der Sicherheit und des Rechts* (Schriftenreihe des Arbeitskreises Europäische Integration, Band 51), (2005), p. 55-73 (72).

5 Article 61 of the EC Treaty.

6 European Council Programme of Tampere.

7 See for instance R. Geimer/R. Schütze, *Europäisches Zivilverfahrensrecht* 2nd ed., (2004); Staudinger/ Rauscher, *Europäisches Zivilprozessrecht*, vol. 1, 2nd. ed. (2006), p. 10-57; P.G. Mayr, D. Czernich, *Europäisches Zivilprozessrecht* (2006).

8 Rules to help Courts' work in cross-border cases, like the Regulation 1348/2000 on the service in the Member States of judicial and extrajudicial documents in civil or commercial matters.

9 Cf. D. Coester-Waltjen, "Die Europäisierung des Zivilprozessrechts", (2006) *Jura* 914-921 (915).

"tertium" (the so-called *Binnenmarktprozess*[10]) between internal procedures and international civil procedures.

2 Competence

Article 65 of the EC Treaty allows the Community to take measures in the field of judicial cooperation, in civil matters having cross-border implications in accordance with Article 67 and insofar as necessary for the proper functioning of the internal market. Among these measures is the elimination of obstacles to the good functioning of civil proceedings, if necessary by promoting the compatibility of the rules on civil procedure applicable in the Member States. The relationship between Article 65 and Article 95 has been a subject of intensive debate because these articles seem to overlap with each other to some extent, as Article 95 establishes that the Council will adopt the measures for the approximation of the provisions laid down by law, regulation or administrative action in Member States which have as their objective the establishment and functioning of the internal market.

Two solutions to this problem have been suggested. On the one hand, Article 65 could have a complementing function to Article 95. Because of its position in Title IV of the EC Treaty, it could only be applied to take measures relating to the free movement of persons, the freedom of establishment and the free movement of workers and services. It would be then only applicable to harmonize the matters expressly excluded in Article 95.2.[11] On the other hand, it seems more reasonable to conceive Article 65 as a *lex specialis* to Article 95, as it empowers the Community to take measures to guarantee the proper functioning of the internal market in general, so not only a reactive harmonization (when a threat to the fundamental liberties or market distortions exists), but an active harmonization, aiming to the achievement of a space of liberty, security and justice.[12] This activity is limited by the principles of subsidiarity and proportionality.

Article III-269.2 of the Treaty establishing a Constitution for Europe would enlarge the competence given to the Union, because it could act particularly when necessary for the proper functioning of the internal market, but also in other occasions.[13]

10 B. Hess, "Der Binnenmarktprozeß", (1998) *JZ* 1021-1032.

11 See for example T. Wiedmann, "Article 65 EGV", in: J. Schwarze, *EU-Kommentar*, 1st. ed. (2000), n. 9.

12 S. Leible, "Die Europäisierung des internationalen Privat- und Prozessrechts", in: S. Sánchez Lorenzo, *La cooperación judicial en materia civil y la unificación del derecho privado en Europa* Madrid (2003), p. 16-20; S. Leible, A. Staudinger, "El Articulo 65 TCE ¿Carta blanca de la Comunidad Europea para la unificación del derecho internacional privado y procesal?", (2001) *Anuario Español de DIPr* 89-115 (106).

13 R. Wagner, "Zur Vereinheitlichung des Internationalen Privat- und Zivilverfahrensrechts sieben Jahre nach In-Kraft-Treten des Amsterdamer Vertrags", (2006) *EuZW* 424-428.

III Four Ways leading to Europeanization of Civil Procedure

1 ECJ Decisions

The voices speaking of an Americanization of European Law[14] are not wholly unfounded, for its maturity is to a great extent due to ECJ Decisions. Through this indirect way, European Law has deeply influenced national procedure rules. In absence of a unitary civil procedure, national Procedure Laws are the instruments which need to comply with the protection offered by the secondary law (that is, the so called principle of procedural autonomy[15]) and the goals set by primary law. The European Court controls in its decisions the respect of the equivalency principle, which itself is a manifestation of the prohibition of discrimination, and of the effectivity principle. This is called negative integration.[16]

According to the first, the procedural conditions governing action at law intended to ensure the protection of the rights which citizens have from the direct effect of community law cannot be less favourable than those relating to similar actions of a domestic nature[17]. The second principle establishes that the rules governing actions for safeguarding rights which individuals derive from de direct effect of Community law must not be render the exercise of rights conferred by Community law virtually impossible or excessively difficult.[18]

Summarizing all the concretions of these principles in the precedents of the ECJ would certainly go beyond the true purposes of this paper,[19] but let us take a look on some examples. First of all, the ECJ has established a doctrine relating to procedural terms. The Court asserts that national laws have to guarantee the correct application of the directives. Therefore, while a directive has not been properly transposed, a defaulting Member State may not rely on an individual's delay in initiating proceedings against it in order to protect rights conferred upon him by the provisions of the directive, and a period laid down by national law, within which proceedings must be initiated, cannot begin to run before that time.[20] Moreover, terms cannot be so short compared with those prescribed in

---

[14] A. Stadler, "Das Europäische Zivilprozessrecht – Wie viel Beschleunigung verträgt Europa?", (2004) *IPRax* 2-11 (5).

[15] Á.J.D. Pérez-Ragone, *Europäisches Mahnverfahren. Prozessrechtliche Abhandlungen*, Heft 120 (2005) p. 324-327.

[16] C. Otero García-Castrillón, *Cooperación judicial civil en la Unión Europea. El cobro de las deudas* (2007), p. 93-97.

[17] C- 33/1976 [1976] ECR I-1989, n. 5 – *Rewe-Zentralfinanz* eG; C- 43/1995 [1996] ECR I-4661, n. 12 – *Data delecta*.

[18] C-312/1993 [1995] ECR I-4599, n. 12 – *Peterbroeck*; C-199/1982 [1983] ECR I-3595 – *San Giorgio*.

[19] About the effectivity principle in the ECJ Decisions, P. Rott, *Effektivität des Verbraucherrechtsschutzes. Rahmenfestlegungen des Gemeinschaftsrechts*, http://www.ble.de/download/pdf/04HS033.pdf.; p. 35 f.

[20] C-208/1990 [1991] ECR I-4269, *Emmott*.

the legal systems of the other Member States that they render excessively difficult or virtually impossible the exercise of rights conferred by Community law.[21]

Two other important decisions referring to the Directive 93/13/EEC are the *Cofidis* Decision[22] and the *Océano* Decision[23]. The national court will have to be able to determine whether a term of a contract in its motion is unfair, when making its preliminary assessment as to whether a claim should be allowed to proceed before the national courts, and fixing a time-limit for the court's power to find that an unfair term is contrary to the objectives of the Directive. To allow the Member States to introduce such time-limits, which might differ from each other, would also be contrary to the principle of the uniform application of Community law.

The ECJ has established clear principles for the national legislators to follow, but it works towards a harmonization only in a subtle way, because it cannot be forgotten that its decisions operate only inter partes. Therefore, once a State has been condemned, the other Member States are not obliged to change their own procedure rules which are also likely to contravene European Law. Thus, there is no true harmonization at this level.

2 Directives on Material Law

On the other hand, a moderate harmonization of the national civil procedures has been achieved with the directives regulating aspects of substantive law which demand measures of a procedural character from the national legislator.[24] A good example is the Directive 2000/35/EC on combating late payment in commercial transactions; Article 5 establishes that Member States have to ensure that an enforceable title can be obtained, irrespective of the amount of the debt, normally within 90 calendar days of the lodging of the creditor's action or application at the court or other competent authority, provided that the debt or aspects of the procedure are not disputed.

Both this Directive and the Directive on unfair terms require the Member States to ensure that, in the interests of consumers and of competitors, adequate and effective means exist to prevent the continued use of terms which are unfair (Directive 93/13) or grossly unfair (Directive 2000/35). As in Article 7 of the Directive on unfair terms (and similarly in Article 3. 5. of the Directive combating late payment) said, these means include provisions whereby persons or organizations, having a legitimate interest under national law in protecting consumers, may take action according to the national law concerned before the courts or before competent administrative bodies. The associations' suit

21 ECJ C-126/1997 [1999] ECR I-3055, n. 45, *Eco Swiss China Time Ltd v Benetton International NV*

22 ECJ C-473/2000 [2002] ECR I-10875, n. 31, *Cofidis.*

23 ECJ C-240/1998 [2000] ECR I-4941, n. 2, *Océano Grupo Editorial S.A.*

24 U. Rörig, "Einfluss des Rechts der Europäischen Gemeinschaft auf das nationale Zivilprozessrecht", (2004) *EuZW* 18-20; Coester-Waltjen (n. 9) 918.

is maybe one of the most important contributions made by the Directives to national Procedure Laws.[25]

Finally, the Directive 98/27/EC on injunctions for the protection of consumers' interests establishes the minimal requirements that the injunctions foreseen in the Directives have to fulfill in the national systems. This norm tries to grant the access to jurisdiction to the consumer, the freedom of movement of the decisions and to harmonize Procedure Laws.

3 European Proceedings

Until recently, the European Regulations on Procedure Law were mainly focused on aspects of international jurisdiction and recognition and enforcement of decisions. Meanwhile, the European legislator has gone further and created also real cross-border proceedings. In 2002, a Green Paper on litigation was published, which demanded two European orders, one for payment procedure and another to simplify and speed up small claims. The Commission intended those two proceedings to be applicable not only in cross-border cases, but also in internal cases, if the litigants had opted for them. It was argued – a very evident attempt to obtain a unification of civil procedures "through the backdoor" – that the cross-border dimension of a case may become apparent only once the creditor proceeds to the stage of enforcement, and that it could also be unjust that plaintiffs in purely internal cases were possibly left with a burdensome ordinary civil procedural system that does not meet their justified needs. Moreover, a marked disequilibrium with regard to the efficiency of the procedural means afforded to creditors from different Member States for the recovery of their claims, be they small or uncontested, could have a direct bearing on the proper functioning of the internal market.[26]

It is true that these arguments are convincing,[27] but it is also true that such a solution would have generated the very uneasy situation in which two parallel proceedings, the national and the European one, would have concurred with each other. Nevertheless, it would be exaggerated to assert that this situation implies the possibility for the parties in a trial to choose Procedural Laws directly, that is, not by means of an agreement concerning jurisdiction as it is foreseen for example in Article 23 of the Brussels I Regulation, which would automatically mean ignoring the commonly accepted principle *lex fori regit processum*.

The creation of uniform proceedings in the frame of the EU in order to grant effective legal protection in all Member States does not signify a breach of this

[25] Cf. H. Koch, "Non-class Group Litigation under EU and German Law", 11 (2001) *Duke J. of Comp. & Int'l L.* 355-367.

[26] COM (2002) 746 final.

[27] Sharing them M. Loredo Colunga, "¿Hacia un Derecho procesal europeo? Reflexiones en torno al proyecto de procedimiento europeo de escasa cuantía", (2006) 1 *InDret* 10.

principle.[28] On the other hand, it is to be considered that one of the arguments given to justify the fact that the judges apply only its own national Procedure Law is the reference to its neutrality.[29] Procedure Law is thought to be neutral and therefore the application of one law or another does not interfere (apparently) with the international harmony of solutions. One could argue that when the Commission considers it unjust that the claimant, in a purely internal case, cannot use the European Proceeding, it is in fact supposing that the latter will be better (more neutral) than a national Procedure, and that cannot be in no way considered a proven fact.

Fortunately, the Commission was forced to rectify its position because of its lack of competence: According Article 65 EC Treaty, the Community can only legislate in civil matters having cross-border implications. As a result, the Regulations 1869/2006 and 861/2007 are expressly limited to cross-border cases.

4 Establishing Minimal Standards

In 2004, the new Regulation creating a European enforcement order for uncontested claims[30] simultaneously suppressed the exequatur and the public policy test which hitherto had been widely used to refuse the recognition of foreign judgments. So the country of origin principle also applies to Procedure Law. Underlying the Regulation is the idea of mutual trust in the administration of justice in the other Member States. Given that not all the Member States have a reliable law of civil procedure[31], this idea is not without danger.[32]

As a counterpart, Chapter III of the same Regulation establishes some minimal conditions that national Procedure Laws have to fulfil in order for the own judgments to be enforced in other Member States. Thus the Community creates a System based on the formula "do ut des", in which every Member State is free to change its Procedure Law in order to reach the European standards, but it accepts that, unless it does its judgment, it will not be a capable of a European enforcement order and that therefore the regime of the Brussels-I Regulation will apply. The particular conditions, set out in Arts. 13 to 17, refer to the form in which the service of the document instituting the proceedings or an equivalent document has to be provided and the minimal content of such a document: the debtor must receive due information about the claim and the procedural steps necessary to contest it.

Although the observation of these conditions is optional, it is clear that with this Regulation the Community is putting an indirect pressure on the different national legislators in order to make them reform, when necessary, their proce-

---

[28] Otero García Castrillón (n. 16), p. 24.

[29] B. von Hoffmann, K. Thorn, *Internationales Privatrecht*, 8th ed. (2005), p. 66-67.

[30] Regulation 805/2004 (Official Journal 2004, L 143/15).

[31] Just remember the Krombach Decision (Judgment of 28th March 2000, [2000] ECR I-1935).

[32] Cf. P. Georganti, *Die Zukunft des ordre public-Vorbehalts im Europäischen Zivilprozessrecht* (2006).

dure norms relating to delivery of documents, because if not doing so, their creditors would be in a disadvantageous position in comparison with creditors from other Member States. Once more, like in the case of directives, the question is why the citizens have to suffer the consequences of the irresolution or the simple laziness of the legislator.[33]

IV Harmonization or Unification?

1 Different Strategies for Different Subjects

Summing up what has been said, it becomes clear that different policies have been followed to achieve the Europeanisation of Civil and Procedure Law. In Civil Law, a progressive rapprochement of the different national laws has been regarded as the best solution by the European legislator, whereas a rather cautious attitude can be observed when mending national civil procedures.

Although the reasons for this different approach have not been clarified, it seems that its origin is to be found in the features of both fields of the law: In Civil Law, and particularly in Contract Law, the States of the civil law tradition share basic institutions which all originated in Roman Law, the main differences are due to mere cultural singularities, and Comparative Law has played a big role in its development.

This is not the case for Procedure Law, because the different national proceedings have evolved without receiving external influences and there is no previous relevant work in the field of Comparative Procedure Law.[34] Even when the same institutions can be observed, their use can be very different, and a good example of that is the default procedure: In England its function is to find out which are the true controversial questions in the trial, whereas in France it is simply understood as an expression of the will of not taking part in the trial.[35]

It cannot be denied that the creation of common standards in Consumer Law by means of directives has been a very important success, though not a resounding one. According to Smits, the acquis created in this way is fragmentary, arbitrary, incoherent and ineffective.[36] The directives have not been transposed, either in a uniform way or simultaneously, and in some cases doubts may arise

33 T. Rauscher, S. Pabst, *Europäisches Zivilprozessrecht* vol. 2. (2006), p. 1443-1444; Stadler (n. 14) 2-11 (4).

34 It seems that this tendency will change in the future, see H. Koch, "Prozessrechtsvergleichung: Grundlage europäischer Verfahrenspolitik und Kennzeichnung von Rechtskreisen, Zeitschrift für Europäisches Privatrecht" 3/2007, p. 735-753.

35 K. Kerameus, "Angleichung des Zivilprozeßrechts in Europa. Einige grundlegende Aspekte", 66 (2002) *RabelsZ* 1-17 (9).

36 J. Smits, "Dret privat europeu: per un ordre jurídic espontani", (2007) 7 *Revista Catalana de Dret Privat* 147-197 (154-157).

as to which of them (that is, which of the acts transposing them) is applicable. For example, in a time-sharing contract which has been negotiated away from business premises, which is the allowed time for the consumer to exercise his or her right of withdrawal? One must regrettably conclude that the existing law is fragmentary, unsteady and without axiological basis.[37] The present efforts to achieve unitary Contract Law are the fact that most clearly reveals that harmonization of substantive Law has not been as successful as expected.

Procedural law is a neutral, technical area of the law. The most fundamental requirements that have to be fulfilled are that it must be internally coherent and respect the fundamental rights of the parties. As long as the different national systems remained enclosed, this coherence was not endangered. However, the situation has gradually changed and therefore it is necessary to know what the right direction to follow is. Not only the ECJ and the Directives are eroding the present national proceedings. The two new European Regulations that have been adopted are influenced by different procedural traditions,[38] and their necessary coordination with national norms can be problematic in the future. The example has shown that a fragmentary harmonization can lead to a worse situation. As a consequence, what is asked for is not a piecemeal approach, but a fundamental reform.

2 *Binnenmarktprozessrecht* as a Model: A Procedural CFR

The creation of a European Civil Code and a European Code of civil procedure seems to be the ultimate step to the implementation of the principles established in the Treaty of Rome. Leaving aside that at the moment the Community does not have the competence to elaborate them, and that its democratic legitimation would under no circumstances be comparable to those of national parliaments, it must be emphasized that there are also sectors in the field of Procedure Law that lend themselves more to unification than others.[39]

These sectors are the most technical ones, which do not pretend to give support to certain tendencies of substantive law. The Community has actually taken steps in this direction by means of the Regulations Brussels I and II, but unfortunately these Regulations only operate within the Internal Market. A counterexample of a norm that has such a strong connection to national substantive law that would make it impossible to Europeanize, is the special proceeding to safeguard the efficacy of real rights foreseen in the Spanish *Ley de Enjuiciamiento Civil*, which is closely related to Article 41 of the *Ley Hipotec-*

[37] Focusing on the problems of existing European Private Law, S. Sánchez Lorenzo, "¿Hacia un Código civil europeo?", in S. Sánchez Lorenzo, *La cooperación judicial en materia civil y la unificación del derecho privado en Europa* (2003), p. 381-405 (385-388).

[38] Consider for instance the fees regime in the Regulation 861/2007, which is closer to the Spanish rules than the German ones.

[39] Kerameus (n. 35) 1-17.

caria.[40] Consequently, a future European Code of civil procedure is unimaginable without unified substantive Law and vice versa.

However, these facts would not hinder a partial unification of the civil procedures in Europe. The creation of cross-border proceedings besides national systems as an option for the parties, a kind of procedural CFR,[41] has recently been suggested. It would be useless here to repeat the arguments here that have already been brought forward against the possibility of a direct choice of the norms governing the trial,[42] but at the same time the increasing importance of the so-called *Binnenmarktprozessrecht*, which is not only contenting itself with the regulation of recognition and enforcement of decisions but is also creating European proceedings, cannot be forgotten. It is not unreasonable to think of a future cross-border (and mandatory) European Civil Procedure in the future. Taking into account how European Procedure Law, and more specific the Brussels Convention, has influenced nationals laws,[43] such a norm could serve as a model for the Member States to follow, thereby giving them the possibility to manage the way in which they Europeanize their own civil procedures without imposing norms from above which could affect its coherence and eventually the rights of the individuals.

The combination of this European proceeding with the future Regulations unifying international private law would make forum shopping disappear from the Union, since the same cross-border case would be decided applying the same substantive law and with the same proceedings in all the Member States, no matter what the Tribunal would decide. Besides, the external costs resulting from the application of foreign Procedure Law would also disappear, and the free movement of lawyers within the Internal Market would be simplified. But this option is not as advantageous as it may seem at first sight. A cross-border proceeding would have to be adapted to all substantive laws, which seems difficult. On the other hand, a partial European cross-border proceeding with remissions to national laws would be also very complicated to put into practise.

Nonetheless, the Spanish legal system is an example of the coexistence of diverse substantive laws with the same civil procedure. For this to be possible, a certain organization of the Tribunals is needed. In the Spanish system, the *Tribunales Superiores de Justicia* are the last instance for the interpretation of foral laws, and they also decide about the appeals concerning procedural infrac-

---

40 About the close relation between substantive and Procedure law see W. Zöllner, "Materielles Recht und Prozeßrecht", 190 (1990) *Archiv für die civilistische Praxis* 471-495.

41 W. Hau, "Zur Entwicklung des Internationalen Zivilverfahrensrechts in der Europäischen Union in den Jahren 2005 und 2006", (2007) *Gemeinschafts-Privatrecht* 93-100.

42 See III. 3.

43 Cf. A. Alsina Naudi, *Die Umsetzung des Europäischen Zivilprozessrechts in Spanien* (2005); H. Schack, "Wechselwirkungen zwischen Europäischen und nationalem Zivilprozeßrecht", 107 (1994) *Zeitschrift für Zivilprozess* 279-299.

tions.[44] After all the remedies of ordinary jurisdiction have been used the so called *recurso en interés de la Ley* can be decided by the *Tribunal Supremo.*[45] But also common standards of protection of the subjective rights of the parties in a trial are necessary, in Spain contained in Article 24 of the Constitution, and a single Tribunal controlling its respect and fixing their development. Let us see now how this protection would be materialised in the context of a European Proceeding.

V Uniform Protection of Subjective Rights in the Trial

1 Judicial Structure

Whereas the relationship between fundamental rights and substantive Law is nowadays a field of debate,[46] there is no doubt about the close connection between Constitutional Law and Procedure Law. This connection is so strong that it can even be said that the procedure itself is nothing more than an expression or a consequence of the right of effective judicial protection and of human dignity. The necessary balance between procedural principles is also fixed by national legislators with regard to constitutional rights. The contents of the constitutional norms granting fundamental rights in the correlative Member States are very alike, and therefore it can be asserted that the level of protection is at least similar,[47] but their development by means of case law can be different to some extent just because judicial decisions are an expression of national sovereignty. If all the judges in the Union applied the same proceeding, it would become necessary to find a solution to this question.

As everybody knows, nowadays the ECJ is not a Court of appeal, so it usually interprets European Law when a case is referred to it for a preliminary ruling by a national judge. But a European civil procedure requires one superior Court having real power to establish uniform case law, and as long as national courts can still decide whether they ask Brussels for advice or they follow their own criteria this will not be possible. Nonetheless, it is not clear that the creation of a kind of "European cassation appeal" focused on the control of procedural infractions would be so positive at all, for the trial would last for a long time and the number of cases would make a structural reform of the Court necessary.

44 Articles 468 and 478 of the Spanish Ley de Enjuiciamiento Civil (LEC).

45 Articles 490-493 LEC.

46 See for example J. Smits, "Private Law and Fundamental Rights: A Sceptical View". Available at SSRN: http://ssrn.com/abstract=928560.

47 But not equal, see III. 4.

2 Protection at Different Levels: Article 6 ECHR vs. Chapter VII of the Charter of Fundamental Rights of the European Union

According to Article 6(2) of the Treaty of Maastricht, the European Union binds herself to respect the fundamental rights contained in the European Convention on Human Rights, being the rights relating to the procedure contained in its Article 6. In addition, the Charter of Fundamental Rights of the European Union is also referred to in the decisions of the ECJ, although it does not have binding character at the moment.[48] But in that respect one must be reminded that just a week ago a final agreement was reached in Lisbon referring to the new Treaty which will be adopted instead of the failed European Constitution. Consequently, the Charter of Fundamental Rights of the European Union will at last be part of the primary law and it will no longer be necessary to resort to the ECHR when implementing European Law, whether this implementation is done on the national or the Community level.[49]

These three levels of protection of the subjective rights (ECHR, Primary Law and national constitutions) will apparently coexist harmoniously. Until now, the judges of Luxemburg and Strasbourg had been reciprocally taking into account each other's decisions, and this situation will continue because Article 53 of the Charter establishes that it must not be interpreted as restricting or adversely affecting human rights and fundamental freedoms as recognized, among others, in the ECHR. This means that, in fact, Article 6 ECHR will keep on setting the standards of protection of subjective rights in the future, not only because its previous development by means of case law is important, but also because the new text of the Charter is almost a literal transcription.

VI Conclusions

The aim of this paper was to find out which of the possible alternatives was the best suited in order to solve the problem of the diverse procedural standards in the Members States in the context of the Europeanization of material law. Unfortunately, the solution to this question is not an easy one, because it requires finding a balance between the developments of material and Procedure Law. On the one hand, there is no doubt that the excessive use of single harmonizing measures can lead to incoherent legal systems, both in the fields of substantive and Procedure Law. It is obviously impossible to be always successful in creating norms which are compatible with all 27 legal systems in the Community and therefore it is necessary to make sure that national procedures preserve their essence. On the other hand, one cannot constantly refuse

[48] For example in ECJ C-432/05.

[49] See Article 51 of the Charter.

these measures because, if European substantive law develops at greater velocity than civil procedure, it is possible that Procedure Law cannot guarantee the accomplishment of the rights conferred by Community law.

A piecemeal approach can endanger the coherence of national systems and can be insufficient if important progress is achieved on the level of substantive law, so the option of a single procedure for all of Europe seems advisable at first sight. But this impression has proven not to be absolutely right. As said before, not all the norms in the procedure can nowadays be successfully unified, so a complete European procedure cannot successfully coexist with split private laws unless an adequate system of remedies is created. The control of fundamental rights in the Union would also need to be reviewed, and national judges would need to become familiar with the Charter of Fundamental Rights when implementing European law. These requirements would not contravene the subsidiarity principle (Article 5 EC Treaty) because at any rate the protection of fundamental rights is to be guaranteed on the Community level.

At the moment the Community is only competent to create cross-border proceedings. It is true that European Procedure Law has served as a model for national legislators, but in my opinion this fact alone does not justify the review of the whole system of remedies and of the relationship of the ECJ with the national courts, which would be a difficult task with unclear results. The development of Procedure Law in Europe depends on the development of substantive law. If substantive law evolves slowly, then a few little changes in national procedures will not be harmful at all. If on the contrary substantial progresses were made, unification of national civil procedures would be both possible and necessary.